Campbell Hardy

**Forest Life in Acadie**

Sketches of Sport and Natural History in the lower Provinces of the Canadian

Dominion

Campbell Hardy

**Forest Life in Acadie**
*Sketches of Sport and Natural History in the lower Provinces of the Canadian Dominion*

ISBN/EAN: 9783337190286

Printed in Europe, USA, Canada, Australia, Japan

Cover: Foto ©ninafisch / pixelio.de

More available books at **www.hansebooks.com**

# FOREST LIFE IN ACADIE.

# FOREST LIFE IN ACADIE,

---

## SKETCHES OF SPORT AND NATURAL HISTORY IN THE LOWER PROVINCES OF THE CANADIAN DOMINION.

BY CAPTAIN CAMPBELL HARDY,

ROYAL ARTILLERY.

AUTHOR OF "SPORTING ADVENTURES IN THE NEW WORLD."

View on Gold River, N.S.

LONDON:

CHAPMAN & HALL, 193, PICCADILLY.

# PREFACE.

THE Author having brought out several years since a work on sporting in Atlantic America, which was favourably received, is induced to present the present volume of more recent experiences, especially as the interval since elapsed has been unmarked by the production of any English publication of a similar kind.

Many inquiries concerning the sports and physical features of the British Provinces bordering on the Atlantic, evidently made by those who meditate seeking a transatlantic home, appear from time to time in the columns of sporting periodicals, and elicit various and uncertain replies.

The Author's sojourn in the Acadian Provinces having extended over a period of fifteen years, he trusts that the information here afforded will prove useful to such querists.

It will appear evident that he has formed a strong attachment to the country, its scenery and wild sports, and by some it will probably be said that the pleasures of forest life are exaggerated in his descriptions of a country possessing neither grandeur of landscape nor inducements to the "sensational" sportsman. There is, however, a quiet, ever-growing charm to be found in the

woodlands or on the waters of Acadie, which those who
have resided there will readily admit. Many who have
touched at its shores as visitors within the Author's
recollection, have made it their home; whilst those of his
vocation who have been called away, have almost invariably expressed a hope of speedy return.

Several of the descriptive sporting scenes found in this
work will be recognised as having appeared in "The
Field," and the Author begs to express his appreciation
of the Editor's courtesy in permitting their republication.
The notices on the natural history of the Elk and Beaver
are reproduced, with slight alterations, from the pages
of "Land and Water," with the kind consent of the
managers, the articles having appeared therein over the
signature of "Alces."

The acknowledgments of the Author are also due to
several old friends across the Atlantic—to "The Old
Hunter," for anecdotes of camp life, and to Dr. Bernard Gilpin for his valuable assistance in describing
the game fish, and in preparing the illustration of the
American Brook Trout.

# CONTENTS.

## CHAPTER VIII.

## CHAPTER IX.

## CHAPTER X.

## CHAPTER XI.

## CHAPTER XII.

## APPENDIX.

# LIST OF ILLUSTRATIONS.

# FOREST LIFE IN ACADIE.

## CHAPTER I.

### THE MARITIME PROVINCES.

PADDLING down a picturesque Nova-Scotian stream called the Shubenacadie some ten years since in an Indian canoe, it occurred to me to ask the steersman the proper Micmac pronunciation of the name. He replied, " We call 'em ' Segéebenacadie.' Plenty wild potatoes—segéeben—once grew here." " Well, ' acadie,' Paul, what does that mean ? " I inquired. " Means— where you find 'em," said the Indian.

The termination, therefore, of acadie, signifying a place where this or that is found, being of frequent occurrence in the old Indian names of places, seems to have been readily adopted by the first permanent settlers in Nova Scotia to designate an extensive district, though one with uncertain limits — the Acadie of the followers of Mons. De Monts in the first decade of the seventeenth century comprising the present provinces of Nova Scotia, New Brunswick, and Prince Edward Island, with a portion of the State of

B

Maine.* The peninsula of Nova Scotia was, however, Acadie proper, and herein was laid the scene of the expulsion of the French neutrals from their settlements by the shores of Minas Basin and elsewhere—an event round which has centred so much misconceived sympathy of authors and poets, but which has since been shown to have been a most justifiable and necessary

---

* Having had access since these lines were written to Dr. Dawson's second edition of "Acadian Geology," recently published by Macmillan and Co., I was at once struck with the author's account of the derivation of the term "Acadie," which he has given in language so similar to my own (even to instancing the Indian name of the same river), that I think it but just to notice this fact—his work being produced some time prior to my own. From this standard work on the Geology of the British Provinces, I will also quote a few passages in further exemplification of the subject.

The author is informed by the Rev. Mr. Rand, the zealous Indian Missionary of the Acadian Indians, who has made their ways and language his whole study for a long period of years, and translated into their tongue the greater portion of Scripture, that "the word in its original form is *Kady* or *Cadie*, and that it is equivalent to region, field, ground, land, or place, but that when joined to an adjective, or to a noun with the force of an adjective, it denotes that the place referred to is the appropriate or special place of the object expressed by the noun or noun-adjective. Now in Micmac, adjectives of this kind are formed by suffixing 'a' or 'wa' to the noun. Thus Segubbun is a ground-nut; Segubbuna, of or relating to ground-nuts; and Segubbuna-Kaddy is the place or region of ground-nuts, or the place in which these are to be found in abundance."

As further examples of this common termination of the old Indian names of places, Dr. Dawson gives the following :—

Soona-Kaddy (Sunacadie). Place of cranberries.

Kata-Kaddy. Eel-ground.

Tulluk-Kaddy (Tracadie). Probably place of residence ; dwelling place.

Buna-Kaddy (Bunacadie, or Benacadie). Is the place of bringing forth ; a place resorted to by the moose at the calving-time.

Segoonuma-Kaddy. Place of Gaspereaux ; Gaspereaux or Alewife river.

Again, "Quodiah or Codiah is merely a modification of Kaddy in the language of the Maliceets " (a neighbouring tribe dwelling in New Brunswick, principally on the banks of the St. John), "and replacing the other form in certain compounds. Thus Nooda-Kwoddy (Noodiquoddy or Winchelsea Harbour) is a place of seals, or, more literally, place of seal-hunting. Pestumoo-Kwoddy (Passamaquoddy), Pollock-ground, &c. &c."

step, from their unceasing plottings with the Indians against British dominancy, receiving, of course, strong support from the French, who still held Louisburg and Quebec.

Most interesting, and indeed romantic, as is the early history of Acadie during her constant change of rulers until the English obtained a lasting possession of Nova Scotia in 1713, and finally in 1763 were ridded of their troublesome rivals in Cape Breton by the cession on the part of the French of all their possessions in Canada and the Gulf of St. Lawrence, a history political and statistical of the Lower Provinces would be quite irrelevant to the general contents of a work like the present. The subject has been ably and exhaustively treated by the great historian of Nova Scotia, Judge Haliburton, and more recently, and in greater bulk, by Mr. Murdoch. Of their works the colonists are justly proud, and when one reads the abundant events of interest with which the whole history of Nova Scotia is chequered, of its steady progress and loyalty as a colony, and of the men it has produced, one cannot wonder at the present distaste evinced by its population on being compelled to merge their compact history and individuality in that of the New Dominion.

An outline sketch of the physical geography of Acadie is what is here attempted, and a description of some of the striking features of this interesting *locale.*

Nova Scotia is a peninsula 256 miles in length, and about 100 in breadth ; a low plateau, sixteen miles wide, connects it with the continental province of New Brunswick. The greatest extension of the peninsula, like that

of similar geographical conformations in all parts of the
earth, is towards the south.   The actual trend of its Atlantic coast is from north-east to south-west—a direction
in which are extended its principal geological formations
agreeing with the course of the St. Lawrence and of the
Apellachian chain of mountains which terminate at Cape
Gaspé.   Its dependency, Cape Breton, is an island, 100
miles long, and eighty broad, separated from Nova Scotia
by the narrow, canal-like Gut of Canseau, in places but
half a mile in width—" a narrow transverse valley," says
the author of " Acadian Geology," " excavated by the
currents of the drift period."   The largest and the greater
proportion of the rivers flow across the province, through
often parallel basins, into the Atlantic, indicating a
general slope at right angles to the longer axis.   The
Shubenacadie is, however, a singular exception, rising
close to Halifax harbour on the Atlantic side of the province, and crossing with a sluggish and even current
through a fertile intervale country to the Bay of Fundy.
The Atlantic coasts of Nova Scotia are indented to a
wonderful extent by creeks and arms of the sea, often
running far inland—miniature representations of the
Scandinavian fiords.   As might be expected, as accom-
paniments to such a jagged coast-line, there are numerous
islands, shoals, and reefs, which render navigation dangerous, and necessitate frequent light-houses.   The
outlines of the western shores are much more regular,
with steep cliffs and few inlets, somewhat similar on
comparison with the same features of the continent itself
as displayed on its Atlantic and Pacific coasts.   To these
harbours and to the fisheries may be attributed the
position of the capital of Halifax on the Atlantic side.

All, or nearly all, the **best portion of the country, in an** agricultural point of view, lies in the interior and to the westward. The old capital, Port Royal, afterwards named by the English Annapolis Royal, has a most picturesque position at the head of a **beautiful bay, termed Anna-polis Basin, on the** western **side of the province, and is** backed by **the garden of Nova Scotia,** the Annapolis Valley, **which extends in a** direction parallel to the coast, sheltered on both **sides by steep** hills crowned with **maple forests** for more than sixty miles, **when** it termi-nates on the shores **of Minas** Basin **in the Grand Pré of** the French Acadians.

**The whole surface of the country is dotted with count-less lakes. Often occurring in** chains, these give **rise to** the larger rivers **which flow into the** Atlantic. **In fact,** all **the rivers issue directly from** lakes **as their head** waters ; these latter, **again,** being supplied by **forest** brooks rising **in elevated swamps. In the hollows of the** high lands are **likewise embosomed lakes of every variety** of form, and often quite isolated. **Deep and intensely** blue, their shores fringed with **rock boulders,** and gene-rally **containing several islands, they do much** to diversify the monotony **of the forest by their** frequency and pic-turesque scenery. **In a paper read before** the Nova-Scotian Institute **in 1865, the writer, Mr. Belt,** believes that the conformation of **the larger lake basins of Nova-Scotia is due** to glaciation, evidenced by **the deep fur-rows and** scratchings on their exposed rocks, the rounding of protuberant **bosses, and the** transportation **of** huge boulders—the Grand Lake **of** the Shubenacadie chain being **a** notable instance.

Although the country is most uneven, sometimes

boldly undulating, at others broken up in extremely irregular forms, the only absolute levels being marginal on the alluvial rivers, there are no lofty mountains in Nova Scotia. The Cobequid Hills, skirting Minas Basin towards the junction of the province with New Brunswick, are the most elevated, rising to 1200 feet above the sea. This chain runs for more than 100 miles nearly due east and west. No bare peaks protrude ; it is everywhere clothed with a tall luxuriant forest, with a predominance of beech and sugar-maple.

Very similar in its general physical features to Nova Scotia, New Brunswick is distinguished by bolder scenery, larger rivers, and greater dimensions of the more important conifers. From the forests in its northern part arise sugar-loaf mountains with naked summits—outlying peaks of the Alleghanies—which occur also in Maine, more frequently, and on a still larger scale. The mountain scenery where the Restigonche divides the Gaspé chain from the high lands of northern New Brunswick is magnificent ; and the aspects of Sussex Vale, and of the long valley of the Miramichi, are as charming as those of the intervales of Nova Scotia.

The little red sandstone island of Prince Edward, lying in a crescent-shape, in accordance with the coast lines of New Brunswick and Nova Scotia, in a deep southern bay of the Gulf of St. Lawrence, is the most fertile of the three provinces, and possesses the attractive scenery of high cultivation pleasantly alternating with wood and water.

The area of the Acadian provinces is as follows :—Of Nova Scotia, with Cape Breton, 18,600 square miles ; of New Brunswick, 27,100 square miles ; and of Prince

Edward Island, 2137 square miles. Their population, respectively, being nearly **332,000, 252,000, and** 81,000.

To the Geologist, the most interesting feature of modern discovery in a country long famous for its mineral wealth, is the wide **dissemination of gold in** the quartz veins **of** the metamorphic **rocks,** which occur on the Atlantic shore of Nova Scotia, stretching from Cape Sable to the Gut of Canseau, and extending to a great distance across **the province.** Its first discovery **is** currently supposed to have been made in 1861 in a brook near Tangier **harbour, about** sixty miles **from Halifax, and to have been** brought about by **a man,** stopping **to drink, perceiving a** particle of **the** precious metal shining amongst the pebbles. This led to an **extended research,** soon rewarded **by discovery of the matrix, and general** operations **accompanied** by fresh discoveries in **widely distant** points, **and thus,** perhaps, was fairly started **gold mining in Nova Scotia.** I believe, **however, that I am right in attributing the** honour of **being the first** gold finder **in the province to** my friend and quondam companion **in** the woods, Captain **C. L'Estrange of the Royal Artillery, and** understand that **his claim to** priority in this matter has been recently fully recognised **by the** Provincial Government ; **it being** satisfactorily **shown** that **he found** and brought in **specimens of gold in quartz from** surface rocks, **when** **moose-hunting in the eastern districts, some time** before the discoveries at Tangier. **The** Oven's **Head** diggings, **near Lunenburg, were discovered during the summer of** **the same year ; and the sea-beach below the cliffs at this** **locality afforded for a short time a golden harvest by** washing the sand and pounded shale **which had been**

silted into the fissures of the rocks below high water
mark. The gold thus obtained had of course come from
the cliff detritus—the result of the incessant dash of
Atlantic waves over a long period of time—and was soon
exhausted: the claims on the cliff, however have proved
valuable. Then followed the discovery of the highly-
prolific barrel-shaped quartz at Allen's farm, afterwards
known as the Waverley diggings, of the Indian Harbour
and Wine Harbour gold-fields on the Eastern Coast
beyond Tangier, and of others to the westward, at Gold
River and La Have. Farther back from the coast, and
towards the edge of the slate formation, the precious
metal has been found at Mount Uniacke, and in the most
northern extension of the granitic metamorphic strata
towards the Bay of Fundy, at a place called Little
Chester.

Though no small excitement naturally attended the
simultaneous and hitherto unexpected discovery of such
extensive gold areas, the development of the Nova-
Scotian gold mines has been conducted with astonishing
decorum and order : the robberies and bloodshed incident
on such a pursuit in wilder parts of America, or at the
Antipodes, have been here totally unknown. The individuals who prospected and took up claims, soon finding
the difficulty of remunerating themselves by their own
unaided labour, disposed of them for often very considerable sums to the companies of Nova-Scotians,
Germans, and Americans, which had been formed to
work the business methodically. Though constantly seen
glistening as specks in the quartz, close to the surface,
the metal was seldom disclosed in nuggets of great value,
and the operation of crushing alone (extracting the gold

by amalgamation with quicksilver) proved remunerative in the long run and when carried out extensively.

At the commencement of this important era in the economical history of Nova Scotia, the interest attached to the pursuit of gold-digging may be well imagined. Farm labourers, and farmers themselves, deserted their summer's occupation and hastened to the localities proclaimed as gold-fields. Shanties, camps, and stores appeared amongst the rough rocks which strewed the wilderness in the depths of the forest. At Tangier, when I visited it (the same summer in which gold was first discovered there),' a street had risen, with some three hundred inhabitants, composed of rude frame houses, bark camps, and tents. Flags flaunted over the stores and groggeries, and the characteristic American " store " displayed its motley merchandise as in the settlements. Anything could be here purchased, from a pickaxe to a crinoline. A similar scene was shortly afterwards presented at the Oven's Head ; whilst at the Waverley diggings, only ten miles distant from the capital of Nova Scotia, a perfect town has sprung up. This latter locality is famous for the singular formation of its gold-bearing quartz lodes, termed " The Barrels." These barrels were discovered on the hill-side at a small distance below the surface, and consisted of long trunk-like shafts of quartz enclosed in quartzite. They were arranged in parallel lines, and looked very like the tops of drains exposed for repair. At first they were found to be exceedingly rich in gold, some really fine nuggets having been displayed ; but subsequent research has proved them a failure, and the barrel formation has been abandoned for quartz occurring in veins of ordinary position. A German com-

pany established here has succeeded in obtaining large
profits, working the quartz veins by shafts sunk to a great
depth.  Their crushing mill, when I visited it, contained
sixteen ponderous "stampers" moved by water power.
Every three or four weeks an ingot was forwarded by
them to Halifax, weighing four or five hundred ounces.
Some beautiful specimens of gold in quartz of the
purest white, from this locality, were exhibited by
the Commissioners at the last great International Exhi-
bition.

Even at the present time it is impossible to form any
just estimation of the value of the Nova-Scotian gold-
fields.  Scientific men have given it as their opinion that
the main seat of the treasure has not yet been touched,
and that the present workings are but surface pickings.
Then, again, we may refer to the immense extent of the
Lower Silurian rocks on the Atlantic coast.  At one end
of the province, stretching back for some fifty miles, the
whole area of the formation has been stated to comprise
about 7000 square miles.  The wide dispersion over this
tract of casual gold discoveries and of the centres of
actual operations naturally lead to the belief that gold
mining is still in its infancy in Nova Scotia.

The yield of gold from the quartz veins is exceedingly
variable : some will scarcely produce half an ounce, others
as much as eight ounces to the ton.  I have seen a large
quartz pebble picked up on the road side between Halifax
and the Waverley diggings, rather larger than a man's
head, which was spangled and streaked with gold in every
direction, estimated in value at nearly one hundred
pounds.  It is curious to reflect for how many years that
valuable stone had been unwittingly passed by by the

needy settler returning from market to his distant farm on the Eastern Road. Now frequent roadside chippings strewed about attest the curiosity of the modern traveller through the gold districts.

Of much greater importance, however, to these colonies than the recently discovered gold-fields are their boundless resources as coal-producing countries, paralysed though their works may be at present by the pertinacious refusal on the part of the United States to renew the Reciprocity Treaty. To this temporary prostration an end must soon be put by the opening up of intercolonial commerce, to be brought about by the speedy completion of an uninterrupted railway communication between the Canadas and the Lower Provinces, and well-established commercial relations throughout the whole of the New Dominion.

The coal-fields of Acadie are numerous and of large area, the carboniferous system extending throughout the province of Nova Scotia, including Cape Breton, bounding the metamorphic belt of the Atlantic coast, and passing through the isthmus, which joins the two provinces, into New Brunswick, where it attains its broadest development. In the latter province, however, the actual coal seams are unimportant; and it is in certain localities in Nova Scotia and Cape Breton where the magnificent collieries of British North America are found, and from which it has been said the whole steam navy of Great Britain might be supplied for centuries to come, as well as the demands of the neighbouring colonies. It is impossible to over-estimate the political importance accruing from so vast a transatlantic storehouse of this precious mineral both to England and the colonists themselves, whilst

singularly enough, on the Pacific side of the continent,
and in British possession, occur the prolific coal-fields of
Vancouver's Island. "That the eastern and western
portals of British America," says Mr. R. G. Haliburton,*
"should be so favoured by nature, augurs well for the
New Dominion, which, possessing a vast tract of magnificent agricultural country between these extreme limits,
only requires an energetic, self-reliant people, worthy of
such a home, to raise it to a high position amongst
nations."

The grand coal column from the main seam of the
Albion mines at Pictou, exhibited at the last Great Exhi-
bition in London, will be long remembered. This seam
is 37 feet in vertical thickness. With iron of excellent
quality found abundantly and in the neighbourhood of
her great coal-fields, and fresh discoveries of various other
minerals of economic value being constantly made, Acadie
has all the elements wherewith to forge for herself the
armour-plated bulwark of great commercial prosperity.
And yet the shrewd capitalists of the Great Republic are
rapidly becoming possessed of the mineral wealth of the
country, almost unchallenged by provincial rivalry.

Considerably removed from the mainland, with a coast
line for some distance conforming to the direction of the
Gulf Stream, the northern edge of which closely approaches
its shores, the climate of Nova Scotia is necessarily most
uncertain; south-westerly winds are continually struggling
for mastery with the cold blasts which blow over the
continent from the north-west. In comparatively fine
weather in summer, the sea fog, which marks the mingling

---

* On the Coal Trade of the New Dominion, by R. G. Haliburton, F.S.A.,
F.R.S.N.A. : from " Proceedings of the N.S. Institute of Nat. Science."

of the warm waters of the great Atlantic current with
the colder stream which courses down the eastern coast
of Newfoundland from the Polar regions, carrying with
it troops of icebergs, is almost always hovering off the
land, from which it is barely repelled by the gentle west
winds from the continent. The funnel-shaped Bay of
Fundy, and the bight in the Nova-Scotian coast which
merges into the long harbour of Halifax are the strong-
holds of this obnoxious pall of vapour. A few miles
inland the west wind generally prevails ; indeed it is
often astonishing with what suddenness one emerges
from the fog on leaving the coast. A point or two of
change in the direction of the wind makes all the difference. I have often made the voyage from Halifax to
Cape Race—the exact course of the northern fog line—
alternating rapidly between sunshine and dismal and
dangerous obscurity as the wind veered in the least
degree on either side of our course. Past this, the south-
easternmost point of Newfoundland, the fog holds on its
way till the great banks are cleared : it seldom works up
the coast to the northward, and is of rare occurrence at
St. John's. St. John, New Brunswick, seems to be especially visited, though it has no footing in the interior of
that province.

Insidiously drawing around the mariner in these
waters in calm summer weather, the fog of the Gulf
Stream is always thickest at this season, although the
stratum of vapour scarcely reaches over the vessel's tops,
the moon or stars being generally visible from the deck
at night. Fog trumpets or lights are to a certain extent
useful precautions, yet even the strictest watch from the
bowsprit is often insufficient to avert collision.

In winter time the propinquity of the Gulf Stream produces frequent moderations of temperature. Deep falls
of snow are perpetually melting under its warm currents
of air when borne inland, though such phases are quickly
succeeded by a reassertion of true North American cold,
with a return of the north-west wind, arresting the thaw,
and encasing the steaming snow with a film of glace ice.

During the spring months again, the Arctic currents,
accompanied by easterly or north-easterly winds, exercise
a chilling influence on the climate of the Atlantic coast
of the Lower Provinces. Immense areas of field ice float
past the Nova-Scotian shores from the mouth of the St.
Lawrence and harbours of the Gulf, often working round
into Halifax harbour and obstructing navigation, whilst
vegetation is thereby greatly retarded.

The mirage observed on approaching these floating ice
plains at sea is very striking—mountains appear to grow
out of them, with waterfalls; towns, castles, and spires,
ever fleeting and varying in form. I have observed very
similar effects produced in summer, off the coast, on a
clear day, on a distant wall of sea fog, by evaporation.
As might be reasonably expected, the commingling of
two great currents emanating from such far distant
sources as do the Gulf and the Polar streams, must be
productive at their point of junction, of phenomena interesting to the ichthyologist. To the student of this
branch of natural history Halifax is an excellent position
for observation, and from the recorded memoranda of
Mr. J. M. Jones we find many curious meetings of
northern and southern types in the same waters—for
instance that of the albicore and the Greenland shark
(Thynnus vulgaris and Scymnus borealis)—the former a

well-known inhabitant of the tropics, the latter a true boreal form. Tropical forms of fish are of frequent occurrence in the Halifax market, and shoals of flying fish have been observed by Admiral Sir Alexander Milne in the Gulf Stream as far as 37 deg. 50 min. N.

A sketch, however slight, of the physical geography of the Acadian Provinces would be incomplete were notice to be omitted of the famous Bay of Fundy tide—a page of modern geological history much to be studied in elucidation of phenomena of ages long past, as pointed out by Dr. Dawson, the well-known author of a valuable scientific work termed " Acadian Geology." On the Atlantic seaboard at Halifax the rise of the spring tide is about six feet, a height attained at high water with but little variation throughout this coast. After passing Cape Sable, the southernmost extremity of the province, the portals of the bay may be said to be gained ; and here an appreciable rise occurs in the tidal wave of about three feet. Farther round, at Yarmouth, sixteen feet is the height at high water in spring tides, reaching to twenty-seven feet at Digby Gut, forty-three feet at Parsboro, and, at the mouth of the Shubenacadie River at the head of Cobequid Bay, occasionally attaining the extraordinary elevation of seventy feet above low water mark. In this, as well as in several other rivers discharging into the bay, the tide rushes up the channel for a considerable distance into the interior with an attendant phenomenon termed " the Bore,"—an advanced wave or wall of surging waters, some four feet above the level of the descending fresh water stream. The spectator, standing on the river bank, presently sees a procession of barges, boats, or Indian canoes, taking advantage

of this natural "Express" from the ocean, whirling past
him at some seven or eight miles per hour, whilst the
long shelving banks of red mud are quickly hidden
by the eager impulsive current. Out, in the open bay,
the eddying "rips" over the flats as the rising waters
cover them, or the tumultuous seas which rise where
the great tide is restrained by jutting headlands afford
still greater spectacles. With a strong wind blowing
in an opposite direction to the tide, the navigation of
the Bay of Fundy is perilous on a dark night, and
many are the victims engulfed with their little fishing smacks in its treacherous and ever-shifting shoals.
It wears a beautiful aspect, however, in fine summer
weather—a soft chalky hue quite different from the
stern blue of the sea on the Atlantic shores, and somewhat approaching the summer tints of the Channel on
the coasts of England. The surrounding scenery too is
beautiful; and the twelve hours' steam voyage from
Windsor, Nova Scotia, to St. John, the capital of New
Brunswick, past the picturesque headlands of Blomidon,
Cape Split, and Parsboro, in fine weather most enjoyable.
The red mud, or, rather, exceedingly fine sand, carried
by the surging waters, is deposited at high tide on the
flats and over the land overflown at the edges of the bay,
and thus have been produced the extensive salt marsh
lands which constitute the wealth of the dwellers by the
bay shores—soils which, never receiving the artificial
stimulus of manure, show no signs of exhaustion though
a century may have elapsed since their utilisation. The
occurrence of submerged forests, the stumps of which
still stand *in situ*, observed by Dr. Dawson, and indicating a great subsidence of the land in modern times, and

the frequent footprints of birds and animals on the successive depositions of mud, dried by the sun, and easily detached with the layers on which they were stamped, are interesting features in connection with the geology of this district.

The Fauna and Flora of the three provinces constituting Acadia (the name, though, is now seldom applied otherwise than poetically) are almost identical with those displayed on the neighbouring portions of the continent, in New England, and the Canadas, though of course, and as might be expected, a few species swell the lists of either kingdom further inland and on receding from the ocean. There are one or two noticeable differences between the provinces themselves. Thus, for instance, whilst the white cedar (Thuya occidentalis) is one of the most common of the New Brunswick coniferæ, frequent up to its junction with Nova Scotia, there are but one or two isolated patches of this tree existing, or ever known to exist, in the latter province, and these not found near the isthmus, but on the shores of the Bay of Fundy, near Granville. Again, not a porcupine exists on the island of Cape Breton, though abundant in Nova Scotia up to the strait of Canseau, in places scarcely half a mile broad. The migratory wild pigeon, formerly equally abundant in New Brunswick and Nova Scotia, has now entirely deserted the latter, though still numerous in summer in the former province.

The Canadian deer (Cervus virginianus), common in New Brunswick, has never crossed the isthmus ; and the wolf (Canis occidentalis), though now and then entering Nova Scotia, apparently cannot make up its mind to stay, though there is an amplitude of wilderness country :

c

seen at long intervals of time in different parts of the
province, and almost simultaneously, it rapidly scours
over the country, and retires to the continent.

There are no deer now indigenous to Prince Edward's
Island, though the cariboo was formerly found there in
abundance. The Morse or Walrus, once numerous on
the coasts, seems to have entirely disappeared even
from the most northern parts of the Gulf : it was once
common in the St. Lawrence as far up as the Saguenay.
Another disappearance from the coast of Nova Scotia
is that of the Snow Goose (Anser hyperboreus), now
seldom seen south of the St. Lawrence.

Of the former presence of the Great Auk (Alca im-
pennis) in the neighbourhood of the Gulf, it is to be
regretted that there are no living witnesses, or even
existing traditions. That it was once a resident on the
shores of Newfoundland is shown by the specimens
found in guano on the Funk Islands entombed under
ice. As has probably happened in the case of this bird,
it is to be feared that the retirement of other members of
the true Boreal Fauna within more Arctic limits forebodes
a gradual, though often inexplicable, progress towards
extinction.

The newly-arrived emigrant or observant visitor cannot fail to be impressed with the similarity of forms in
both the animal and the vegetable kingdoms to those
of western Europe, here presented. To the Englishman
unaccustomed to northern fir forests and their accompanying flora, the woods are naturally the strangest
feature in the country—the density of the stems in the
jagged forest lines which bound the settlements, the long
parallel-sided openings, cut out by the axe, which mark

the new clearings, where crops are growing rankly amongst
the stumps, roots, and rock boulders which still strew
the ground, and the wild tanglement of bushes and briars
on half-reclaimed ground—but in the fields and uplands
of a thoroughly cleared district he is scarcely reminded
of a difference in the scene from that to which he has
been accustomed. In the pastures he sees English
grasses, with the buttercup, the ox-eye, and the dandelion;
the thistle and many a well known weed are recognised
growing by the meadow-side, with the wild rose and the
blackberry, as in English hedge-rows. Though the house-
sparrow and the robin are missed, and he is surprised to
find the latter name applied everywhere to the numerous
red-breasted thrushes which hop so fearlessly about the
pastures, he finds much to remind him of bird life at
home. Swallows and martins are as numerous, indeed
more so ; the tit-mouse, the wren, and the gold-crest are
found to be almost identical with those of the old
country, the former being closely analogous in every
respect to the small blue tit, and many of the warblers
and flycatchers have much in common with their Transatlantic representatives. The rook is not here, but its place
is taken by flocks of the common American crow, often
as gregarious in its habits as the former, whilst the
various birds of prey present most striking similarities
of plumage when compared with those of Europe; and
the appropriateness of calling the American species the
same common names as are applied to the goshawk,
sparrowhawk, or osprey, is at once admitted. The wasp,
the bee, and the house-fly, present no appreciable differences, nor can the visitor detect even a shade of distinction in many of the butterflies.

The seafaring man arriving from Europe will find even less of divergence amongst the finny tribes and the sea-fowl on these coasts, and indeed will not pretend to assert a difference in most cases.

The very interesting question thus readily suggests itself to the naturalist—in what light are many analogous forms in Western Europe and Atlantic North America to be regarded in reference to each other? The identity of the species which almost continuously range the circum-arctic zoological province is perfectly well established in such instances as those of the arctic fox, the white bear, and of many of the Cetaceæ and Phocidæ amongst mammals; of the eiders, common and king, the pintail and others of the Anatidæ, and of the sturgeon, capelin, herring, and probably the sea-salmon amongst fishes. Nor could the fact be reasonably doubted in the case of creatures which are permanent residents of a limited circumpolar zone, or even in that of the migratory species which affect polar regions for a season, and thence regularly range south-wards over the diverging continents. The question, how-ever, which is offered for solution is respecting those analogous forms which have apparently permanent habi-tats in the Old and New Worlds, and have always remained (as far as is known) geographically isolated. With regard to the arctic deer the author's considerations will be found given at some length, but there are many other analogies in the fauna and flora of the two hemi-spheres, which, on comparison, naturally lead to a dis-cussion on the subject of local variation, and as to how far the system of classification is to be thus modified.

Buffon's idea that many of the animals of the New World were the descendants of Old World stock would

seem not only to be set aside but reversed in argument
by a new and growing belief that transmission of species
has extensively occurred from America to Europe and
Asia. "America," says Hugh Miller, "though emphati-
cally the New World in relation to its discovery by
civilized man, is, at least in these regions, an old world
in relation to geological type, and it is the so-called old
world that is in reality the new one. Sir Charles Lyell,
in the "Antiquity of Man," states that "Professors
Unger and Heer have advanced, on botanical grounds
the former existence of an Atlantic continent, during
some part of the tertiary period, as affording the only
plausible explanation that can be imagined of the
analogy between the miocene flora of Central Europe and
the existing flora of Eastern America. Other naturalists,
again, have supposed this to have been effected through
an overland communication existing between America
and Eastern Asia in the direction of the Aleutian
Islands. Sir George Simpson has stated that almost
direct proof exists of the American origin of the
Tchuktchi of Siberia; whilst it would appear that
primitive customs and traditions in many parts of the
globe are being traced to aboriginal man existing in
America.

Professor Lawson, of Dalhousie College, Halifax, N.S.,
in referring to the recent and well-established discovery
of heather (Calluna vulgaris) as indigenous to the
Acadian provinces, observes, "The occurrence of this
common European plant in such small quantities in
isolated localities on the American continent is very in-
structive, and obviously points to a period when the heath
was a widely-spread social plant in North America, as it is

still in Europe where oft-recurring fires are yearly lessen-
ing its range. In Calluna we have probably an example
of a species on the verge of extinction as an American
species, while maintaining a vigorous and abundant
growth in Europe. If so, may not Europe be indebted
to America for Calluna, and not America to Europe ?"

With such scanty data, however, valuable indeed as
they are in building up theories, but few and uncertain
steps can be made towards solving so important a question. An irresistible conclusion is however forced on the
mind of the naturalist that in many of the analogies he
meets with in animal or vegetable life in this portion of
the New World it is not fair to call them even types of
those of the Old ; they are analogous species.

# CHAPTER II.

A GLANCE at a physical map of the country will serve to show the relative position of the main bodies of the North American forest, the division of the woods where the wedge-shaped north-western corner of the plains comes in, and their well-defined limit on the edge of the barren grounds, coincident with the line of perpetual ground frost.

Characterised by a predominance of coniferous trees, the great belt of forest country which constitutes the hunting grounds of the Hudson's Bay Company, has its nearest approach to the Arctic Ocean in the Mackenzie Valley, becoming ever more and more stunted and monotonous until it merges at length into the barren waste.

In its southern extension, on meeting the northern extremity of the prairies, it branches into two streams— the one directed along the Pacific coast line and its great mountain chain ; the other crossing the continent diagonally between the boundaries of the plains and Hudson's Bay towards the Atlantic. On this course the forest soon receives important accessions of new forms of trees, gradually introduced on approaching the lake district, and loses much of its sterner character.

The oak, beech, and maple groves of the Canadas are equally characteristic of the forest scenery of these regions, with the white pine or the hemlock spruce.

On approaching the Atlantic seaboard, the forest is again somewhat impoverished by the absence of those forms which seem to require an inland climate. In the forests of Acadie many Canadian trees found farther westward in the same latitude are wanting, or of so rare occurrence as to exercise no influence on the general features of the country, such as the hickory and the butternut. "In Nova Scotia," says Professor Lawson, "the preponderance of northern species is much greater than in corresponding latitudes in Canada, and many of our common plants are in Western Canada either entirely northern, or strictly confined to the great swamps, whose cool waters and dense shade form a shelter for northern species."

Though certain soils and physical conformations of the country occasionally favour exclusive growths of either, the woods of the Lower Provinces display a pleasing mixture of what are locally termed hard and soft wood trees—in other words, of deciduous and evergreen vegetation. Broken only by clearings and settlements in the lines of alluvial valleys, roads, or important fishing or mining stations, the forest still obtains over large sections of the country, notwithstanding continued and often wanton mutilation by the axe, and the immense area annually devastated by fire. The fierce energy of American vegetation, if allowed, quickly fills up gaps, and the burnt, blackened waste is soon re-clothed with the verdure of dense copses of birch and aspen.

The true character of the American forest is not to

be studied from the road-side or along the edges of
the cleared lands.   To read its mysteries aright, we must
plunge into its depths and live under its shelter through
all the phases of the seasons, leaving far behind the sound
of the settler's axe and the tinkling of his cattle-bells.
The strange feelings of pleasure attached to a life
in the majestic solitudes of the pine forests of North
America cannot be attained by a merely marginal
acquaintance.

On entering the woods, the first feature which naturally strikes us is the continual occurrence of dense copses
of young trees, where a partial clearing has afforded a
chance to the profusely sown germs to spring up and
perpetuate the ascendancy of vegetation, though of
course, in the struggle for existence, but few of these
would live to assert themselves as forest trees.   As we
advance we perceive a taller and straighter growth, and
observe that many species, which in more civilised
districts are mere ornamental shrubs, throwing out their
feathery branches close to the ground, now assume the
character of forest trees with clean straight stems,
though somewhat slender withal, engendering the belief
that, left by themselves in the open, they would offer but
a short resistance to wintry gales.   The foliage predomi-
nates at the tree top ; the stems (especially of the
spruces) throw out a profusion of spikes and dead
branchlets from the base upwards.   Unhealthy situations, such as cold swamps, are marked by the utmost
confusion.   Everywhere, and at every variety of angle,
trees lean and creak against their comrades, drawing a
few more years of existence through their support.   The
foot is being perpetually lifted to stride over dead stems,

sometimes so intricately interwoven that the traveller
becomes fairly pounded for the nonce.

This tangled appearance, however, is an attribute of
the spruce woods ; there is a much more orderly arrangement under the hemlocks. These grand old trees seem
to bury their dead decently, and long hillocks in the
mossy carpet alone mark their ancestors' graves, which
are generally further adorned by the evergreen tresses
of the creeping partridge-berry, or the still more delicate
festoons of the capillaire.

The busy occupation of all available space in the
American forest by a great variety of shrubs and herbaceous plants, constitutes one of its principal charms—the
multitudes of blossoms and delicate verdure arising from
the sea of moss to greet our eyes in spring, little maple
or birch seedlings starting up from prostrate trunks or
crannies of rock boulders, with wood violets, and a host
of the spring flora. The latter, otherwise rough and
shapeless objects, are thus invested with a most pleasing
appearance—transformed into the natural flower vases of
the woods. The abundance of the fern tribe, again, lends
much grace to the woodland scenery. In the swamp the
cinnamon fern, O. cinnamomea, with O. interrupta, attain
a luxuriant growth ; and the forest brook is often almost
concealed by rank bushes of royal fern (O. regalis).
Rocks in woods are always topped with polypodium,
whilst the delicate fronds of the oak fern hang from their
sides. Filix fœmina and F. mas are common everywhere, and, with many others of the list, present apparently inappreciable differences to their European representatives.

There is a beauty peculiar to this interesting order

especially pleasing to the eye when studying details of a landscape in which the various forms of vegetation form the leading features. The luxuriant mosses and great lichens which cover or cling to everything in the forest act a similar part. Even the dismal black swamps are somewhat enlivened by the long beards of the Usnea; fallen trees are often made quite brilliant by a profusion of scarlet cups of Cladonia gracilis.

But now let us examine further into the specific character of at least some of the individuals of which the forest is composed. As we wander on we chance, perhaps, to stumble upon what is called, in woodsman's *parlance*, a "blazed line"—a broad chip has been cut from the side of a tree, and the white surface of the inner wood at once catches the eye of the watchful traveller; a few paces farther on some saplings have been cut, and, keeping the direction, we perceive in the distance another blazed mark on a trunk. It may be a path leading from the settlement to some distant woodland meadow of wild grass, or a line marking granted property, or it may lead to a lot of timber trees marked for the destructive axe of the lumberer—perhaps a grove of White Pine. This is the great object of the lumberer's search. Ascending a tree from which an extensive view of the wild country is commanded, he marks the tall overbearing summits of some distant pine grove (for this tree is singularly gregarious, and is generally found growing in family groups), and having taken its bearings with a compass, descends, and with his comrades proceeds on his errand of destruction. In the neighbourhood of the coast, or on barren soil, the pine is a stunted bushy tree, its branches feathering nearly to the ground; but the pine of the forest ascends as a straight

tower to the height of some 120 feet, two or three massive branches being thrown out in twisted and fantastic
attitudes.  As if aware of its proud position as monarch
of the forest, it is often found on the summit of a precipice ; and these conspicuous positions, which it seems to
prefer, have doomed this noble specimen of the cone-
bearing evergreens to ultimate extermination as certain
as that of the red man or the larger game of this continent.  Some half-century since, the pine was found on
the margins of all the large lakes and streams, but of late
the axe and devastating fires have, as it were, driven the
tree far back into the remoter solitudes of the forest, and
long and expensive expeditions must be undertaken ere
the head-quarters of a gang of lumber-men can be fixed
upon for a winter employment.  At the head waters of
some insignificant brook, and in the neighbourhood of
good timber, these hardy sons of the forest fell the trees,
and cut and square them into logs, dragging them to the
edge of the stream, into whose swollen waters they are
rolled at the breaking up of winter and melting of the
snow, to find their way through almost endless difficulties
to the sea.  That most useful animal in the woods, the
ox, accompanies the lumberers to their remote forest
camps, and drags the logs to the side of the stream.  It
is really wonderful to watch these animals, well managed,
performing their laborious tasks in the forest : urged on
and directed solely by the encouraging voice of the team-
ster, the honest team drag the huge pine-log over the
rough inequalities of the ground, over rocks, and through
treacherous swamps and thickets, with almost unaccountable ease and safety, where the horse would at once become confused, frightened, and injured, besides failing on

THE LUMBERER'S CAMP IN WINTER

the score of comparative strength. Slowly but surely the ox performs incredible feats of draught in the woods, and asks for no more care than the shelter of a rough shed near the lumberers' camp, with a store of coarse wild hay, and a drink at the neighbouring brook.

This aristocrat of the forest, Pinus strobus, refuses to grow in the black swamp or open bog, which it leaves to poverty-stricken spruces and larches, nor in its communities will it tolerate much undergrowth. Pine woods are peculiarly open and easy to traverse. Bracken, and but little else, grows beneath, and the foot treads noiselessly on a soft slippery surface of fallen tassels. A peculiarly soft subdued light pervades these groves—a ray here and there falling on the white blossoms of the pigeon berry (Cornus Canadensis) in summer, or, later, on its bright scarlet clusters of berries, sets frequent sparkling gems in our path. That beautiful forest music termed *soughing* in Scotland, in reference to the sound of the wind passing over the foliage of the Scotch fir, is heard to perfection amongst the American pines.

The white pine, according to Sir J. Richardson, ranges as far to the northward as the south shore of Lake Winipeg. "Even in its northern termination," he says, " it is still a stately tree."

The Hemlock, or Hemlock Spruce (Abies Canadensis of Michaux), is a common tree in the woodlands of Acadie, affecting moist mossy slopes in the neighbourhood of lakes, though generally mixing with other evergreens in all situations. It is found, however, of largest growth (80 feet), and growing in large groves, principally in the former localities, where it vies with the white pine in its solid proportions. The deeply grained columnar

trunk throws off its first branches some 50 feet above the
ground, and the light feathery foliage clings round the
summit of an old tree in dense masses, from which protrude the bare twisted limbs which abruptly terminate
the column.

Perched high up in its branches may be often seen in
winter the sluggish porcupine, whose presence aloft is
first detected by the keen eye of the Indian through the
scratches made by its claws on the trunk in ascending its
favourite tree to feed on the bark and leaves of the
younger shoots.

Large groves of hemlock growing on woodland slopes
present a noble appearance ; their tall columns never
bend before the gale. There is a general absence of
undergrowth, thus affording long vistas through the
shady grove of giants ; and the softened light invests the
interior of these vast forest cathedrals with an air of
solemn mystery, whilst the even spread of their mossy
carpet affords appreciable relief to the footsore hunter.
The human voice sounds as if confined within spacious
and lofty halls.

Hawthorne, describing the wooded solitudes in which
he loved to wander, thus speaks of a grove of these
trees :—" These ancient hemlocks are rich in many things
beside birds. Indeed, their wealth in this respect is
owing mainly, no doubt, to their rank vegetable growths,
their fruitful swamps, and their dark, sheltered retreats.

" Their history is of an heroic cast. Ravished and
torn by the tanner in his thirst for bark, preyed upon by
the lumberman, assaulted and beaten back by the settler,
still their spirit has never been broken, their energies
never paralysed. Not many years ago a public highway

passed through them, but it was at no time a tolerable road ; trees fell across it, mud and limbs choked it up, till finally travellers took the hint and went around ; and now, walking along its deserted course, I see only the footprints of coons, foxes, and squirrels.

"Nature loves such woods, and places her own seal upon them. Here she shows me what can be done with ferns and mosses and lichens. The soil is marrowy and full of innumerable forests. Standing in these fragrant aisles, I feel the strength of the vegetable kingdom and am awed by the deep and inscrutable processes of life going on so silently about me.

"No hostile forms with axe or spud now visit these solitudes. The cows have half-hidden ways through them, and know where the best browsing is to be had. In spring the farmer repairs to their bordering of maples to make sugar ; in July and August women and boys from all the country about penetrate the old Barkpeeling for raspberries and blackberries ; and I know a youth who wonderingly follows their languid stream casting for trout.

"In like spirit, alert and buoyant, on this bright June morning go I also to reap my harvest,—pursuing a sweet more delectable than sugar, fruit more savoury than berries, and game for another palate than that tickled by trout." *

Hemlock bark, possessing highly astringent properties, is much used in America for tanning purposes, almost

---

* There is no mistaking the authorship of this passage from the note-books of Nathaniel Hawthorne. It is not embodied in the recently published English edition of his notes ; I found it in a contribution of his to an American periodical many years since, and preserved it as a gem.

entirely superseding that of the oak. Its surface is very
rough with deep grooves between the scales. Of a light
pearly gray outside, it shows a madder brown tint when
chipped. The sojourner in the woods seeks the dry and
easily detached bark which clings to an old dead hemlock as a great auxiliary to his stock of fuel for the camp
fire ; it burns readily and long, emitting an intense heat,
and so fond are the old Indians of sitting round a small
conical pile of the ignited bark in their wigwams, that
it bears in their language the sobriquet of "the old
Grannie."

The hemlock, as a shrub, is perhaps the most ornamental of all the North American evergreens. It has
none of that tight, stiff, old-fashioned appearance so generally seen in other spruces : the graceful foliage droops
loosely and irregularly, hiding the stem, and, when each
spray is tipped with the new season's shoot of the
brightest sea-green imaginable, the appearance is very
beautiful. The young cones are likewise of a delicate
green.

This tree has a wide range in the coniferous woodlands of North America, extending from the Hudson's
Bay territory to the mountains of Georgia. The great
southerly extension of the northern forms of trees on the
south-east coast, is due to the direction of the Allegha-
nian range, which, commencing in our own province of
vegetation, carries its flora as far south as 35 degrees
north latitude, elevation affording the same conditions of
growth as distance from the equator.

It would appear that this giant spruce has no analogous form in the Old World as have others of the genus
Abies found in the New. All the genera of conifers,

however, here contain a larger number of trees, which, though they are exceedingly similar in general appearance, are specifically distinct from their European congeners.

Under the Arctic circle, as pointed out by Sir J. Richardson, and beyond the limits of tree growth, but little appreciable difference exists in circumpolar vegetation, and so we recognise in the luxuriant cryptogamous flora of the forests we are describing most of the mosses and lichens found across the Atlantic, which here attain such a noticeable development. As with nobler forms, America, however, adds many new species to the list.

The Black Spruce is one of the most conspicuous and characteristic forest trees of North-Eastern America, forming a large portion of the coniferous forest growth, and found in almost every variety of circumstance. Sometimes it appears in mixed woods, of beautiful growth and of great height, its numerous branches drooping in graceful curves from the apex towards the ground, which they sweep to a distance of twenty to thirty feet from the stem, whilst the summit terminates in a dense arrow head, on the short sprays of which are crowded heavy masses of cones. At others, it is found almost the sole growth, covering large tracts of country, the trees standing thick, with straight clean stems and but little foliage except at the summit. Then there is the black spruce swamp, where the tree shows by its contortions, its unhealthy foliage, and its stem and limbs shaggy with usnea, the hardships of its existence. Again on the open bog grows the black spruce, scarcely higher than a cab-

bage sprout *—the light olive-green foliage living on
the compressed summit only, whilst the grey dead twigs
below are crowded with pendulous moss ; yet even here,
amidst the cold sphagnum, Indian cups, and cotton grass,
the tree lives to an age which would have given it a
proud position in the dry forest.   Lastly, in the fissure of
a granite boulder may be seen its hardy seedling ; and
the little plant has a far better chance of becoming a tree
than its brethren in the swamp; for, one day, as frost and
increasing soil open the fissure, its roots will creep out and
fasten in the earth beneath.

In unhealthy situations a singular appearance is frequently assumed by this tree.   Stunted, of course, it
throws out its arms in the most tortuous shapes, suddenly terminating in a dense mass of innumerable
branchlets of a rounded contour like a beehive, display-
ing short, thick, light green foliage.   The summit of
the tree generally terminates in another bunch.   The
stem and arms are profusely covered with lichens and
usnea.   As a valuable timber tree the black spruce ranks
next to the pine, attaining a height of seventy to a hundred feet.   Being strong and elastic, it forms excellent
material for spars and masts, and is converted into all
descriptions of sawed lumber—deals, boards, and scant-
lings.   From its young sprays is prepared the decoction,

---

* Indeed these miniature trees in bogs where the sphagnum perpetually
bathes their roots with chilling moisture, have a very similar appearance to
Brussels sprouts on a large scale.   The water held in the moss is always
cold : on May 5th, 1866, the tussacs of sphagnum were frozen solidly
within two or three inches of the surface.   The centre of these bogs, often
called cariboo bogs by reason of this deer frequenting them in search of
the lichen, Cladonia rangiferinus, is generally quite bare of spruce clumps,
which fringe the edge of the surrounding forest, the trees increasing in
height as they recede from the open bog.

fermented with molasses, the celebrated spruce beer of the American settler, a cask of which every good farmer's wife keeps in the hot, thirsty days of haymaking. To the Indian, the roots of this tree, which shoot out to a great distance immediately under the moss, are his rope, string and thread. With them he ties his bundle, fastens the birch-bark coverings to the poles of his wigwam, or sews the broad sheets of the same material over the ashen ribs of his canoe.

For ornamental purposes in the open and cultivated glebe the black spruce is very appropriate. The numerous and gracefully curved branches, the regular and acute cone shape of the mass, its clear purplish-grey stem, and the beautiful bloom with which its abundant cones are tinged in June, all enhance the picturesqueness of a tree which is long-lived, and, moreover, never outgrows its ornamental appearance, unless confined in dense woodland swamps.

The bark of the black spruce is scaly, of various shades of purplish-grey, sometimes approaching to a reddish hue, hence, doubtless, suggesting a variety under the name of red spruce, which is in reality a form depending on situation. In the latter, the foliage being frequently of a lighter tinge of green, strengthens the supposition. No specific differences have, however, been detected between the trees.

The White Spruce or Sea Spruce of the Indians (Abies alba, Mich.) is a conifer of an essentially boreal character. Indeed in its extension into our own woodlands it appears to prefer bleak and exposed situations. It thrives on our rugged Atlantic shores, and grows on exposed and brine-washed sands where no other vegetation ap-

pears, and hence is very useful, both as a shelter to the
land, and as holding it against the encroachment of the
sea. Its dark glaucous foliage assumes an almost impene-
trable aspect under these circumstances. I have seen
groves of white spruce on the shore, the foliage of which
was swept back over the land by prevailing gales from
the south-west, nearly parallel to the ground, and so
compressed and flattened at the top that a man could
walk on them as on a platform, whilst the shelter beneath was complete.

The Balsam Fir growing in these situations assumes a
very similar appearance in the density and colour of its
foliage and trunk to the white spruce, from which, however, it can be quickly distinguished, on inspection, by
the pustules on the bark and its erect cones. In the
forest the white spruce is rare in comparison with the
black, whose place it however altogether usurps on the
sand hills bordering the limit of vegetation in the far
north-west. The former tree prefers humid and rocky
woods.

Our Silver Fir (Abies balsamea, Marshall) is so like the
European picea that they would pass for the same
species were it not for the balsam pustules which characterise the American tree. Both show the same silvery
lines under the leaf on each side of the mid-rib, which,
glistening in the sun as the branches are blown upwards
by the wind, give the tree its name. We find it in moist
woods—growing occasionally in the provinces to a height
of sixty feet where it has plenty of room—a handsome,
dark-foliaged tree ; short-lived, however, and often falling
before a heavy gale, showing a rotten heart.

The silver fir is remarkable for the horizontal regularity

of its branches, and the general exact conical formation of the whole tree. An irregularity in the growth of the foliage, similar to that occurring in the black spruce, is frequently to be found in the fir. A contorted branch, generally half-way up the stem, terminates in a multitude of interlaced sprays which are, every summer, clothed with very delicate, flaccid, light-green leaves, forming a beehive shape like that of the spruce. It may be noticed, however, that whilst this bunch foliage is perennial in the case of the latter tree, that of the fir is annually deciduous. Up to a certain age the silver fir in the forest is a graceful shrub. Its flat delicate sprays form the best bedding for the woodman's couch; the fragrance of its branches, when long cut or exposed to the sun, is delicious, and their soft elasticity is most grateful to the limbs of the wearied hunter on his return to camp. The bark of the larger trees, peeling readily in summer, is used in sheets to cover the lumberer's shanty, which he now takes the opportunity to build in prospect of the winter's campaign.

The large, erect, sessile cones of the balsam fir are very beautiful in the end of May, when they are of a light sea-green colour, which, changing in June to pale lavender, in August assumes a dark slaty tint. They ripen in the fall; and the scale being easily detached, the seeds are soon scattered by the autumnal gales, leaving the axis bare and persistent on the branch for many years. In June each strobile is surmounted with a large mass of balsam exudation.

A casual observer, on passing the edges of the forest, cannot help remarking the brown appearance of the spruce tops in some seasons when the cones are unusually abundant. They are crowded together in bushels, and often kill the upper part of the tree and its leading shoot, after which a new leader appears to be elected amongst the nearest tier of branchlets to continue the upward growth. From such a crop the Indians augur an unusually hard winter, through much the same process of reasoning as that which the English countryman adopts in prophesying a rigorous season from an abundant crop of haws and other autumnal hedge fruits, and generally with about the same chance of fulfilment.

No less majestic than the coniferæ are many of the species of deciduous trees, or "hard woods," which, intermingled with the former, impart such a pleasing aspect to the otherwise gloomy fir forests of British North America. Growing, as the firs, with tall straight stems, and struggling upwards for the influence of the sunlight on their lofty foliage, the yellow and black birches aspire to the greatest elevation, attaining a height of seventy or eighty feet. Mixed with these are beeches and elms; and in many districts the country is covered with an almost exclusive growth of the useful rock or sugar-maple.

In these "mixed woods," as they are locally termed (indicative, it is said, of a good soil), the prettiest contrast is afforded by the pure white stems of the canoe birch (Betula papyracea) against the spruce boughs; and, as these are generally open woods, the latter come sweeping down to the ground. The young stems of the yellow birch (B. excelsa) gleam like gilded rods in sunlight; their shining yellow bark looks as though it had been fresh coated with varnish.

These American birches are a beautiful family of trees,

particularly the canoe or paper **birch, so called from the** readiness with which its folds of bark will **separate from** the stem like thick sheets of paper. Smooth and round, without a knot or branch for some **forty feet from the** ground, is the tree which the Indian anxiously looks for; it affords him the broad sheets of bark which cover his **wigwam and the frame of his canoe,** and long journeys does he often undertake **in search of it.** The bark is thick as leather, **and as** pliable, and in the summer can readily **be** separated for any distance up the stem. From it the Indians make the boxes and curiosities, **by** the sale of which these poor creatures endeavour to earn a livelihood. Their fanciful goods **cannot,** however, **compete** with the useful productions of civilised labour, **and are** only bought by the stranger and the charitable. **The** white birch of the forest **is as** closely connected with the interests of the Indian **as the pine is** with those of **the** lumberer, and the former dreads the **ultimate comparative** scarcity of the birch as the latter does that of the noble timber-tree.

From the mountains of Virginia, on the south-east, this important tree ranges **northwardly in** Atlantic America far **into** the interior of Labrador, whilst in the **extreme north-west it ascends the valley of the Mackenzie** as far as 69 degrees **N. lat.**

In travelling the forest in summer **it is quite refreshing** to enter the bright sheen of a birch-covered hill, exchanging the close resinous atmosphere of heated fir-woods **for** its cool open vaults. **The transition** is often **quite sudden** —the scene changing from **gloom** to brightness with a magical effect. Such a **contrast is presented to** the marked lights and **shades** of the pine forest! The silvery

stems with their light canopy of sunlit leaves, through
the breaks in which the blue sky shows quite dark as a
background, the innumerable lights falling on the light
green undergrowth of plants and shrubs beneath, and the
general absence of appreciable lines of shadow everywhere, stamp these hard-wood hills with an almost fairy-
land appearance.

If at all near the borders of civilisation, we soon strike
a "hauling road," leading from such localities into the
settlements—a track broad enough for a sled and pair of
oxen to pass over when the farmer comes in winter to
transport his firewood over the snow.  And a goodly
stock indeed he requires to battle with the cold of a
North American winter in the backwoods ; logs, such as
it would take two men to lift, of birch, beech or maple,
are piled on his ample hearth ; the abundance of fuel
and the readiness with which he can bring it from the
neighbouring bush, is one of his greatest blessings.  He
deserves a few comforts, for perhaps his lifetime, and that
of his father, has been spent in redeeming the few acres
round the dwelling from the fangs of gigantic stumps
and boulders of rock.  A patch of potatoes, an acre or
so of buckwheat, and another of oats, and a few rough-
looking cattle, are his sources of wealth, or perhaps a
rough saw mill, constructed far up in the forest brook,
and the whirr of whose circular saw disturbs only the
wild animals of the surrounding woods.

How vividly is recalled to my memory the delight
experienced on many occasions by our tired, belated
party, returning from a hunting camp through unknown
woods, on finding one of these logging roads, anticipating
in advance the kindly welcome of the invariably hospit-

able backwoods farmer, towards whose clearings it was sure to trend. Perhaps for hours before **we** had almost despaired of quitting the forest by nightfall. **On sending** the Indians into tree-tops to reconnoitre, the disheartening cry would be, "Woods all round as far as we can **see.**" Further on, perhaps, we should hear that there **were** "Lakes **all round** !" **Worse again,** for then a wearisome detour must be made. But at last some one finds signs of chopping, then a stack **of cord-wood,** and then we strike a regular blazed line. Now **the** spirits of every one revive, and we soon emerge on the **forest road with** its clean-cut track, corduroy platforms through swamps, and rude log bridges over the brooks, **which brings us** within the welcome sound **of** cattle bells, and at length to the broad glare of the clearings.

Before leaving the woods, however, we may not **omit** to notice those characteristic trees of the American **forest,** the maples, particularly that most important member of the family, the rock or sugar maple—Acer saccharinum. Found generally interspersed with other hard-wood trees, this tree is seen of largest and most frequent growth in the Acadian forests on the slopes of the Cobequid hills, and other similar ranges in Nova Scotia, often growing together in **large clumps.** Such groves are termed "Sugaries," **and are yearly visited by** the settlers for the plentiful supply of sap which, in the early spring, courses between the bark and the wood, and from which the maple sugar **is** extracted. Towards the end of March, when winter is relaxing its hold, and the hitherto **frozen** trees begin to feel **the** influence of the sun, **the** settlers, old and young, turn into the woods with their axes, sap-troughs, and boilers, and commence the operation of sugar-making. A fine young maple is selected; an oblique incision made by two strokes of the axe at a few feet from the ground, and the pent-up sap immediately begins to trickle and drop from the wound. A wooden spout is driven in, and the trough placed underneath; next morning a bucketful of clear sweet sap is removed and taken to the boiling-house. Sometimes two or three hundred trees are tapped at a time, and require the attention of a large party of men. At the camp, the sap is carefully boiled and evaporated until it attains the consistency of syrup. At this stage much of it is used by the settlers under the name of "maple honey, or molasses." Further boiling; and on pouring small quantities on to' pieces of ice, it suddenly cools and contracts, and in this stage is called "maple-wax," which is much prized as a sweetmeat. Just beyond this point the remaining sap is poured into moulds, in which as it cools it forms the solid saccharine mass termed "maple sugar." Sugar may also be obtained, though inferior in quality, from the various birches; but the sap of these trees is slightly acidulous, and is more often converted into vinegar.

White or soft maple (A. dasycarpum), and the red flowering maple (A. rubrum), are equally common trees. Both contribute largely to the gorgeous colouring of the fall, and the latter species clothes its leafless sprays in the spring almost as brilliantly with scarlet blossoms. Before these fade, a circlet of light green leaves appears below, when a terminal shoot has a fitting place in an ornamental bouquet of spring flowers.

As a rule, all the Aceraceæ are noted for breadth of leaf, and, being even more abundant than the birches in

the forests of Acadie, the solid appearance of the rolling
hard-wood hills is thus accounted for.   These great
swelling billows in a sea of verdure form the grandest
feature of American forest scenery.   In Vermont and
New Hampshire, to the westward of our provinces, they
become perfectly tempestuous.   The black arrow-heads
of the spruces, or the slanting tops of the pines, pierce
through them distinctly enough, but the summits of the
hard-woods are blended together in one vast canopy of
light green foliage, in which the eye vainly seeks to trace
individual form.

Amongst the varieties of scenery presented by our
wild districts, I would notice the burnt barrens.   These
sometimes extend for many miles, and are most dreary in
their appearance and painfully tedious to travel through.
Years ago, perhaps, some fierce fire has run through the
evergreen forest, and its ravages are now shown in the
spectacle before us.   Gaunt white stems stand in groups,
presenting a most ghost-like appearance, and pointing
with their bleached branches at the prostrate remains of
their companions, which, strewed and mixed with matted
bushes and briars, lie beneath, rendering progress almost
impossible to the hunter or traveller.

In granitic districts, where the scanty soil—the result
of ages of cryptogamous vegetation and decay—has been
clean licked up by the fire, even the energetic power of
American vegetation appears utterly prostrated for a
period, as if hopeless of again assimilating the desert to
the standard of surrounding features.

As a contrast to such a scene, and in conclusion to
our dissertation on the forests, turn we to the smiling
intervale scenery of her alluvial valleys, for which

Acadie is so famous.    Many of the rivers, coursing
smoothly through long tracts of the country, are broadly
margined by level meadows with rich soils, productive
of excellent pasture.    The banks are adorned with orange
lilies; and the meadows, which extend between the
water and the uplands, shaded by clumps of elm (Ulmus
americana).

Almost the whole charm of these intervales (in an
artistic point of view) is due to the groups of this
graceful tree, by which they are adorned.    Its stem,
soon forking and diverging like that of the English horn-
beam, nevertheless carries the main bulk of the foliage
to a good elevation, the ends of the middle and lower
branches bending gracefully downwards.    The latter often
hang for several yards, quite perpendicularly, with most
delicate hair-like branchlets and small leaves.    We have
but one elm in this part of America; yet no one at first
sight would ever connect the tall trunk and twisted top
branches of the forest-growing tree with the elegant
form of the dweller in the pasture lands.

Whether from appreciation of its beauty, or in view of
the shade afforded their cattle, which always congregate
in warm weather under its pendulous branches, the
settlers agree in sparing the elm growing in such situations.

These long fertile valleys are further adorned by
copses of alders, dogwood, and willows—favourite haunts
of the American woodcock, which here alone finds
subsistence, the earth-worm being never met with in the
forest.

ELMS IN AN INTERVALE.

# CHAPTER III.

———•———

## THE MOOSE.

*(Alce, Hamilton Smith ; Alce Americanus, Jardine.)*

Muzzle very broad, produced, covered with hair, except a small, moist, naked spot in front of the nostrils. Neck short and thick ; hair thick and brittle ; throat rather maned in both sexes ; hind legs have the tuft of hair rather above the middle of the metatarsus ; the males have palmate horns. The nose cavity in the skull is very large, reaching behind to a line over the front of the grinders ; the inter-maxillaries are very long, but do not reach to the nasal. The nasals are very short.

In the foregoing diagnosis, taken from "Gray's Knowsley Menagerie," are summed up the principal characteristics of the elk in the Old and New Worlds. In colour alone the American moose presents an unimportant difference to the Swedish elk; being much darker ; its coat at the close of summer quite black, when the males are in their prime. The European animal varies according to season from brown to dark mouse-grey. In old bulls of the American variety the coat is inclined to assume a grizzly hue. The extremities only of the hairs are black ; towards the centre they become of a light ashy-grey, and finally, towards the roots, dull white—the difference of colour in the hair of the two varieties thus

being quite superficial. The males have a fleshy appen-
dage to the throat, termed the bell, from which and the
contiguous parts of the throat long black hair grows
profusely. A long, erect mane surmounts the neck
from the base of the skull to the withers. Its bristles
are of a lighter colour than those of the coat, and
partake of a reddish hue. At the base of the hair
the neck and shoulders are covered with a quantity of
very fine soft wool, curled and interwoven with the hair.
Of this down warm gloves of an extraordinarily soft
texture are woven by the Indians.

Moose hair is very brittle and inelastic. Towards its
junction with the skin it becomes wavy, the barrel of
each hair suddenly contracting like the handle of an oar
just before it enters the skin.*

Gilbert White, speaking of a female moose deer which
he had inspected, says : " The grand distinction between
this deer and any other species that I have ever met
with consisted in the strange length of its legs, on which
it was tilted up, much in the manner of birds of the
grallæ order." This length of limb is due, according to
Professor Owen, " to the peculiar length of the cannon
bones (metacarpi and metatarsi)."

The other noticeable peculiarities of the elk are the

---

* In "Anatomical Descriptions of Several Creatures Dissected by the
Royal Academy of Sciences at Paris, by Alexander Pitfield, F.R.S., 1688,"
the above peculiarity is thus described :—"The hair was three inches long,
and its bigness equalled that of the coarsest horsehair ; this bigness grew
lesser towards the extremity, which was pointed all at once, making, as it
were, the handle of a lance. This handle was of another colour than the
rest of the hair, being diaphanous like the bristles of a hog. It seems that
this part, which was finer and more flexible than the rest of the hair, was
so made to the end, that the hair which was elsewhere very hard might
keep close and not stand on end. This hair, cut through the middle,
appeared in the microscope spongy on the inside, like a rush."

great length of the head and ear, and the muscular
development of the upper lip ; the movements of which,
directed by four powerful muscles arising from the maxillaries, prove its fitness as a prehensile organ.   In form it
has been said to be intermediate between the snout of
the horse and of the tapir.   I am indebted to Mr. Buckland for the following description of a skull, which had
been forwarded to him from Nova Scotia :—

"This splendid skull weighs ten pounds eleven ounces,
and is twenty-four inches and a-half in length.   The
inter-maxillary bones are very much prolonged, to give
attachment to the great muscle or upper prehensile lip,
and the foramen in the bone for the nerve, which
supplies the 'muffle' with sensation, is very large.   I
can almost get my little finger into it.   The ethmoid
bone, upon which the nerves of smelling ramify themselves, is very much developed.   No wonder the hunter
has such difficulty in getting near a beast whose nose
will telegraph the signal of 'danger' to the brain, even
when the danger is a long way off, and the 'walking
danger,' if I have read the habits of North American
Indians, is in itself of a highly odoriferous character.   The
cavities for the eyes are wide and deep.   I should say the
moose has great mobility of the eye.   The cavity for the
peculiar gland in front of the eye is greatly scooped out.
The process at the back of the head for the attachment
of the ligamentum nuchæ—the elastic ligament which,
like an india-rubber spring, supports the weight of the
massive head and ponderous horns without fatigue to the
owner, is much developed.   The enamel on the molar
teeth forms islands with the dentine somewhat like the
pattern of the tooth of the common cow."

The height of the elk at the withers but little exceeds that at the buttock ; the back consequently has not that slope to the rear so often misrepresented in drawings of the animal. The appearance of extra height forwards is given by the mane, which stands out from the ridge of the neck, something like the bristles of an inverted hearth-broom. The ears, which are considerably over a foot in length in the adult animal, are of a light brown, with a narrow marginal dark-brown rim ; the cavity is filled with thick whitish-yellow hair. The naked skin fringing the orbit of the eye is a dull pink ; the eye itself of a dark sepia colour. Under the orbit there is an arc of very dark hair. The lashes of the upper lid are full, and rather over an inch in length. A large specimen will measure six feet six inches in height at the shoulder ; length of head from occiput to point of muffle, following the curve, thirty-one inches ; from occiput to top of withers in a straight line, twenty-nine inches ; and from the last point horizontally to a vertical tangent of the buttocks, fifty-two inches. A large number of measurements in my possession, for the accuracy of which I can vouch, show much variation of the length of back in proportion to the height, thus probably accounting for a commonly received opinion amongst the white settlers of the backwoods that there are two varieties of the moose.

## THE PAST HISTORY OF THE ELK.

The study of northern zoology presents a variety of considerations interesting both to the student of recent nature and to the palæontologist. Taking as well known

instances the reindeer and musk-ox, there are forms yet
inhabiting the arctic and sub-arctic regions which may
be justly regarded as the remains of an ancient fauna
which once comprised many species now long since
extinct, and which with those already named, occupied a
far greater southerly extent of each of the continents
converging on the pole than would be possible under the
present climatal conditions of the world. With those
great types which have entirely disappeared before man
had recorded their existence in the pages of history, including the mammoth (Elephas primigenius), the most
abundant of the fossil pachyderms, whose bones so crowd
the beaches and islands of the Polar Sea that in parts the
soil seems altogether composed of them, the Rhinoceros
tichorinus, and others, were associated genera, a few
species of which lived on into the historic period, and
have since become extinct, whilst others, occupying
restricted territory, are apparently on the verge of disappearance. "All the species of European pliocene
bovidæ came down to the historical period," states Professor Owen in his "British Fossil Mammals," "and the
aurochs and musk-ox still exist; but the one owes its
preservation to special imperial protection, and the other
has been driven, like the reindeer, to high northern latitudes." Well authenticated as is the occurrence of the
rangifer as a fossil deer of the upper tertiaries, the
evidence of its association in ages so remote, with Cervus
Alces, has been somewhat a matter of doubt. The elk
and the reindeer have always been associated in descriptions of the zoology of high latitudes by modern naturalists, as they were when the boreal climate, coniferous
forests, and mossy bogs of ancient Gaul brought them

E

under notice of the classic pens of Cæsar, Pausanias, and
Pliny.   And there is a something in common to both of
these singular deer which would seem to connect them
equally with the period when they and the gigantic
contemporary genera now extinct roamed over so large
a portion of the earth's surface in the north temperate
zone, where the fir-tree—itself geologically typical of a
great antiquity—constituted a predominant vegetation.

The presence of the remains of Cervus Alces in association with those of the mammoth, the great fossil musk-ox
(Ovibos), the fossil reindeer, and two forms of bison in
the fossiliferous ice-cliffs of Eschscholtz Bay, as described
by Sir John Richardson, would seem to be an almost
decisive proof of its existence at a time when the temperature on the shores of the Polar Sea was sufficiently
genial to allow of a vegetation affording browse and
cover to the great herds of mammals which have left
their bones there, with buried, fossilised trees, attesting
the presence of a forest at a latitude now unapproached
save by shrubs, such as the dwarf birch, and by that only
at a considerable distance to the south.   The elk of the
present day, as we understand his habits, unlike the
musk-ox and reindeer, for which lichens and scanty
grasses in the valleys of the barren grounds under the
Polar circle afford a sufficient sustenance, is almost
exclusively a wood-eater, and could not have lived at
the locality above indicated under the present physical
aspects of the coasts of Arctic America, any more than
the herds of buffaloes, horses, oxen and sheep, whose
remains are mentioned by Admiral Von Wrangell as
having been found in the greatest profusion in the
interior of the islands of New Siberia, associated with

mammoth bones, could now exist in that icy wilderness.
On these grounds a high antiquity is claimed for the
sub-genus Alces, probably as great as that of the reindeer.

As a British fossil mammal, the true elk has not yet
been described, though for a long time the remains of
the now well-defined sub-genus Megaceros were ascribed
to the former animal. There is a statement, however, in
a recent volume of the "Zoologist" to the effect that the
painting of a deer's head and horns, which were dug out
of a marl pit in Forfarshire, and presented to the Royal
Society of Edinburgh, is referable to neither the fallow,
red, nor extinct Irish deer, but to the elk, which may be
therefore regarded as having once inhabited Scotland.
The only recorded instance of its occurrence in England
is the discovery, a few years since, of a single horn at the
bottom of a bog on the Tyne. It was found lying on,
*not in*, the drift, and therefore can be only regarded as
recent.

Passing on to prehistoric times, when the remains of
the species found in connexion with human implements
prove its subserviency as an article of food to the hunters
of old, we find the bones of Cervus Alces in the Swiss
lake dwellings, and the refuse-heaps of that age ; whilst
in a recent work on travel in Palestine by the Rev. H.
B. Tristram, we have evidence of the great and ancient
fauna which then overspread temperate Europe and Asia
having had a yet more southerly extension, for he discovers a limestone cavern in the Lebanon, near Beyrout,
containing a breccious deposit teeming with the *débris* of
the feasts of prehistoric man—flint chippings, evidently
used as knives, mixed with bones in fragments and teeth,

assignable to red or reindeer, a bison, and an elk. "If,"
says the author, "as Mr. Dawkins considers, these teeth
are referable to those now exclusively northern quadrupeds,
we have evidence of the reindeer and elk having been
the food of man in the Lebanon not long before the
historic period; for there is no necessity to put back to
any date of immeasurable antiquity the deposition of
these remains in a limestone cavern. And," he adds,
with significant reference to the great extension of the
ancient zoological province of which we are speaking,
"there is nothing more extraordinary in this occurrence
than in the discovery of the bones of the tailless hare of
Siberia in the breccias of Sardinia and Corsica."

The first allusion to the elk in the pages of history is
made by Cæsar in the sixth book "De Bello Gallico"—
"*sunt item quæ appellantur Alces,*" etc. etc., a description of an animal inhabiting the great Hercynian forest
of ancient Germany, in common with some other remarkable feræ, also mentioned, which can refer to no other,
the name being evidently Latinised from the old Teutonic
cognomen of elg, elch, or aelg, whence also our own term
elk. He speaks of the forest as commencing near the
territories of the Helvetii, and extending eastward along
the Danube to the country inhabited by the Dacians.
"Under this general name," says Dr. Smith, "Cæsar
appears to have included all the mountains and forests
in the south and centre of Germany, the Black Forest,
Odenwald, Thüringenwald, the Hartz, the Erzgebirge, the
Riesengebirge, etc., etc. As the Romans became better
acquainted with Germany, the name was confined to
narrower limits. Pliny and Tacitus use it to indicate
the range of mountains between the Thüringenwald and

the Carpathians. The name is still preserved in the
modern Harz and Erz." Gronovius states that the
German word was Hirtsenwald, or forest of stags. In
an old translation of the Commentaries I find the word
"alces" rendered "a kind of wild asses," and really a
better term could hardly be applied, had the writer,
unacquainted with the animal, caught a passing glimpse
of an elk, especially of a young one without horns. But
it is evident that Cæsar alludes to a large species of deer,
and, although he compares them to goats (it is nearly
certain that the original word was "capreis," "caprea"
being a kind of wild goat or roebuck), and received from
his informants the story of their being jointless—an
attribute, in those days of popular errors and super-
stitions, ascribed to other animals as well—the very fact
of their being hunted in the manner described, by
weakening trees, so that the animal leaning against them
would break them down, involving his own fall, proves
that the alce was a creature of ponderous bulk.

The descriptive paragraph alluded to contains one of
the fallacies which have always been attached to the
natural history of the elk, ancient and modern ; and,
even now-a-days the singular appearance of the animal
attempting to browse on a low shrub close to the ground,
his legs not bent at the joint, but straddling stiffly as he
endeavours to cull the morsel with his long, prehensile
upper lip, might impart to the ignorant observer the idea
that the stilt-like legs were jointless. The fabrication of
their being hunted in the way described was, of course,
based on the popular error as to the formation of their
limbs. "*Mutilæque sunt cornibus*" may imply that
Cæsar, or more likely some of his men, had either seen a

female elk, or—as might be more acceptably inferred—a
male which had lost one horn, and consequently late in
the autumn, as it is well known that the horns are not
shed simultaneously.  Pausanias speaks of the elk as
intermediate between the stag and the camel, as a most
sagacious animal, and capable of distinguishing the odour
of a human being at a great distance, taken by hunters
in the same manner as is now pursued in the "skall" of
north Europe, and as being indigenous to the country of
the Celtæ; whilst Pliny declares it to be a native of
Scandinavia, and states that at his time it had not been
exhibited at the Roman games.  At a later period the
animal became better known, for Julius Capitolinus
speaks of elks being shown by Gordian, and Vopiscus
mentions that Aurelian exhibited the rare spectacle of the
elk, the tiger, and the giraffe, when he triumphed over
Zenobia.

In these few notices is summed up all that has been
preserved of what may be termed the ancient history of
the European elk.  An interesting reflection is suggested
as to what were the physical features of central Europe in
those days.  It seems evident that ancient France, then
called Gaul, was a region of alternate forests and
morasses in which besides the red and the roe, the reindeer abounded, if not the elk; that in crossing the Alps,
a vast, continuous forest, commencing on the confines of
modern Switzerland, occupied the valleys and slopes of
the Alps, from the sources of the Rhine to an eastern
boundary indicated by the Carpathian mountains, and
embraced, as far as its northern extension was known,
the plateau of Bohemia.  Strange and fierce animals,
hitherto unknown to the Romans—accustomed as they

had been to seeing menageries of creatures brought from
other climes, dragged in processions and into the arena
—were found in these forests. The urus or wild bull,
now long extinct, " in size," says Cæsar, "little less than
the elephant, and which spares neither man nor beast
when they have been presented to his view." The savage
aurochs yet preserved in a Lithuanian forest, the elk and
the reindeer were their denizens, and formed the beef and
venison on which the fierce German hunters of old subsisted. "The hunting of that day" may be well imagined
to have been very different to the most exciting of
modern field sports, and continued down to the thirteenth
century, as is shown by the well-known passage from the
Niebelungen poem, where the hero, Sifrid, slays some of
the great herbivoræ—the bison, the elk, and the urus—
as well as "einen grimmen Schelch," about the identity
of which so much doubt has arisen, though the conjecture
has been offered by Goldfuss, Major Hamilton Smith,
and others, that the name refers to no other than the
great Irish elk or megaceros.

The recent notices of the elk contained in some curious
old works on the countries of northern Europe and their
natural history are valuable merely as indicating the
presence and range of the animal in certain regions. The
errors and extravagances of the classic naturalists still
obtained, and tinged all such writings to the commencement of the great epoch of modern natural history
ushered in by St. Hilaire and Cuvier. A confused
account of the animal is given by Scaliger, and it is
mentioned by Gmelin in his Asiatic travels. Olaus
Magnus, the Swedish bishop, says, "The elks come from
the north, where the inhabitants call them elg or elges."

Scheffer, in his history of Lapland, published in 1701, speaks of that country "as not containing many elks, but that they rather pass thither out of Lithuania." Other writers mention it, but, whenever a scientific description is attempted it is full of credulous errors, such as its liability to epileptic fits—a belief entertained not only by the peasants of northern Europe, but likewise, with regard to the moose, by the North American Indians ; its attempt to relieve itself of the disease by opening a vein behind the ear with the hind foot, whence pieces of the hoof were worn by the peasants as a preventive against falling sickness ; and its being obliged to browse backwards through the upper lip becoming entangled with the teeth.[*] There are also ample notices of the elk in the works of Pontoppidan and Nilsson ; Albertus Magnus and Gesner state that in the twelfth century it was met with in Sclavonia and Hungary. The former writer calls it the equicervus or horse hart. In 1658 Edward Topsel published his "History of Four-footed Beasts and Serpents : to be procured at the Bible, on Ludgate-hill, and at the Key, in Paul's Churchyard." At page 165 he treats of the elk : "They are not found but in the colder northern regions, as Russia, Prussia, Hungaria, and Illyria, in the wood ; Hercynia, and among the Borussian Scythians, but most plentiful in Scandinavia, which Pausanias calleth the Celtes."

---

[*] Mr. Buckland, referring to the above statement in "Land and Water," says :—"Of course some part of the elk was used medicinally. Our ancestors managed to get a 'pill et haustus' out of all things, from vipers up to the moss in human skulls. The Pharmacopœia of the day prescribes a portion of the hoof worn in a ring ; 'it resisteth and freeth from the falling evil, the cramp, and cureth the fits or pangs.' Fancy an hysterical lady being told to take 'elk's hoof' for a week, to be followed by 'hart's horn.' "

The accounts given by the earlier American voyagers
of Cervus Alces—there found under the titles of moose
(Indian) or *l'original* (French)—were also highly exaggerated ; though, considering that they received their
descriptions from the Indians, who to this day believe in
many romantic traditions concerning the animal, they
are excusable enough.   From the writings of Josselyn,[*]
Denys, Charlevoix, Le Hontan, and others, little can be
learnt of the natural history of the moose.   Suffice it to
say, that they represented it as being ten or twelve feet
in height, with monstrous antlers, stalking through the
forest and browsing on the foliage at an astonishing
elevation.   It was consequently long believed that the
American animal was much larger than his European
congener ; and when the gigantic horns of the Megaceros
were first ascribed to an elk, it was to the former that
they were referred by Dr. Molyneux.

---

## RECENT NATURAL HISTORY OF THE SPECIES.

Commencing its modern history, let us now briefly
trace the limits within which the elk is found in Europe,
Asia, and—regarding the moose as at least congeneric—
America.   It is to the sportsmen and naturalists who

---

[*] " The moose or elke is a creature, or rather, if you will, a monster of
superfluity ; a full grown moose is many times bigger than an English
oxe ; their horns, as I have said elsewhere, very big and brancht out into
palms, the tops whereof are sometimes found to be two fathoms asunder
(a fathom is six feet from the tip of one finger to the tip of the other, that
is four cubits), and in height from the toe of the fore feet to the pitch of
the shoulder twelve foot, both of which hath been taken by some of my
*sceptique* readers to be monstrous lies."—*Josselyn's Voyages to New England*,
pub. 1674.

have recently written on the field sports of the Scandinavian Peninsula that we are indebted for nearly all our
information on the natural history of this animal, and its
geographical distribution in northern Europe. The works
of Messrs. Lloyd and Barnard contain ample notices.
"At the present day," says the latter author, " it is found
in Sweden, south of the province of East Gothland.
Angermannland is its northernmost boundary." The late
Mr. Wheelwright, in " Ten Years in Sweden," which contains an admirable synopsis of the fauna and flora of that
country, places the limits of the elk in Scandinavia
between 58° North lat. and 64°. Mr. Barnard states that
"it likewise inhabits Finland, Lithuania, and Russia,
from the White Sea to the Caucasus. It is also found in
the forests of Siberia to the River Lena, and in the neighbourhood of the Altai mountains." Von Wrangel met
with the elk—though becoming scarce, through excessive
hunting and the desolation of the forest by fire—in the
Kolymsk district, in the almost extreme north-east of
Siberia. Erman, another eminent scientific traveller in
Siberia, describes it as abundant in the splendid pine
forests which skirt the Obi, and mentions it on several
occasions in the narrative of his journey eastward through
the heart of the country to Okhotsk. It has been recently
noticed amongst the mammalia of Amoorland, and as
principally inhabiting the country round the lower
Amoor. It is thus seen that the domains of the elk
in the Eastern Hemisphere are immensely extensive,
lying between the Arctic Circle—indeed, approaching the
Arctic Ocean, where the great rivers induce a northern
extension of the wooded region—and the fiftieth parallel
of north latitude, from which, however, as it meets

greater civilisation in the western portion of the Russian empire, it recedes towards the sixtieth.

In the New World, it would appear from old narratives that the moose (as we must unfortunately continue to call the elk, whose proper title has been misappropriated to Cervus canadensis) once extended as far south as the Ohio. Later accounts represent its southern limit on the Atlantic coast to be the Bay of Fundy, the countries bordering which—Nova Scotia, New Brunswick, and the State of Maine—appear to be the most favourite abode of the moose ; for nowhere in the northern and western extension of the North American forest do we find this animal so numerous as in these districts. Absent from the islands of Prince Edward, Anticosti, and Newfoundland, it is found on the Atlantic sea-board, and to the north of New Brunswick, in the province of Gaspé ; across the St. Lawrence, not further to the eastward than the Saguenay, though it was met with formerly on the Labrador as far as the river Godbout. The absence of the moose in Newfoundland appears unaccountable ; for, although a large portion of this great island is composed of open moss-covered plateaux and broad savannahs —favourite resorts of the cariboo or American reindeer— yet it contains tracts of forest, principally coniferous, of considerable extent, in which birch, willow, and swamp-maple are sufficiently abundant to afford an ample subsistence to the former animal, which is stated by Sir J. Richardson to ascend the rivers in the northwest of America nearly to the Arctic Circle—as far, in fact, as the willows grow on the banks.

Assuming that the moose is still found in New Hampshire and Vermont, where it exists, according to Audubon and Bachman, at long intervals, we may therefore define its limits on the eastern coasts of North America as lying between 43° 30′ and the fiftieth parallel of latitude.

In following the lines of limitation of the species across the continent, we perceive an easy guide in considering its natural vegetation. As regards the general features of the forests which the moose affects, we find them principally characterised by the presence of the fir tribe and their associations of damp swamps and soft open bogs, provided that they are sufficiently removed from the region of perpetual ground-frost to allow of the requisite growth of deciduous shrubs and trees on which the animal subsists. The best indication, therefore, of the dispersion of the moose through the interior of the continent is afforded by tracing the development of the forest southwards from the northern limit of the growth of trees.

The North American forest has its most arctic extension in the north-west, where it is almost altogether composed of white spruce (Abies alba), a conifer which, when met with in far more genial latitudes, appears to prefer bleak and exposed situations. Several species of Salix fringe the river banks, and feeding on these we first find the moose, even on the shores of the Arctic Sea, where Franklin states it to have been seen at the mouth of the Mackenzie, in latitude 69°. Further to the eastward Richardson assigns 65° as the highest limit of its range ; and in this direction it follows the general course of the coniferous forest in its rapid recession from the arctic circle, determined by the line of perpetual ground-frost, which comes down on the Atlantic sea-board to the fifty-ninth parallel, cutting off a large section of Labrador. To the northward of this line are the treeless wastes, termed barren-grounds, the territory of the small arctic cariboo.

The monotonous character and paucity of species of the evergreen forest in its southern extension continues until the valley of the Saskatchewan is reached, where some new types of deciduous trees appear—balsam-poplar, and maple—forming a great addition to the hitherto scanty fare of the moose. Here, however, the forest is divided into two streams by the north-western corner of the great prairies—the one following the slopes of the Rocky Mountains, whilst the other edges the plains to the south of Winipeg and the Canadian lakes. In the former district, and west of the mountains, the Columbia river is assigned as the limit of the moose. On the other course the animal appears to be co-occupant with the wapiti, or prairie elk, of the numerous spurs of forest which jut out into the plains, and of the isolated patches locally termed moose-woods. Constantly receiving accession of species in its south-westerly extension, the Canadian forest is fully developed at Lake Superior, and there exhibits that pleasing admixture of deciduous trees with the nobler conifers—the white pine and the hemlock spruce—which conduces to its peculiarly beautiful aspect. This large tract of forest, which, embracing the great lakes and the shores of the St. Lawrence, stretches away to the Atlantic sea-board, and covers the provinces of New Brunswick, Nova Scotia, and Prince Edward's Island, including a large portion of the Northern States, has been termed by Dr. Cooper, in his excellent monograph on the North American forest-trees, the Lacustrian Province, from the number of its great lakes ; it is chiefly characterised by the predominance of evergreen coniferæ. It was all at one time plentifully occupied by the moose, which is now but just frequent enough in its almost inaccessible retreats in the Adirondack hills to be classed amongst the quadrupeds of the State of New York. The range of the animal across the continent is thus indicated, and its association with the physical features of the American forest. As before remarked, the neighbourhood of the Bay of Fundy appears to be its present most favoured habitat ; and it seems to rejoice especially in the low-lying, swampy woods, and innumerable lakes and river-basins of Nova Scotia and New Brunswick.

The scientific diagnosis of the Alcine groups (Hamilton Smith) having been detailed already, we pass on to describe the habits of the American moose—the result of a long period of personal observation in the localities last mentioned. First, however, a few remarks on the specific identity of the true elks of the two hemispheres seem as much called for at this time as when Gilbert White, writing exactly a century ago, asks, " Please to let me hear if my female moose " (one that he had inspected at Goodwood, and belonging to the Duke of Richmond) " corresponds with that you saw ; and whether you still think that the American moose and European elk are the same creature ? " In reference to this interesting question, my own recent careful observations and measurements of the Swedish elks at Sandringham compared with living specimens of moose of the same age examined in America, convince me of their identity ; whilst the late lamented Mr. Wheelwright, with whom I have had an interesting correspondence on the subject, states in " Ten Years in Sweden " : " The habits, size, colour, and

form of our Swedish elk so precisely agree with those of
the North American moose in every respect, that unless
some minute osteological difference can be found to exist
(as in the case of the beavers of the two countries), I
think we may fairly consider them as one and the same
animal."[*] The only difference of this nature that I ever
heard of as supposed to exist, consisted in a greater
breadth being accredited to the skull, at the most protuberant part of the maxillaries, in the case of the European elk. This I find is set aside in the comparative
diagnosis at the Museum of the Royal College of Sur-

---

[*] The following corroborative statement has appeared in "Land and
Water," from the pen of a correspondent whose initials are appended :—
" I beg to state my opinion that the elk of North America and of Northern
Europe are identical. Having lived four years in New Brunswick and
Nova Scotia, and having had the opportunity since I have been living in
Prussia of seeing the interesting paintings of the elk of East Prussia,
executed by Count Oscar Krochow, I have very little doubt on the subject ;
indeed, the differences are so trifling and so manifestly the result of climatic
influences, that as a sportsman I have no doubts whatever. The elk (Elend
thier, Elenn thier, Elech or Elk in German) is still found in the forest
lying between the Russian frontier and the Curische Huff, in the govern-
mental district of Gumbinnen, where it is strictly preserved, and where
its numbers have considerably increased in late years. I think that only
six stags are allowed to be shot yearly in this district, and permission is
only to be obtained on very particular recommendation to high authorities
in Berlin. The best German sporting authorities and sporting naturalists
consider the moose deer of North America and the elk of Northern Europe
to be identical. The elk was not extinct in Saxony till after the year 1746,
and is still found in Prussia, Livonia, Finland, Courland (where it is called
Halang), in the Ural, and in Siberia. Perhaps the greatest numbers are
found in the Tagilsk forests in the Ural, where the elk grows to an
enormous size. The size and weight, shape of the antlers, its having
topmost height at the shoulder, the shape and mode of carrying the head,
prolongation of the snout to what is called (in North America) 'the mooffle,'
the awkward trotting gait, and also its power of endurance and the distances which it travels when alarmed, all concur in establishing the identity
of the North American and Northern European elks. The elk of Northern
Europe goes with young forty weeks ; the rutting season commences in
Lithuania (East Prussia) about the end of August, and lasts through
September. As well as can be established by recent observation, the
duration of life is from sixteen to eighteen years."—B. W. (Berlin).

geons, in which no grounds of distinction whatever are evidenced.

I consider that this and the other arctic deer—the rangifers (excepting, perhaps, in the latter instance the small barren-ground cariboo, which is probably a distinct species)—owe any differences of colour or size, or even shape of the antler, to local variation, influenced by the physical features of the country they inhabit. There is more variation in the woodland cariboo of America in its distribution across the continent than I am able to perceive between the elks of the Old and New World. As migratory deer, occupying the same great zoological province, almost united in its arctic margin, we need not look for difference of species as we do in the case of animals whose zones of existence are more remote from the Pole, and where we find identical species replaced by typical.

The remark of an old writer that the elk is a " melancholick beast, fearful to be seen, delighting in nothing but moisture," expresses the cautious and retiring habits of the moose, and the partiality which it evinces for the long, mossy swamps, where the animal treads deeply and noiselessly on a soft cushion of sphagnum. These swamps are of frequent occurrence round the margins of lakes, and occupy low ground everywhere. They are covered by a rank growth of black spruce (Abies nigra), of stunted and unhealthy appearance, their roots perpetually bathed by the chilling water which underlies the sphagnum, and their contorted branches shaggy with usnea. The cinnamon fern (Osmunda cinnamomea) grows luxuriantly ; and its waving fronds, tinged orange-brown in the fall of the year, present a pleasing contrast to the light seagreen carpet of moss from which they spring profusely.

A few swamp-maple saplings, withrod bushes (viburnum), and mountain-ash, occur at intervals near the edge of the swamp, where the ground is drier, and offer a mouthful of browse to the moose, who, however, mostly frequenting these localities in the rutting season, seldom partake of food. Here, accompanied by his consort, the bull remains, if undisturbed, for weeks together ; and, if a large animal, will claim to be the monarch of t' e swamp, crashing with his antlers against the tree stems should he hear a distant rival approaching, and making sudden mad rushes through the trees that can be heard at a long distance. At frequent intervals the moss is torn up in a large area, and the black mud scooped out by the bull pawing with the fore-foot. Round these holes he continually resorts. The strong musky effluvia evolved by them is exceedingly offensive, and can be perceived at a considerable distance. They are examined with much curiosity by the Indian hunter (who is not over particular) to ascertain the time elapsed since the animal was last on the spot. A similar fact is noticed by Mr. Lloyd in the case of the European elk, " grop " being the Norse term applied to such cavities found in similar situations in the Scandinavian forest.

The rutting season commences early in September, the horns of the male being by that time matured and hardened. An Indian hunter has told me that he has called up a moose in the third week of August, and found the velvet still covering the immature horn ; however, the connexion between the cessation of further emission of horn matter from the system owing to strangulation of the ducts at the burr of the completed antler, with the advent of the sexual season, is so well established as a fact in the natural history of the Cervinæ that such an instance must be regarded as exceptional. The first two or three days of September over, and the moose has worked off the last ragged strip of the deciduous skin against his favourite rubbing-posts—the stems of young hacmatack (larch) and alder bushes, and with conscious pride of condition and strength, with clean hard antlers and massive neck, is ready to assert his claims against all rivals. A nobler animal does not exist in the American forest ; nor, whatever may have been asserted about his ungainliness of gait and appearance, a form more entitled to command admiration, calculated, indeed, on first being confronted with the forest giant, to produce a feeling of awe on the part of the young hunter. To hear his distant crashings through the woods, now and then drawing his horns across the brittle branches of dead timber as if to intimidate the supposed rival, and to see the great black mass burst forth from the dense forest and stalk majestically towards you on the open barren, is one of the grandest sights that can be presented to a sportsman's eyes in any quarter of the globe. His coat now lies close, with a gloss reflecting the sun's rays like that of a well-groomed horse. His prevailing colour, if in his prime, is jet black, with beautiful golden-brown legs, and flanks pale fawn. The swell of the muscle surrounding the fore-arm is developed like the biceps of a prize-fighter, and stands well out to the front. I have measured a fore-arm of a large moose over twenty inches in circumference. The neck is nearly as round as a barrel, and of immense thickness. The horns are of a light yellowish white stained with chestnut patches ; the tines rather darker ; and the base of the horn, with the lowest group of prongs projecting forwards, of a dark reddish brown.

At this season the bulls fight desperately. Backed by the immense and compact neck, the collision of the antlers of two large rivals is heard on a still autumnal night, like the report of a gun. If the season is young, the palm of the horn is often pierced by the tines of the adversary, and I have picked up broken fragments of tines where a fight has occurred. Though at other seasons they rarely utter a sound, where moose are plentiful they may be heard all day and night. The cows utter a prolonged and strangely-wild call, which is imitated by the Indian hunter through a trumpet of rolled-up birch-bark to allure the male. The bull emits several sounds. Travelling through the woods in quest of a mate, he is constantly "talking," as the Indians say, giving out a suppressed guttural sound—quoh! quoh! —which becomes much sharper and more like a bellow when he hears a distant cow. Sometimes he bellows in rapid succession ; but when approaching the neighbourhood of the forest where he has heard the call of the cow moose, and for which he makes a bee line at first, he becomes much more cautious, speaking more slowly, constantly stopping to listen, and often finally making a long noiseless *détour* of the neighbourhood, so as to come up from the windward, by which means he can readily detect the presence of lurking danger These latter cautious manœuvres on the part of the moose are, however, more frequently exercised in districts where they are much hunted ; in their less accessible retreats the old bulls will often rush up to the spot without hesitation. The suspicious and angry bull will often go into a thick

swamp and lay about him amongst the spruce stems right
and left, now and then making short rushes—the dead
sticks flying before him with reports like pistol shots.   I
have often heard a strange sound produced by moose
when "real mad," as the Indians would say—a half-
choked sound as if there was a stoppage in the wind-pipe,
which might be expressed—hud-jup, hud-jup!   When
with his mate, his note is plaintive and coaxing—cooah,
cooah !

A veteran hunter, now dead, well-known in Nova
Scotia as Joe Cope—to be regretted as one of the last
examples of a thorough Indian, and gifted with extraordinary faculties for the chase—thus described to me,
over the camp-fire, one of his earlier reminiscences of the
woods—the subject being a moose fight.

It was a bright night in October, and he was alone,
calling, on an elevated ridge which overlooked a great
extent of forest land.   " I call," said he, " and in all my
life I never hear so many moose answer.   Why, the place
was bilin' with moose.   By-and-by I hear two coming
just from opposite ways—proper big bulls I knew from
the way they talked.   They come right on, and both
come on the little hill at same time—pretty hard place,
too, to climb up, so full of rocks and windfalls.   When
they coming up the hill, I never hear moose make such
a shockin' noise, roarin', and tearin' with their horns.   I
just step behind some bushes, and lay down.   They meet
just at the top, and directly they seen one another, they
went to it.   Well, Capten, you wouldn't b'lieve what a
noise—just the same as if gun gone off.   Well, they
ripped away, till I couldn't stand it no longer, and I shot
one of the poor brutes ; the other he didn't seem to mind

the gun one bit—no more noise than what he been makin', and he thought he killed the moose ; so I just loaded quick, and I shot him too. What fine moose them was—both layin' together on the rocks ! No moose like them now-a-days, Capten."

It is not long since that an animated controversy appeared in the columns of a sporting paper under the heading " Do stags roar ? " It was decided, I believe, that such was the case with the red-deer of the Scottish hills, by the testimony of many sportsmen. I can testify that such is also a habit of the moose, and many will corroborate this statement. On two occasions in the fall I have heard the strange and, until acquainted with its origin, almost appalling sound emitted by the moose. It is a deep, hoarse, and prolonged bellow, more resembling a feline than a bovine roar. Once it occurred when a moose, hitherto boldly coming up at night to the Indians' call, had suddenly come on our tracks of the previous evening when on our way to the calling-ground. On the other occasion I followed a pair of moose for more than an hour, guided solely by the constantly repeated roarings of the bull, which I shot in the act.

Young moose of the second and third year are later in their season than the old bulls. Before the end of October, when their elders have retired, though they will generally readily answer the Indians' call from a distance, they show great caution in approaching—stealthily hovering round, seldom answering, and creeping along the edges of the barren or lake so as to get to leeward of the caller, making no crashing with their horns against the trees as do the older bulls, and always adopting the moose-paths. In consequence they are seldom called up.

When the moose wishes to beat a retreat in silence, his
suspicions being aroused, he can effect the same with
marvellous stealth.   Not a branch is heard to snap, and
the horns are so carefully carried through the densest
thickets that I believe a porcupine or a rabbit would
make more noise when alarmed.

In the fall the bull moose, forgetting his hitherto cautious habits of moving through the forest, seems, on the
contrary, bent on making himself heard, " sounding " (as
the Indians term it) his horns against a tree with a peculiar metallic ring.   Sometimes the ear of the hunter,
intently listening for signs of advancing game, is as-
sailed by a most tremendous clatter from some distant
swamp or burnt-wood, "just (as my Indian once aptly
expressed it) as if some one had taken and hove down a
pile of old boards."   It is the moose, defiantly sweeping
his forest of tines right and left amongst the brittle
branches of the ram-pikes, as the scathed pines, hardened
by fire, are locally termed.   The resemblance of the
sound of the bull when he answers at a great distance off
to the chopping of an axe is very distinct ; and even the
practised ear of the sharpest Indian is often exercised in
long and anxiously criticising the sound before he can
make up his mind from which it emanates.   There are
of frequent occurrence, in districts frequented by these
animals, what are termed moose-paths — well-defined
lines of travel and of communication between their feeding
grounds which, when seeking a new browsing country,
or when pursued, they invariably make for and follow.
These paths, which in some places are scarcely visible, at
other times are broad enough to afford a good line of
travel to a man ; they are also used by bears and wild

cats. Sometimes they connect the little mossy bogs which often run in chains through a low-lying evergreen forest; at others they traverse the woods round the edges of barrens, skirting lakes and swamps. I have often observed that moose, chased from a distance into a strange district, will at once and intuitively take to one of these moose-paths.

With the exception of the leaves and tendrils of the yellow pond lily (Nuphar advena), eaten when wallowing in the lakes in summer, and an occasional bite at a tussack of broad-leaved grass growing in dry bogs, the food of the moose is solely afforded by leaves and young terminal shoots of bushes. The following is a list of trees and shrubs from which I picked specimens, showing the browsing of moose, on returning to camp one winter's afternoon. Red maple, white birch, striped maple, swamp maple, balsam fir, poplar, witch hazel, mountain ash. The withrod is as often eaten, and apparently relished as a tonic bitter, as the mountain ash; but the young poplar growing up in recently burnt lands in small groves, with tender shoots, appears to form the most frequently sought item of diet. In winter young spruces are often eaten, as, also, is the silver fir; in the latter case the Indians say the animal is sick. The observant eye of the Indian hunter can generally tell in winter, should drifting snow cover up its tracks, the direction in which the moose has proceeded, feeding as he travels, by the appearance of the bitten boughs; as the incisors of the lower jaw cut into the bough, the muscular upper lip breaks it off from the opposite side, leaving a rough projection surmounting a clean-cut edge, by which the position of the passing animal is indicated. The wild

meadow hay stacked by the settlers back in the woods is
never touched by moose, though I have seen them eat
hay when taken young and brought up in captivity.   A
young one in my possession would also graze on grass,
which, vainly endeavouring to crop by widely straddling
with the forelegs he would finally drop on his knees to
eat, and thus would advance a step or two to reach
further, and in a most ludicrous manner.

To get at the foliage out of reach of his mouffle the
animal resorts to the practice of riding down young
trees, as shown in the accompanying woodcut.

The teeth of the moose are arranged according to the
dental formula of all ruminants, though I once saw a
lower jaw containing nine perfect incisors.   The crown
of the molar is deeply cleft, and the edges of the enamel
surrounding the cutting surfaces very sharp and hard as
adamant—beautifully adapted to reduce the coarse
sapless branches on which it is sometimes compelled to
subsist in winter, when accumulated snows shut it out
from seeking more favourable feeding grounds.   I have
often heard it asserted by Indian hunters that a large
stone is to be found in the stomach of every moose.
This, of course, is a fable ; but a few years since I was
given a calculus from a moose's stomach which I had
sawn in two.   The concentric rings were well defined,
and were composed of radiating crystals like needles.   The
nucleus was plainly a portion of a broken molar tooth
which the animal had swallowed.   A short time afterwards I obtained another bezoar taken from a moose.
The rings were fewer in number than in the preceding
case, but the nucleus was a very nearly perfect and entire
molar.

MOOSE RIDING-DOWN A TREE.

The young bull moose grows his first horn (a little dag), of a cylindrical form, in his second summer, *i.e.*, when one year old. Both these and the next year's growth, which are bifurcate, remain on the head throughout the winter till April or May. The palmate horns of succeeding years are dropped earlier, in January or February—a new growth commencing in April. The full development of the horn appears to be attained when the animal is in its seventh year.*

As a means of judging age, no dependence is to be placed on the number of the tines, but more upon the colour and perfect appearance of the antler. In an old moose, past his prime, the horns have a bleached appearance, and the tines are not fully developed round the edge of the palm. It is my impression that when moose are much disturbed, and are not allowed to "breed" their horns in quiet, contorted and undersized horns most frequently occur. Double and even treble palms,

---

* Old Winckell, perhaps the best authority among the Germans on sporting zoology, says on this point :—" In the first year of life, and indeed earlier than the red deer, the elk calf shows knobby projections on that part of the head where the horns grow, which by September attain an inch in height. In the spring of the second year the true knobs appear, forming single points seven or eight inches in length. These are covered with dark brown velvet. In the latter part of April, or beginning of May in the year following, these are cast, and are replaced either by longer single points or by forked antlers, according to which the young elk is called either 'spiesser' or 'gabler.' These again are cast early in April, and are replaced by heavier forks, or by shorter but six-pointed antlers, when the elk obtains the designation of 'geringer hirsch.' In the fifth year the horns are cast in March, and the new ones lose their velvet also at a correspondingly earlier date. These are cast in February of the sixth year. I should have previously remarked that they had already developed into branches, which form they retain from henceforth, the number of points on the broad shovel-shaped branches increasing with age. From this time forth the elk casts in December and January, the complete reproduction of the great antlers, which attain a weight of from 30 to 40 lb., not being completed till June. The antlers of the young are light, those of the full-grown elk are dark brown."—B. W.

folded back one layer upon the other, are not uncommon ; and sometimes an almost entire absence of palmation occurs, in which case I have seen a pair of moose horns ascribed to the cariboo. Structural irregularity of the antler is frequently the result of constitutional injury. A friend in Nova Scotia, well known there as "the Old Hunter," recently gave me a pair of horns of most singular appearance, the original possessor of which he had shot a few falls previous. They were of a dead-white colour, without palmation, and with immense and knotted burrs and long bony excrescences sprouting from the shafts of the antlers like stalactites. The horn matter, instead of flowing evenly over the surface, had been impeded in its course, and had burst out at the base of the horn. The animal, an unusually large and old bull, when shot showed evident signs of having been in the wars during the previous season. Several of his ribs were broken, and the carcass bore many other marks of injury. The very bones appeared affected by disease, and were dried up and marrowless.

Even when badly wounded, the moose is seldom known to attack a man unless too nearly approached. There are instances, however, recorded to the contrary. An old Indian, long since dead, called "Old Joe Cope" (not the Joe previously mentioned), was for years nearly bent double by a severe beating received from the fore-foot of a wounded moose which turned on him. For safety, there being no tree near, he jammed himself in between two large granite boulders which were near at hand. The aperture did not extend far enough back to enable him to get altogether out of the reach of the infuriated bull.

Whatever may be said about the mild eyes of the dying moose, a wounded animal, unable to get away, assumes a very "ugly" expression. The little hazel eye and constricted muscles of the mouffle speak volumes of concentrated hate. Such scenes I have lost no time in terminating by a quick *coup de grâce*. When the moose faces the hunter, licking his lips, it is a caution to stand clear.

Portions of skeletons, the skulls united by firmly locked antlers, are not unfrequently found in the wilderness arena where a deadly fight has occurred, and the unfortunate animals have thus met a lingering and terrible death, to which may be applied the well-known lines of Byron in illustration—the contest, indeed, being prolonged beyond the original intention :—

> " Friends meet to part : love laughs at faith ;
> True foes, once met, are joined till death !"

A splendid pair of locked horns of the American moose now adorn the Museum of the Royal College of Surgeons.

In hot weather the moose appears much oppressed and lazy ; he will scarcely stir, and a little exertion causes him to pant and the tongue to hang out. Cold weather, on the contrary, braces him up, and we always find that on a frosty night and morning in the fall of the year the moose is more inclined to travel and answer the hunter's call than on a close night, though in the height of the season. The best time for calling is on a cold frosty morning just before sunrise, when a rime frost whitens the barrens, and the air holds a death-like stillness, the constant hooting of the cat-owls (Bubo Virginianus) portending the approach of a storm.

Except in the height of the rutting season, the great ear of the moose is ever on the alert to detect danger ; the slightest snap of a dead bough trodden on by the advancing hunter, and he is off in a long swinging trot for many a mile. He readily perceives the difference of sounds occasioned by the presence of his human foe to those produced by the animals or birds of the forest, or by the approach of his own species. " The only way you can fool a moose," says my Indian, " is when the drops of rain are pattering off the trees on to the dead leaves ; then he don't know nothing."

The presence of the moose is so difficult to detect, except by tracks and signs of browsing, that habitual silence and caution in walking through the forest becomes a leading trait in the moose hunter, whose eyes are ever glancing around through the forest. By observing this strictly, and from long habit, I shot my last moose unexpectedly. On our road to the calling ground, a picturesque little open bog of a hundred acres or so in the middle of a heavily-wooded evergreen forest, we had passed through a descending valley under tall hemlock woods on the soft mossy carpet which makes travelling so easy and grateful to the moccasined foot. Not a word had been spoken save in cautious undertones, and debouching on the bog, we walked up to a little pile of rocks and dead trees near the centre, where we were to try our luck with the moose-call on the approach of evening, and quietly deposited our loads—blankets and camp-kettle. Lighting our pipes, we sat still for a few moments, scanning the edges of the woods. It was perfectly calm ; not a sound except the cry of the jay or the woodpecker's tap. Presently the Indian, who lay in the

bushes close by, gave a little warning "hist;" and, looking up, I saw a fine moose standing about eighty yards
off, and slowly looking about him.   He had come out of
the woods close to our point of exit, and we must have
been passed by him quite handy.   I was capped; and in
a few minutes crowds of moose-birds had assembled to
share the hunter's feast.   But for our caution we should
never have seen or heard him.

In November, the rutting season over, the bull moose
again seeks the water and recovers his appetite: remaining, nevertheless, in poor condition throughout the
winter.   He may be now seen standing listless and
motionless for hours together, and seeming to take but
little notice of the approach of danger unless his nostrils
are invaded by the scent of a human being, which will
start a moose under any circumstances.   About this
time the cows, young bulls, and calves congregate in
small parties of three to half a dozen, and affect open
barrens and hill sides, where there is a plentiful supply
of young wood of deciduous trees, constituting what is
termed a "moose-yard."   If undisturbed they will remain
on such spots, feeding round in an area more or less limited
in extent, for several weeks; when, the supply of provender failing, they break up camp and proceed in search
of fresh ground.   When the weather and state of the
snow permits, these shifts are practised throughout the
winter.   In Canada, however, and in Northern New
Brunswick, the moose is a far less migratory animal than
he is in Nova Scotia, owing to the great depth of the
snow; once he chooses his yard he has to remain in it,
and is quite at the mercy of the hunter who may have
discovered the locality, and who can invade his domains

at any time and at his own convenience. The old bulls become very solitary in their habits, and, indeed, seem to avoid the society of their species, living in the roughest and most inaccessible districts, on hill sides strewn in the wildest confusion with bleached granite boulders, and windfalls where some forest fire has passed over and left the land thus desolate.

In severe snow-storms the moose seeks shelter from the blinding drift (*poudre*) in fir thickets. In the yard, the animal spends the day in alternately lying down for periods of about two hours, and rising to browse on the bushes near at hand. About ten o'clock in the morning, and again in the afternoon, they may generally be found feeding, or standing, chewing the cud, with their heads listlessly drooping. At noon they always lie down ; and the Indian hunter knows well that this is the worst time of day to approach a yard, as the animal is then keenly watching, with its wonderful faculties of scent and hearing on the alert, for the faintest taint or sound in the air which would intimate coming danger. I have waited motionless for an hour at a time, knowing the herd was reposing close at hand, and anxiously expecting a little wind to stir the branches so as to cover my advance, which would otherwise be quite futile. The snapping of a little twig, or the least collision of the rifle with a branch in passing, or the crunching of the snow under the moccasin, though you planted your footsteps with the most deliberate caution, would suffice to start them.

The moose is not easily alarmed, however, by distant sounds, nor does he take notice of dogs barking, the screams of geese, or the choppings of an axe—sounds, emanating from some settler's farm, which are borne through the air on a clear frosty morning to an astonishing distance in America. Indeed, I once was lying in the bushes in full view of a magnificent bull when the cars passed on a provincial railway at a distance of four or five miles, and the deep discordant howl of the American engine-whistle, or rather trumpet, woke echoes from the hill-sides far and near. Once or twice he raised his ears and slowly turned his head to the sound, and then quietly and meditatively resumed the process of rumination.

In April, about the time of the sap ascending in trees, the moose horns begin to sprout, the old pair having fallen two months previously. The latest date that I have ever seen a bull wearing both horns was on the 29th of January. The cylindrical dag of the moose in his second year, and the two-pronged and still impalmate horn of the next season are, however, retained till April. In the middle of this month the coat is shed, and for some time the moose presents a very rugged appearance. Towards the end of May the cow drops one or two calves (rarely three), by the margin of a lake, often on one of the densely-wooded islands, where they are more secure from the attacks of the black bear or of the bull moose themselves. It has been affirmed as one of the distinctive traits of the Arctic deer that the fawns are not spotted. Though faint, there are decided dapples on the sides and flanks of the young moose ; in the cariboo they are quite conspicuous. In May the plague of flies commences, driving the more migratory cariboo to the mountains and elevated lands, and inducing the moose to pass much of his time in the lakes, where they may be frequently seen browsing on water-lilies near the shore, or swimming from point to point. Besides the clouds of mosquitoes and black flies (Simulium molestum) which swarm round everything that moves in the woods, there are too large Tabani, or breeze flies, that are always about moose, a grey speckled fly, and one with yellow bands. The former is locally termed moose-fly, and is very troublesome to the traveller in the woods in summer, alighting on an exposed part, and quickly delivering a sharp painful thrust with its lance-like proboscis. A tick (Ixodes) affects the moose, especially in winter and early spring. The animal strives to free itself from their irritation by striding over bushes and brambles. The ticks may often be seen on the beds in the snow where moose have lain down, and whence they are quickly picked up by the ever-attendant moose birds, or Canada jays (Corvus canadensis). These vermin will fasten on the hunter when backing his meat out of the woods. The Indian says : " Bite all same as a piece of fire."

So many are the Indian tales illustrating the supposed power that the moose possesses of being able to hide himself from his pursuers by a complete and long-sustained submergence below the surface of the water, that one is almost inclined to believe that the animal is gifted with an unusual faculty of retaining the breath. I know that moose will feed upon the tendrils and roots of the yellow pond lily by reaching for them under water. An instance occurring in the same district in Nova Scotia that I was hunting in, and at the same time, which was related to me, will serve as a sample of the oft-repeated stories bearing on this point. We had crossed a fresh moose track of that morning's date on proceeding to our hunting grounds on the Cumberland hills in search of cariboo. Not caring to kill moose we left it; but shortly after the track was taken up and followed on light new-fallen snow by a settler. Having started the animal once or twice without getting a shot, he followed its track to the edge of a little round pond in the woods whence he could not find an exit of the trail. Sitting down to smoke his pipe before giving it up to return, his gun left against a tree at some distance, he was astonished to see the animal's head appear above the surface in the middle of the pond. On jumping up, the moose quickly made for the opposite shore, and, emerging from the water, regained the shelter of the forest ere he could get round in time for a shot. The Indians have a tradition that the moose originally came from the sea, and that in times of great persecution, some half-century since, when no moose tracks could be found in the Nova Scotian woods, they resorted to the salt water, and left for other lands. An old hunter, now dead, told me he was present when his father shot the first moose that had been seen since their return; that great were the rejoicings of the Indians on the occasion, and that two were shot on the beach by a settler who had seen them swimming for shore from open water in the Bay of Fundy. I can vouch for an instance of a moose, when hunted, taking to the sea and swimming off to an island considerably over a mile from the mainland. Such tales are evidently intimately connected with the powers of the animal in the water, in which, as has been previously stated, it passes much of its existence during the hot weather. A similar hunter's story to the one related above is quoted by Mr. Gosse in the "Canadian Naturalist."

In conclusion, it is with regret that the conviction must be expressed that this noble quadruped, at no very distant period, is destined to pass away from the list of the existing mammalia. The animal has fulfilled its mission ; it has afforded food and clothing to the primitive races who hunted the all-pervading fir forests of Central Europe and Asia to subarctic latitudes, whilst, until very recently, its flesh, with that of the cariboo, formed the sole subsistence of the Micmacs and other tribes living in the eastern woodlands of North America. To these the beef of civilisation—*wenju-tecamwée*, or French moose-meat, as the Indian calls it—but ill and scantily supplies the place of their once abundant venison. It has enabled the early and adventurous settler to push back from the coast and open up new clearings in the depths of the forest. With a barrel of flour and a little tea, rafted up the lakes or drawn on sleds over the snow to his rude log hut, he was satisfied to leave the rest to the providence of nature ; and the moose, the salmon, and the trout, with the annual prolific harvest of wild berries, contributed amply to the few wants of the fathers of many a rising settlement. With but few and exceptional instances, the moose or the elk has not become subservient to man as a beast of burden as has the reindeer ; neither is it, like the latter, still called upon to afford subsistence to nomade tribes of savages who live entirely apart from civilisation. Being an inhabitant of more temperate regions, it is brought more constantly within the influences of the permanent neighbourhood of man, and thus, whilst its extinction is threatened by slaughter, a sure but certain alteration is being effected in the physical features of its native forest regions. The often purposeless destruction of woods by the axe, and the constant devastation of large areas of forest by fires, too frequently the result of carelessness, are reducing the moisture of the American wilderness, removing the sponge-like carpet of mosses by which the water was retained, and rendering the latter a less fitting abode for the moose. Restriction of his domains and constant disturbance are undoubtedly slowly dwarfing the species. We no longer hear of examples of the monster moose of the old times of which Indian tradition still speaks, and when the well-authenticated diminution in the size of the red deer of the Scottish hills is remembered, an appearance of less exaggeration than is usually attributed to them marks the tales of the early American voyageurs concerning the moose.

When the Russian aurochs and the musk-sheep of Arctic America shall have disappeared, it is to be feared that Cervus Alces of the Old and New Worlds, his fir forests levelled, his favourite swamps drained, and unable to exist continuously in the broad glare and radiation of a barren country, will follow, to be regretted as one of the noblest and most important mammals of a past age; his bones will be dug from peat-bogs by a future generation of naturalists, and prized as are now those of the Great Auk of the islands of the North Atlantic, or of the Struthiones of New Zealand, which have perished within the ken of the scientific record of modern natural history.

# CHAPTER IV.

## MOOSE HUNTING.

SUCCESSFUL in the chase, or on the contrary, it must be premised that many a sportsman who essays the sport of moose-hunting in the North-American woods finds but little excitement therein. The toil and monotony of the long daily rambles through a wilderness country, strewed with rocks and fallen trees, and covered with tangled vegetation, with the uncertainty of obtaining even a distant sight of (much less a shot at) these cautious animals, whose tracks one is apparently constantly following to no purpose, drive not a few would-be hunters from the woods in a state of supreme disgust.

There is no country in the world where wild sports are pursued, in which the goddess of hunting exacts so much perseverance and labour from her votaries as the fir-covered districts of North America, or bestows so scanty a reward. The true and persistent moose-hunter (never a poacher or a pot-hunter) is generally animated by other sentiments, and achieves success through an earnest appreciation of the external circumstances which attend the sport. He loves the solitude of the forest, and admires its scenery ; is charmed with the ready resources and wild freedom of camp life, and, instead of listlessly following in the tracks of his Indian guides in a state of semi-disgust, **derives** the greatest **pleasure in watching** their wonderful powers of tracking, their **sagacity in** finding the game, and general display of woodcraft.

It is, perhaps, to this art of tracking or "creeping" that the sport itself owes all its excitement ; and it is in the **lower provinces** (Nova Scotia especially) that it is carried out to perfection by the Indian hunters ; a race, however, which, **it must be regrettingly stated**, is fast disappearing **from** the country.

In Nova Scotia the moose may not be legally shot after the last day **of December, and are thus protected, by the** absence **of deep snow in the woods during the open** season, from such ruthless **invasions** of their **restricted** "yards," **and wanton massacres as** are of frequent occurrence in New **Brunswick and Lower** Canada. Moose hunting in the deep **snows** which choke the **forests to-**wards the close of **winter—the** hunter being able to move freely over the **surface by the aid of** his snow-shoes, whilst the animals are huddled **together, spiritless, and in** wretched condition—is a stupid **slaughter, and** decidedly deserves the imputation often cast **upon it,** that it has no more merit of sport than the being led up to a herd **of cattle in a farmyard.**

The light **snow-storms, however, of** the first winter months cover the ground just **sufficiently to bring out** the art of creeping to its perfection, **whilst the moose** cannot be run down, and snow shoes are never required. The dense deciduous foliage of the hard woods is **now all** removed, and **the** woods afford clear open vistas **in which** game may be far more readily detected than in **the cover** of autumn ; **a** wounded animal seldom escapes the hunter to die a lingering death ; and, lastly, there cannot be the

slightest excuse for leaving in the woods the spoils which
it becomes the imperative duty of the hunter, for many
reasons, to remove.

At the same time fall-hunting has likewise its advantages. There is a double chance of sport now presented, as creeping may be pursued by day, whilst at
sunrise and sunset, and, indeed, throughout the night
when the moon is round, the " call " may be resorted to.
Much, too, in the way of camp equipage may be dispensed
with at this season. One may travel till sundown and
camp in one's tracks amongst the rank ferns and bushes
of the upland barrens with but one rug or blanket for
cover, and sleep soundly and comfortably in the open,
though a rime frost sparkles on every spray next morning. And if, perhaps, the supply of firewood *has* been
somewhat short towards dawn, the excitement of hearing
an answer in the still morning air warms you to action ;
a mouthful of Glenlivet from the flask, and a hasty
snatch of what small amount of caloric may be excited
by the Indian's breath amongst the embers of the night
fire, and you are ready for the " morning call."

And then, when the sun dispels the vapours, raises the
thin misty lines which mark the water courses and forest
lakes, and, finally, mellows the scenery with the hazy
atmosphere of a warm autumnal day, what a glorious
time it is to be in the woods! Give me the fall for
moose hunting, and the stealthy creep through glowing
forests on an Indian summer's day, when the air in the
woods holds that peculiar scent of decaying foliage which
to my nostrils conveys an impression as pleasing as that
produced by the blossom-scented zephyrs of May.

Perhaps one of the most singular of the experiences

which the new hand meets with in moose hunting, and
the one which teaches him to lean entirely for assistance
upon his Indian guide, is the extreme unfrequency with
which an accidental sight of game is obtained in the
forest. Moose tracks are perhaps plentiful, also signs of
fresh feeding on the bushes, and impressed forms of the
animals, where they have rested on the moss, or amongst
ferns, but how seldom do we see the animals themselves by
chance. Suddenly emerging from thick cover on the edge
of an extensive barren occupying several thousand acres,
the eye of the hunter rapidly scans the open in eager
quest of a moving form, but meets with continual disappointment. Not a sign of life, perhaps, but the glancing
flight of a woodpecker or the croak of a raven. One is
prone to believe that the country is deserted by large
game. Presently, however, your Indian, who, leaving
you to rest on a fallen tree and enjoy a few whiffs of the
hunter's solace, makes a cast round for his own satisfaction, returns to tell you that there are moose within
(possibly) a few hundred yards of you. You discredit
it, but are presently induced to believe his assertion
when you are shown the freshly-bitten foliage (anyone
can soon learn to distinguish between a new-cropped
bough and a bite over which a few hours have passed),
or, perhaps, the mud still eddying in a little pool in
which the animal has stepped. You may listen, too, by
the hour together for some token of their whereabouts,
but hear no sounds but those of the birds or squirrels.

If there is daylight, and the wind propitious, your
guide will probably in half an hour or so point to a
black patch seen between tree stems, indicating a portion
of the huge body of a moose, unless you have bungled

the whole affair by an unlucky stumble over a brittle windfall, or clanked your gun-stock against a tree-stem. It will thus be readily seen that success in moose hunting entirely depends upon the excellence of the Indian hunter who accompanies the sportsman. His art, or " gift," is hardly to be comprehended by description ; it is as evidently the result of long practice—not, perhaps, individual practice, but of the skill which he has inherited from his forefathers, who before the advent of Eastern civilisation, regularly "followed the woods"—as is the high state of perfection to which the various breeds of sporting dogs have been brought by artificial means.

Soon confused in the maze of woods through which your Indian leads you after moose, you chance to ask him at length where camp lies. He will tell you within half a point of the compass, and without hesitation, though miles away from the spot. The slightest disarrangement of moss or foliage, a piece of broken fern, or a scratch on the lichens of a granite plateau, are to him the sign-posts of the woods ; he reads them at a glance, running. Should you rest under a tree or by a brook-side, leaving, perhaps, gloves, purse, or pouch behind, next day he will go straight to the spot and recover them, though the country is strange. Under the snow he will find and show you what he has observed or secreted during the previous summer. He is the closest observer of nature, and can tell you the times and seasons of everything ; and there is not an animal, bird, or reptile whose voice he cannot imitate with marvellous exactness.

A faithful companion, and always ready to provide beforehand for your slightest necessities, the Micmac hunter will never leave you in the woods in distress ; and should you cut yourself with an axe, meet with a gun accident, or be taken otherwise sick, will carry you himself out of the woods.* Under his guidance we will now introduce the reader to the sport of moose hunting.

Old Joe Cope, the Indian hunter, is still to the fore :† his little legs, in shape resembling the curved handle of pliers, carry him after the moose nearly as trustily as ever. Perhaps his sight and hearing are failing him, and he generally hunts in company with his son Jem as an assistant ; and Jem, being a lusty young Indian, does most of the work in " backing out" the moose-meat from the woods.

" Joe," said I, on meeting the pair one morning late in September, a few falls ago, at the country-market at Halifax, where they were selling a large quantity of moose-meat, Joe's eyes beaming with ferocious satisfaction

* The following anecdote—a scrap from the note-book of an old comrade in the woods—is an interesting example of the Indian's reflective powers :— " At length Paul, who is leading, stops, and, turning towards us, points towards a cleared line through the forest. ' A road, a road !' and we give three *such* cheers. It is a logging-road, leading from the settlements into the forest ; but which is the way to the clearings ! If we turn in the wrong direction it will delay us another day, and we have only a little tea left and six small biscuits. It is soon settled ; we turn to the left, and presently find a wisp of hay dropped close to a tree. Now comes out a piece of Indian '*cuteness.*' Paul has observed that when a tree knocks off a hand-ful of hay from a load, it falls on that side of the tree to which the cart is going : the hay is on our side of the tree, so we are going in the direction whence the cart came. But it might be wild hay, brought in from a natural meadow. They taste and smell it ; it is salt (in this country the farmers salt the meadow hay to keep it, but not the wild hay) : hence this was hay carted from the settlements for the use of oxen employed in haul-ing out lumber. We are, therefore, going in the direction whence the cart came, and towards the settlements."

† Since this was written, poor Joe has for ever left the hunting grounds of Acadie, having shot his last moose but a few weeks before he rested from a life of singular adventure and toil. *Requiescat in pace.*

as he pocketed the dollars by a ready sale. "Joe, I think I must come and look at your castle, at Indian Lake; they say you have exchanged your camp for a two-storey frame-house, and are the squire of the settlement. Do you think you have left a moose or two in your preserves?"

"Well, Capten, I very glad to see you always when you come along my way. I most too old, though, to hunt with gentlemen—can't see very well."

"We will make out somehow, Joe; and Jem there will help you through, if you come to a stand-still."

"Oh, never fear," replied Mr. Cope (he always speaks of himself as Mr. Cope), laughing; "that Jem, he don't know nothing; I guess I more able to put him through yet."

And so we closed the bargain; to wit, that we should have a day or two's hunting together in what Joe fully regarded as his own preserves and private property—the woods around Indian Lake, distant twenty miles from Halifax.

What would the old Indians, at the close of the last century, have said, if told that in a short time a stage-coach would ply through their broad hunting-grounds between the Atlantic and the Bay of Fundy? Think of the astonishment of Mr. Cope and his comrades of the present age, perhaps just stealing on a bull-moose, when they first heard the yell of the engine and rattle of the car-wheels! This march has been accomplished; the old Windsor coach, with its teams of four, after having flourished for nearly half a century, has succumbed to the iron-horse, and the discordant sounds of passing trains re-echo through the neighbouring woods, to the no

small disgust of Mr. Cope and those of his race in the
same interest.

Joe said that in the country we were going to hunt,
every train might be distinctly heard as it passed ; "and
yet," said he, "the poor brutes of moose don't seem to
mind it much ; they know it can't hurt them."

A settler's waggon took our party over an execrable
road to the foot of Indian Lake. It had been raining
heavily all the morning, and we turned in to warm ourselves at the settler's shanty, whilst the old Indian went
off by a path through the dripping bushes to his camp,
for the purpose of sending his canoe for me. This, and
a few scattered houses in the neighbourhood, was called
the Wellington settlement ; and here, as at the Hammond's Plains settlement, which we had passed through
that morning, the principal occupation of the inhabitants
seemed to be in making barrels for the fishery trade.
They make them very compact, as they are intended for
herring or mackerel in pickle. The staves are spruce,
and are bound with bands of birch. The barrel is sold for
a trifle more than an English shilling. The Hammond's
Plains people are all blacks, a miserable race, descendants
of those who were landed in Nova Scotia at the conclusion of the American war in 1815. Their wretchedness
in winter is extreme, and in the summer they earn a hand-
to-mouth livelihood by bringing in to the Halifax market
a few vegetables grown in the small cleared patches
round their dwellings, bunches of trout from the brooks,
and the various berries which grow plentifully in the
wild waste lands round their settlement.

Presently the canoe was signalled, and, going down to
the water's edge, I embarked, and in a few minutes stood

before Joe's castle. It **was a substantial** frame-house, evidently built by some settler who had a notion of making his fortune by the aid of a small stream which flowed into the lake close by, and over which stood a saw-mill. An old barn was attached, and from its rafters hung moose-hides of all sizes, ages, and in all stages of decomposition; horns, legs, and hoofs; porcupines deprived of their quills, which are used for ornamental work by the women; and, in fact, a very similar collection, only on a grander scale, to that which is often displayed on the outside of a gamekeeper's barn in England.

A rush of lean, hungry-looking curs was made through the door as Joe opened it to welcome me. "Walk in, Capten—ah, you brute of dog, *Koogimook!* Mrs. Cope from home, visiting his friends at Windsor. Perhaps you take some dinner along with me and Jem before we start up lake?"

"All right, Joe; I'll smoke a pipe till you and Jem are ready," I replied, not much relishing the appearance of the parboiled moose-meat which Jem was fishing out of a pot. "No chance of calling to-night, I'm afraid, **Joe;** we shall have a wet night."

"I never see such weather for time of year, Capten; everything in woods so wet—can't hardly make fire; but grand time for creeping—oh, grand! Everything, you see, so soft, don't make no noise. What sort of moccasin you got?"

"A good pair of the moose-shanks you sold me, last winter, Joe; they are the best sort **for** keeping out the wet, and they are so thick and warm."

The moose-shank moccasin is cut from the hind leg of the moose, above and below the hock; it is in shape like an ankle-boot, and is sewn up tightly at the toe, and, with this exception, being without seam, is nearly water-tight. The interior of Cope Castle was not very sweet, nor were its contents arranged in a very orderly manner —this latter fact to be accounted for, perhaps, by the absence of the lady. Portions of moose were strewed everywhere; potatoes were heaped in various corners, and nothing seemed to have any certain place of rest allotted to it. Smoke-dried eels were suspended from the rafters, in company with strings of moose-fat and dried cakes of concrete blue-berries and apples. Joe had, however, some idea of the ornamental, for parts of the *Illustrated News* and *Punch* divided the walls with a number of gaudy pictures of saints and martyrs.

The repast being over, the Indians strided out, replete, with lighted pipes, and paddles in hand, to the beach. Some fresh moose-meat was placed in the canoe, with a basket of Joe's "'taters," which, Jem said, "'twas hardly any use boiling, they were so good, they fell to pieces." A little waterproof canvas camp was spread over the rolls of blankets, guns, camp-kettles, and bags containing the grub, which were stowed at the bottom; and, having seated myself beside them, the Indians stepped lightly into the canoe and pushed her off, when, propelled by the long sweeping strokes of their paddles, we glided rapidly up the lake.

Indian Lake is a beautiful sheet of water, nearly ten miles in length, and, proportionally, very narrow—per-haps half a mile in its general breadth. Rolling hills, steep, and covered with heavy fir and hemlock wood, bounded its western shore; those on the opposite side showing large openings of dreary burnt country. The maple-bushes, skirting the water, were tinged with their brightest autumnal glow; and in the calm water, in coves and nooks, on the windward side of the lake, the reflections were very beautiful. I longed for a cessation of the rain, and a gleam of sunshine across the hill-tops, if only to enjoy the scenery as we passed; and certainly a seat in a canoe is a very pleasant position from which to observe the beauties of lake or river scenery, the spectator being comfortably seated on a blanket or bunch of elastic boughs in the bottom of the canoe—legs stretched out in front, back well supported by rolls of blankets, and elbows resting on the gunwales on either side.

"Ah! here is the Halfway rock, what the old Indians call the Grandmother," said Joe, steering the canoe so as to pass close alongside a line of rocks which stood out in fantastic outlines from the water close to the western shore of the lake. "Here is the Grandmother—we must give him something, or we have no luck."

To the rocks in question are attached a superstitious attribute of having the power of influencing the good or bad fortune of the hunter. They are supposed to be the enchanted form of some genius of the forest; and few Indians, on a hunting mission up the lake, care to pass them without first propitiating the spirit of the rocks by depositing a small offering of a piece of money, tobacco, or biscuit.

"That will do, Capten; anything a'most will do," said Joe, as one cut off a small piece of tobacco, and another threw a small piece of biscuit or a potato on to the rock. "Now you wouldn't b'lieve, Capten, that when you come back you find that all gone. I give you my word that's true; we always find what we leave gone." Whereupon

Joe commenced a series of illustrative yarns, showing the dangers of omitting to visit " the Grandmother," and how Indians, who had passed her, had shot themselves in the woods, or had broken their legs between rocks, or had violent pains attack them shortly after passing the rock, and on returning, and making the presents, had immediately recovered.

" It looks as if it were going to be calm to-night, Joe," said I, as we neared the head of the lake; " which side are we to camp on ? Those long mossy swamps and bogs which run back into the woods on the western side, look likely resorts for moose."

" No place handy for camp on that side," said Joe ; " grand place for moose, though—guess if no luck to-morrow mornin', we cross there. I got notion of trying this side first." And so, having beached the canoe, turned her over, and drawn her into the bushes secure from observation, we made up our bundles, apportioning the loads, and followed Joe into the forest, now darkened by the rapidly closing shades of evening. In a very short time the dripping branches, discharging their heavy showers upon us as we brushed against them, and the saturated moss and rank fern, made us most uncomfortably wet ; and as the difficulties of travelling increased as the daylight receded, and the tight wet moccasin is not much guard to the foot coming in painful contact with an unseen stump or rock, we were not sorry when the weary tramp up the long wooded slope from the lake was ended, and a faint light through the trees in the front showed that we had arrived at the edge of the barrens. " It's no use trying to make call to-night, that sartin," said Joe ; " couldn't see moose if he came. Oh, dear me, I sorry for this weather! Come, Jem, we try make camp right away." It was a cheerless prospect, as we threw off our bundles on the wet ground; it was quite dark, and, though nearly calm, the drizzling rain still fell and pattered in large drops, falling heavily from the tree-tops to the ground beneath. First we must get up a good fire—no easy thing to an unpractised hand in woods saturated by a week's rain. However, it can be done, so seek we for some old stump of rotten wood, easily knocked over and rent asunder, for we may, perhaps, find some dry stuff in the heart. Joe has found one, and, with two or three efforts, over it falls with a heavy thud into the moss, and splits into a hundred fragments. The centre is dry, and we return to the spot fixed upon with as much as we can carry. The moss is scraped away, and a little carefully-composed pile of the dead wood being raised, a match is applied, and a cheerful tongue of flame shoots up, and illumines the dark woods, enabling us to see our way with ease. Now is the anxious time on which depends the success of the fire. A hasty gathering of more dry wood is dexterously piled on, some dead hard-wood trees are felled, and split with the axe into convenient sticks, and in a few moments we have a rousing fire, which will maintain its ground and greedily consume anything that is heaped upon it, in spite of the adverse element. A few young fir saplings are then cut, and placed slantingly against the pole which rests in the forks of two upright supports; the canvas is unrolled and stretched over the primitive frame, and our camp has started into existence. The branches of the young balsam firs, which form its poles, are well shaken over the fire, and disposed in layers beneath, to form the bed ; blankets are unrolled and stretched over the boughs, and finding, to my joy, that the rain had not reached the change of clothes packed in my bundle, I presently recline at full length under the sheltering camp, in front of a roaring fire, which is rapidly vaporising the moisture contained in my recent garments, suspended from the top of the camp in front. Joe is still abroad, providing a further stock of firewood for the night, whilst his son is squatting over the fire with a well-filled frying-pan, and its hissing sounds drown the pattering of the rain-drops.

After our comfortable meal followed the fragrant weed, of course, and a discussion as to what we should do on the morrow. The barrens we had come to were of great extent, and of a very bad nature for travelling, the ground being most intricately strewed with the dead trees of the forest which once covered it, and the briars and bushes overgrowing and concealing their sharp broken limbs and rough granite rocks, often cause a severe bruise or fall to the hunter. It was, as Joe said, a "grand place" for calling the moose, as in some spots the country could be scanned for miles around, whilst the numerous small bushes and rock boulders would afford a ready conceal-ment from the quick sight of this animal. However, time would show. If calling could not be attempted next morning, it would most likely be suitable for creeping ; so, hoping for a calm morning and a clear sky, or, at all events, for a cessation of the rain, we stretched ourselves for repose ; and the pattering drops, the crackings and snappings of the logs on the fire, and the hootings of the owls in the distant forest, became less and less heeded or heard, till sleep translated us to the land of dreams.

H

To our disgust it still rained when we awoke next
morning ; the wind was in the same direction, and the
same gloomy sky promised no better things for us that
day.   The old Indian, however, drew on his moccasins,
and started off to the barren by himself to take a survey
of the country whilst the breakfast was preparing, and I
gloomily threw myself back on the blanket for another
snooze.   After an hour or so's absence, Joe returned, and
sat down to his breakfast (we had finished ours, and were
smoking), looking very wet and excited.   "Two moose
pass round close to camp last night," said he ; " I find
their tracks on barren.   They gone down the little valley
towards the lake, and I see their tracks again in the
woods quite fresh.   You get ready, Capten; I have notion
we see moose to-day.   I see some more tracks on the
barren going southward ;   however, we try the tracks
near camp first,—maybe we find them, if not started by
the smell of the fire."

We were soon at it, and left our camp with hopeful
hearts and in Indian file, stepping lightly in each other's
tracks over the elastic moss.   Everything was in first-rate
order for creeping on the moose ; the fallen leaves did
not rustle on the ground, and even dead sticks bent without snapping, and we progressed rapidly and noiselessly
as cats towards the lake.   Presently we came on the
tracks, here and there deeply impressed in a bare spot of
soil, but on the moss hardly discernible except to the
Indian's keen vision.   They were going down the valley ;
a little brook coursed through it towards the lake, and
from the mossy banks sprung graceful bushes of moose-
wood and maple, on the young shoots of which the moose
had been feeding as they passed.   The tracks showed that

they were a young bull and a cow, those of the latter being
much longer and more pointed. Presently we came to
an opening in the forest, where the brook discharged
itself into a large circular swamp, densely grown up with
alder bushes and swamp maple, with a thick undergrowth
of gigantic ferns. Joe whispered, as we stood on the
brow of the hill overlooking it, " Maybe they are in there
lying down; if not, they are started;" and, putting to
his lips the conical bark trumpet which he carried, he
gave a short plaintive call—an imitation of a young bull
approaching and wishing to join the others. No answer
or sound of movement came from the swamp. " Ah, I
afraid so," said Joe, as we passed round and examined
the ground on the other side. " I 'most all the time fear
they started ; they smell our fire this morning while Jem
was making the breakfast." Long striding tracks, deeply
ploughing up the moss, showed that they had gone off in
alarm, and at a swinging trot, their course being for the
barrens above. It was useless to follow them, so we went
off to another part of the barrens in search of fresh
tracks. The walking in the open was most fatiguing
after the luxury of the mossy carpeting of the forest.
Slipping constantly on wet smooth rocks, or the slimy
surfaces of decayed trees; for ever climbing over masses
of prostrate trunks, and forcing our way through tangled
brakes, and plunging into the oozing moss on newly-
inundated swamps, we spent a long morning without
seeing moose, though our spirits were prevented from
flagging by constantly following fresh tracks. The moose
were exceedingly "yary," as Joe termed it, and we started
two or three pairs without either hearing or seeing them,
until the same exclamation of disappointment from the

H 2

Indian proclaimed the unwelcome fact. At length we reached the most elevated part of the barren. We could see the wooded hills of the opposite shore of the lake looming darkly through the mist, and here and there a portion of its dark waters. The country was very open; nothing but moss and stunted huckleberry bushes, about a foot and a half in height, covered it, save here and there a bunch of dwarf maples, with a few scarlet leaves still clinging to them. The forms of prostrate trunks, blackened by fire, lying across the bleached rocks, often gave me a start, as, seen at a distance through the dark misty air, they resembled the forms of our long-sought game—particularly so when surmounted by twisted roots upheaved in their fall, which appeared to crown them with antlers.

"Stop, Capten! not a move!" suddenly whispered old Joe, who was crossing the barren a few yards to my left; "don't move one bit!" he half hissed and half said through his teeth. "Down—sink down—slow—like me!" and we all gradually subsided in the wet bushes.

I had not seen him; I knew it was a moose, though I dared not ask Joe, but quietly awaited further directions. Presently, on Joe's invitation, I slowly dragged my body through the bushes to him. "Now you see him, Capten—there—there! My sakes, what fine bull! What pity we not a little nearer—such open country!"

There he stood—a gigantic fellow—black as night, moving his head, which was surmounted by massive white-looking horns, slowly from side to side, as he scanned the country around. He evidently had not seen us, and was not alarmed, so we all breathed freely. This success on our part was partly attributable to the sudden-

ness and caution with which we stopped and dropped when
the quick eye of the Indian detected him, and partly to
the haziness of the atmosphere. His distance was about
five hundred yards, and he was standing directly facing
us, the wind blowing from him to us. After a little de-
liberation, Joe applied the call to his lips, and gave out a
most masterly imitation of the lowing of a cow-moose, to
allure him towards us. He heard it, and moved his head
rapidly as he scanned the horizon for a glimpse of the
stranger. He did not answer, however; and Joe said,
as afterwards proved correct, that he must have a cow
with him somewhere close at hand. Presently, to our great
satisfaction, he quietly lay down in the bushes. " Now we
have him," thought I ; " but how to approach him ? "
The moose lay facing us, partially concealed in bushes,
and a long swampy gully, filled up with alders, crossed
the country obliquely between us and the game. We
have lots of time, as the moose generally rests for a
couple of hours at a time. Slowly we worm along towards the edge of the alder swamp ; the bushes are pro-
vokingly short, but the mist and the dull grey of our
homespun favour us. Gently lowering ourselves down
into the swamp, we creep noiselessly through the dense
bushes, their thick foliage closing over our heads. Now
is an anxious moment—the slightest snap of a bough, the
knocking of a gun-barrel against a stem, and the game
is off.

" Must go back," whispered Joe, close in my ear ;
" can't get near enough this side—too open ;" and the
difficult task is again undertaken and performed without
disturbing the moose. What a relief, on regaining our
old ground, to see his great ears flapping backwards and

forwards above the bushes! Another half-hour passes in
creeping like snakes through the wet bushes, which we
can scarcely hope will conceal us much longer. It seems
an age, and often and anxiously I look at the cap of my
single-barrelled rifle. I am ahead, and at length, judging
one hundred and twenty yards to be the distance, I can
stand it no longer, but resolve to decide matters by a
shot, and fire through an opening in the bushes of the
swamp. Joe understands my glance, and placing the call
to his lips, utters the challenge of a bull-moose. Slowly
and majestically the great animal rises, directly facing
me, and gazes upon me for a moment; a headlong stagger
follows the report, and he wheels round behind a clump
of bushes.

"Bravo! you hit him, you hit sure enough," shouts
Joe, levelling and firing at a large cow-moose which had,
unknown to us, been lying close beside the bull. "Come
along," and we all plunge headlong into the swamp.
Dreadful cramps attacked my legs, and almost prevented
my getting through—the result of sudden violent motion
after the restrained movements in the cold wet moss and
huckleberry-bushes. A few paces on the other side, and
the great bull suddenly rose in front of us, and strided
on into thicker covert. Another shot, and he sank life-
less at our feet. The first ball had entered the very
centre of his breast and cut the lower portion of the
heart.

Late that night our canoe glided through the dark
waters of the lake towards the settlement. The massive
head and antlers were with us.

"Ah, Grandmother," said Joe, as we passed the indistinct outlines of the spirit rocks, "you very good to us

this time, anyhow; very much we thank you, Grandmother."

"It's a pity, Joe," I observed, "that we have not time to see whether our offerings of yesterday are gone or not; but mind, when you go up the lake again to-morrow to bring out the meat, you don't forget your Grandmother, for I really think she has been most kind to us."

## MOOSE-CALLING.

Few white hunters have succeeded in obtaining the amount of skill requisite in palming off this strange deceit upon an animal so cautious and possessing such exquisite senses as the moose. It is a gift of the Indian, whose soft, well modulated voice can imitate the calls of nearly every denizen of the forest.

As has been stated before, September is the first month for moose-calling, the season lasting for some six weeks. I have seen one brought up as late as the 23rd of October.

The moose is now in his prime; the great palmated horns, which have been growing rapidly during the summer, are firm as rock, and the hitherto-protecting covering of velvet-like skin has shrivelled up and disappeared by rubbing against stumps and branches, leaving the tines smooth, sharp, and ready for the combat.

The bracing, frosty air of the autumnal nights makes the moose a great rambler, and in a short time districts, which before would only give evidence of his presence by an occasional track, now show countless impressions in the swamps, by the sides of lakes, and on the mossy bogs.  He has found his voice, too, and, where moose are numerous, the hitherto silent woods resound with the plaintive call of the cow, the grunting response of her mate, and the crashings of dead trees, as the horns are rapidly drawn across them to overawe an approaching rival.

This call of the cow-moose is imitated by the Indian hunter through a trumpet made of birch bark rolled up in the form of a cone, about two feet in length ; and the deceit is generally attempted by moonlight, or in the early morning in the twilight preceding sunrise—seldom after.  Secreting himself behind a sheltering clump of bushes or rocks, on the edge of the forest barren, on some favourable night in September or October, when the moon is near its full, and not a breath of wind stirs the foliage, the hunter utters the plaintive call to allure the monarch of the forest to his destruction.  The startling and strange sound reverberates through the country; and as its echoes die away, and everything resumes the wonderful silence of the woods on a calm frosty night in the fall, he drops his birchen trumpet in the bushes, and assumes the attitude of intense listening.  Perhaps there is no response ; when, after an interval of about fifteen minutes, he ascends a small tree, so as to give greater range to the sound, and again sends his wild call pealing through the woods.  Presently a low grunt, quickly repeated, comes from over some distant hill, and snappings of branches, and falling trees, attest the approach of the bull ; perhaps there is a pause—not a sound to be heard for some moments.  The hunter, now doubly careful, knowing that his voice is criticised by the exquisite ear of the bull, kneels down, and, thrusting the mouth of his

MOOSE-CALLING BY NIGHT.

"call" into the bushes close to the ground, gives vent to a lower and more plaintive sound, intended to convey the idea of impatience and reproach. It has probably the desired effect; an answer is given, the snappings of branches are resumed, and presently the moose stalks into the middle of the moonlit barren, or skirts its sides in the direction of the sound. A few paces further—a flash and report from behind the little clump of concealing bushes, and the great carcass sinks into the laurels and mosses which carpet the plains.

Whatever may be adduced in disfavour of moose-calling on the score of taking the animal at a disadvantage, it is confessedly one of the most exciting of forest sports. The mysterious sounds and features of night life in the woods, the beauty of the moonlight in America—so much more silvery and bright than in England—the anxious suspense with which the hunter regards the last flutterings of the aspens as the wind dies away, and leaves that perfect repose in the air which is so necessary to the sport, and the intense feeling of sudden excitement when the first distant answer comes to the wild ringing call, are passages of forest life acknowledged by all who have experienced them as producing a most powerful effect on the imagination, both when experienced and in memory.

But few moose are shot in this manner—very few in comparison with the numbers tracked or crept upon—for the per centage of animals that are thus brought up, even by the best Indian caller, is very small, and it is the attribute of native hunters in every wild country where there are large deer—as the moose, reindeer, or sambur—to attain their object by imitation of their voices.

Another method of calling which has fallen into disuse was formerly practised by the Indians of the Lower Provinces in the fall. The hunter secretes himself in a swamp—one of those damp mossy valleys in which the moose delights at this season ; no moon is required, and his companion holds an immense torch, made of birch bark, and a match ready for lighting it. The moose comes to the call far more readily than when the hunter is on the open barren or bog, and, when within distance, the match is applied to the torch ; the resinous bark at once flares brightly, illuminating the swamp for a long distance round, and discovers the astonished moose standing amongst the trees, and apparently incapable of retreat. The Indians say that he is fascinated by the light, and though he may walk round and round, he cannot leave it, and of course offers an easy mark to the rifle.

It is no easy matter to make sure of a moose, even should he be within pistol range, in the uncertain moonlight ; chalk is sometimes used, the better to show when the barrel is levelled. A highly-polished silver bead is the best for a fore-sight, as it catches the light, and is readily discerned when the alignment is obtained.*

Moose-calling is always a great uncertainty. Some seasons there are when the moose will not come so readily as in others, but stop after advancing for a short distance, and remain in the forest for hours together, answering the call whenever it is made, and tearing the branches with their horns ; the hunter, his patience worn out, and

* " The old Bushman " recommended for shooting large game at night a V-shaped forked stick to be bound on the muzzle, stating that he found it of great service. Get the object in the field of view between the horns of the V and you are pretty sure to hit.

stiff with cold and from lying so **long** and motionless in
the damp bushes, at last gives it up, and retires to **his**
camp. Should there **be the** slightest wind, moose **will**
always take advantage of it in coming up **to the caller,**
and endeavour to get his scent. The capacious nostrils
of the moose, up which a man **can** thrust his arm, show
the fine powers **of** that **organ ; and** should the hunter
have crossed the barren or the forest intervening betwixt
him and the approaching bull at any time during the
day, unless **heavy** rain **has occurred and** obliterated the
smell of his track, the game is **up ; not** another sound is
heard from the moose, who at **once beats a retreat, and so**
noiselessly, that the hunter often **believes him** to be still
standing, quietly listening, when, in fact, he is **in full**
retreat, and miles away. In districts where moose are
very numerous, a number of bulls will reply to the call **at**
the same time from different parts of the surrounding
**woods ; and in such cases it becomes, as the Americans**
express it, " a regular jam ;" they fear one another; and,
unless one of them is a *real old 'un,* and **cares** for nobody,
cannot be induced to come out boldly, though they do
sometimes try to cheat one another, and sneak round the
edge of the woods very quietly.

Your patriarch moose, however, scorns a score of rivals,
and goes in for a fight on every fitting occasion ; indeed,
you have only to approach him when with his partner in
the thick swamp, and, cracking **a** bough or two, put the
call to your lips and utter **the** challenge-note **of a** bull.
With mad fury he leaves his mate and crashes **through**
**the** forest towards you, and then—shoot him, **or else**
stand clear. I have known this plan to be successfully
carried out **when** moose have been started, and are in full

flight ; the imitation of a rival bull has brought the moose suddenly round to meet his doom ; and it is a very common practice for the Indian to adopt, when a moose answers but will not come to the call, and he has every reason to believe that he is already accompanied by a cow.

A few falls since I was in the woods with a companion and an excellent Indian, who is still at the head of his profession, John Williams. We were in a hunting district not containing many moose, being too much surrounded by roads and settlements, but very accessible from Halifax, and one which would always afford a few days' hunting if the ground had not recently been disturbed. We were not much incumbered with baggage ; the nature of our movements prevented our taking much into the wood beyond the actual necessaries, *i.e.*, a small blanket apiece, which, rolled into a bundle, Indian fashion, and carried across the back by a strap passing over the chest and shoulders, contained the ammunition, a couple of pairs of worsted socks, brushes, combs, &c., and a few packages of tea, sugar, and such light and easily-stowed portions of the commissariat. The Indian carried in his bundle the heavier articles—the half dozen pounds of fat pork, about twice that amount of hard pilot bread, . the small kettle with a couple of tin pint cups thrust inside, they in their turn being filled with butter, or salt and pepper, or perhaps lucifers—anything, in fact, which could find a place and fit in snugly ; and lastly, and as a matter of course, a capacious frying-pan, made more portable by unshipping the handle. A large American axe, its head cased in leather, passed through his belt, from which were suspended the broad hunting-knife in an ornamented moose-skin sheath, and the tobacco-pouch of

otter or mink-skin. **Our suits were all of the strong grey**
homespun of the country, an almost colourless **material,**
and on that account, as well as for its tendency to dry
quickly when wet, owing to its porosity, very **valuable**
to the hunter as a universal cloth for every garment.

Thus accoutred, we marched through the forest in **file,**
laying down **our** bundles **now and then to** follow recent
moose-tracks which might cross our path, and to ascertain
**the** whereabouts of the game with regard to the barrens
towards which we were wending our way with the object
of calling the moose. **The previous night had been**
passed under the shelter of a grove of enormous hemlocks, where we had halted on **our** journey **from the**
settlements, night overtaking us. All night the **owls had**
hooted around our little primitive encampment—a sure
sign of coming rain ; and their melancholy **predictions**
were this morning verified, for a damp, misty drizzle **beat**
in our faces as we emerged from the forest on a **grassy**
meadow, which stretched away in a long valley, **and was**
dotted with stacks of wild meadow hay. It was one of
those miniature woodland prairies which afford the settler
such plentiful supplies for feeding his stock in winter, and
which are the result of the labours of the **once** abounding
beaver, **and** enduring monuments **of its industry.**

In crossing the meadows we came upon traces of a very
recent struggle between a young moose and a bear : the
bear had evidently taken advantage of the long grass to
steal upon the moose, and take him at a disadvantage in
the treacherous bog. The grass was much beaten down,
**and** deep furrows in the black **soil** below showed how
energetically the unfortunate moose had striven to escape
from his powerful assailant. There was a broad track,

plentifully strewed with moose hair, showing how the
moose had struggled with the bear towards the woods,
where no doubt the affair was ended, and the bear dined.
The full-grown moose is far too powerful an animal to
dread the attack of the bear ; it is only the unprotected
calf, separated from its parent, which is occasionally
pounced upon.

We reached the barren that afternoon, wet and uncomfortable, and were right glad when a roaring fire
rose up in front of the little gipsy-like camp, partly
of cut bushes and partly of birch bark, which the
Indian constructed for us in the middle.   We did
not care for the possibility of disturbing any stray
moose that might be in the immediate neighbourhood ;
the wind was rising and chasing away the murky
clouds from the northward, and there was no chance of
calling that night, so we passed the afternoon in drying
ourselves, and keeping up the fire, which was no easy
matter, as the woods skirting the barren were at some
distance, and the barren itself offered nothing but clumps
of wet green bushes, moss-tufts, ground laurels, and rocks.
The night was clear and frosty, as is generally the case
after rain ; it was so cold that we could not sleep much,
and our wood failed us.   Once, on going out to search for
some sticks, I heard a moose calling in the thick forest
through which we were to proceed in the morning, in
search of more distant hunting-grounds.

The prospect from our little grotto of bushes, as we
breakfasted next morning, was charming ; the tops of the
maple-covered hills, which sloped down towards the
barren on either side, were delicately tinged with warm
brownish-red, deepened by the frost of the previous night ;

and the bushes which skirted a little lake in front of us, over which hung a stationary line of mist, were painted with every hue, warmed and gilded at their summits by the slanting sun-rays. There was the delicate rose-colour varying to blood-red and deep scarlet, of the smaller maples, which are always brightest in swampy low situations, and the bright golden of the birches, poplars, and beeches. Sometimes a maple was wholly painted with the darkest claret, whilst in another a branch or two were vermilion, and the rest of the foliage of vernal greenness.

The rank patches of rhodora were tinged with a light pinkish tint, a pretty contrast to the rich shining green leaves of the myrica growing with the former shrub in damp spots. The flora of the fall, comprising asters, golden rods and wild-everlastings were all out, encircling the pearly grey rocks which strewed the barren, and every bush was wreathed with lines and webs of little spiders, marked by the myriads of minute dew-drops with which they were strung. Gradually warmed by the rays of the sun when, overcoming the surrounding barrier of the forest, they poured over the whole face of the scene, the little barren sparkled like fairy-land, the morning resolving itself into one of those glorious days for which the fall of the year is noted ; days when the light seems to bring out colours on objects which you would never see at other times; when all nature seems brightened up by the peculiar state of the atmosphere ; when the trees seem more beautiful, rocks more shapely, and water more pellucid ; when the sky has a greater softness and depth than commonly, and one's own feelings are in unison with all around.

On such a morning the clear, affecting notes of the hermit thrush seem more joyous than at his spring advent, and other lingering songsters—the white-throated sparrow, the red-breasted grosbeak, and the well-known robin—pour forth their strains as if in praise for the blessing of renewed summer life.

Our hunt through the neighbouring woods that forenoon was unsuccessful; all the tracks, though recent, showed that the moose had left the immediate vicinity. The "going" was bad, and, returning to camp, we determined to start immediately with our loads for some extensive barrens, of which the Indian knew, at a few miles' distance.

Our path lay through a large evergreen forest, and the walking on soft feather-moss was most refreshing after the painful morning's trudge over rocks and wind-falls. The ground was gently descending; and in the valley were little circular swamps and bogs where the firs showed evidences of the unhealthy situation by their scant foliage, and the profuse moss-beards which clung to them.

A dense covert of fern, coloured a golden brown in its autumnal decay, grew in the swamp : here and there a bunch of bright scarlet leaves of swamp-maple glowed amongst the colourless stems of rotted trees.

In situations like this the moose likes to dwell in the fall, and frequent tracks attested the very recent presence of these animals in the valley through which we were travelling.   Here and there the moss was scraped up in barrows-full, and the dark soil beneath hollowed out in a pit, giving out a strongly offensive odour as we passed ; in fact, the moose had, as Williams told us, only that morning passed, and we might come on them at any moment. We now travelled with great caution; any little blunder committed, such as a slight snap caused by stepping on a rotten stick, or grazing a gun-barrel against a tree-stem, was invested with a plausible appearance by the Indian, who would immediately apply the call to his lips, and utter a low grunt, as it were a moose walking through the woods. At last the forest opened ahead, the gloom of the pines gave place to brighter light, and we stood on the edge of the barren sought for. Below us lay the swamp through which we had followed the moose, and we had the satisfaction of seeing, on crossing the stagnant brook which separated it from our present position, the mud still circling where the animals had passed. They had just crossed it before us, and taken to the barren.

The barren, which was at some elevation above the swampy forest we had recently quitted, sloped from us in an undulating wilderness of tangled brakes and dead trees, whose tall, bleached forms reared themselves like ghosts in the fast approaching twilight. It was quite calm—a delightful evening for "calling"—and we disencumbered ourselves of the loads, and sat down in the bushes to smoke and converse in low tones until the moon should rise and mellow the twilight.

Everything was perfectly still, except the occasional tap of the woodpecker on the decayed trunk of some distant rampike. As the sun sank below the horizon, the gentle breeze gradually diminished, and now not a leaf on the poplar and maple bushes around us flutters.

" Now, John," I whispered to the Indian, " it is almost time to try your voice. We will make the moose hear

I

us to-night, if there are any in these woods. Ah ! did
you hear that ?    Listen."

We all heard it plainly—a heavy crash of branches on
the barren right in front of us ; then another, followed by
a rush through the bushes of some evidently large animal;
then came the call of the cow-moose, followed by the
grunting of bulls.

"Two or three of 'em," said John ; " whole crew
fighting in little swamp just ahead.   Grand chance this.
Put the bundles down behind the rock there, so as moose
can't see them, and look at your caps."

It was just the time to commence calling—the daylight had quite died out, and the young moon, nearly
half grown, shed an uncertain light over the gray rocks
and bare gaunt rampikes of the barren.   We moved on
to a little knoll a few yards ahead, whence was obtained
a view through the rocks and dead trees for over a hundred yards in the direction of the moose, and lay down
a few paces apart in the thick bushes which grew some
two or three feet high everywhere.

The Indian crouched behind a massive trunk near us,
and we anxiously awaited his first challenge to the
moose, which were in a swampy hollow in the barren,
not more than 500 yards distant, though the thickly
standing rampikes and rocks, and the unevenness of the
ground, prevented us from seeing them.   He seemed to
wait long and hesitatingly ; so much would depend upon
the skilfulness of his first call, and several times the bark
trumpet was withdrawn from his lips before he made up
his mind to the effort.

At length he called ; softly, and with a slight quaver,
the plaintive sound was drawn forth, apparently from the

lowest parts of his throat, checked in the middle, then again resumed, and its prolonged cadences allowed gradually to die away. It was a masterly performance ; and our pulses beat high as the echoes returned from the sides of the thick forest which skirted the barren, and we listened for some reply from the moose.

Then followed a prolonged crashing, as if a whole army of giants was forcing its way through the brittle rampikes ; it seemed impossible that a moose could have caused such a tremendous uproar—then a pause, and the moose answered the call—Quoh ! quofh ! He was evidently close at hand, though still concealed by the closeness of the covert ; and we were, moreover, lying crouched as flatly as possible on the ground, and behind a little rise in the barren, which intervened most conveniently. Here he remained for some moments, occasionally drawing his antlers with great rapidity and violence against the dead stems on either side, and making the brittle branches fly in all directions ; then another advance, though with less noise, and his grunts became less frequent ; at last, a dead stop, and not a sound for some moments. He was evidently becoming suspicious, not seeing the object of his desire on the barren before him where he had expected, for moose have a wonderful faculty of travelling through the woods towards a sound if only once heard. I have known them to come for miles, and straight as an arrow, to the exact spot where the Indian had been calling an hour or more previously, having left it in consequence of not hearing the answer.

There was a slight rustle just behind us, and, looking round, I perceived the Indian rapidly worming his way through the bushes, gliding like a snake. He beckoned

with his hand for us to remain quiet, and I at once
divined his object; he was making for the edge of the
woods, some hundred yards or so from the direction of
the moose. Presently a few loud snappings of dead
branches, purposely broken by the Indian as soon as he
had reached the covert, was followed by the well-coun-
terfeited call. The ruse succeeded; the suspicions of
the bull were allayed, and the horns were again dashed
against the stems as he unhesitatingly advanced towards
our ambush. At length we can plainly hear his footsteps,
and the rustling of the little bushes; every now and then
he utters a low, satisfied grunt to himself, as he winds up
the ascent. Now our pulses and hearts beat so, that it
becomes a wonder they do not scare the moose, and we
grasp the stocks of our rifles tightly as we wait for his
appearance. Here he comes! The moonlight just catches
the polished surfaces of his great spreading horns; a black
mountain seems to grow out of the barren in front, and
the bull stands immediately before us, his gigantic proportions standing out in bold relief against the sky, and
clouds of hot vapour circling from his expansive nostrils,
as he pauses for a moment to gaze forward from the
acquired elevation. He must see the glitter of the moonlight on our barrels as they are raised to the shoulder,
but it is too late for retreat; the sharp cracks of the two
rifles proclaim his doom, and as they are lowered the
great moose falls heavily over, without a pace accomplished in retreat, instantaneously dead. Our wild yell
of triumph was echoed by the Indian from the woods
behind, who hastened to join us; the echoes, so strangely
and rudely evoked from the distant forest, gradually fade
away, and all is again still, save where a distant crack

marks the flight of **the startled moose, the late comrades** of our noble bull.

" Pretty handy on to five feet," said John, as he with difficulty raised the ponderous head from the **bushes, to** display the breadth of the antlers ; " that's a great moose, old feller, that ; hind-quarters weigh goin' on for a hundred and **fifty weight each ; we have** to get two or three smart hands to back him out."

The night **was now far advanced, and it was with well-earned** satisfaction **that we stretched** ourselves in front of a roaring fire, wrapping **our blankets tightly round us.** Though **frosty, it was clear and calm ; we** needed no camp, and John dragged up log after **log of** the dead dry timber, **which** was strewed in **plentiful** confusion over the **barren,** until we had a fire **large** enough to have roasted our moose whole. The kettle, filled from **the brook below in the** swamp, soon **boiled,** and after a **refreshing cup and** a biscuit a-piece, we finally tightened our blankets round our forms, and, **with pipes** in our mouths, **gradually dozed off.**

Towards the morning is the coldest time of **the night,** and **I more** than once awoke **from the cold, and went** on the barren for fresh fuel **to supply** the quickly-decaying embers. There **was** the same **solemn** stillness over the **face of that wild scene : the moon was** down long since, **but a few** brilliant **streamers of** the aurora played in the clear sky in the north, and by their light I could **just** discern the great dark **form of the** moose in the **bushes,** all covered **with the thick rime frost, and** guarded **by** two colossal stems, which pointed sternly at the **victim** with their whitened branches, as if to demand vengeance **for** the death **of the** forest monarch. At intervals the

melancholy and deep-toned hoot of the eagle-owl came
from the recesses of the woods, and at length the effect
became so unbearingly solemn and mysterious, that I felt
a relief on stepping back into our little circle, and blew
the embers lustily until spires of flame seized hold of the
fresh wood, and the brilliant fire-light shut out the som-
breness of the dismal night scene.

The sun was long up, and shone brightly in our faces
ere we awoke the next morning, and certain indistinct
sounds of frying and savoury odours were mingled with
tha latter portions of our dreams.

" Come on, Capten," said John ; " come on, and eat
some moose.   This moose be very tender ; little later in
the fall not so good, though ; soon get tough and black."

It was excellent, not partaking of the rank musky
flavour which later in the autumn pervades the whole
carcase.   John fried some liver for himself, and we all
felt more inclined to bask out the day in the sun than to
prepare for a start homewards.   However, a couple of
hours found us plodding through the forest, the Indian
bearing across his shoulders the broad antlers, which
necessitated great management to insinuate through the
denser thickets.   John, however, knew a lumberer's path,
leading out towards the settlement, and we soon had
easy walking.   Once or twice a stream must be crossed,
and it was most interesting on such occasions to watch
the ease and dexterity with which the Indian would
fell a large tree to serve for a bridge, and, heavily bur-
dened as he was, cross on the stem, lopping off the inter-
posing branches as he proceeded, to prepare it for our
passage.   Poor Williams ! no assistance could be procured
at the settlement ; and, as we left him and started home-

wards with our trophy, he had undertaken to retrace his
steps alone to the carcase of the moose, and by degrees
bring out every pound of the meat on his own back.
And this feat he performed, though the distance was
fully five miles ; and the four quarters, exclusive of the
head, skin, and the massive neck, would weigh more
than five hundred pounds. We far from envied him his
task and the long trudge in the lonely forest.

# CHAPTER V.

## THE CARIBOO.

(*Rangifer*, Hamilton Smith ; *Rangifer Caribou*, Audubon and Bachman.)

Muzzle entirely covered with hair ; the tear bag small, covered with a
pencil of hairs. The fur is brittle ; in summer, short; in winter
longer, whiter ; of the throat longer. The hoofs are broad, depressed,
and bent in at the tip. The external metatarsal gland is above the
middle of the leg. Horns, in both sexes, elongate, subcylindric, with
the basal branches and tip dilated and palmated ; of the females
smaller. Skull with rather large nose cavity ; about half as long as
the distance to the first grinder ; the intermaxillary moderate, nearly
reaching to the nasal ; a small, very shallow, suborbital pit.

THE above diagnosis, taken from Dr. Gray's article on
the Ruminantia in the Knowsley menagerie, seems to
embrace the chief characteristics of the reindeer of the
sub-arctic regions. The colour, habits, &c., of the variety
designated above will be found succeeding the following
general considerations. As a species subject to but slight
local variation (with one possible exception in the case
of the barren ground cariboo) the reindeer, Cervus
tarandus of Linnæus, rangifer of Hamilton Smith, inhabits both the old and the new worlds under similar
circumstances of climate and natural productions. Its
range across the Northern continents of Asia, Europe and
America is almost unbroken ; whilst in the North

Atlantic, which presents the only serious interruption to its circumpolar continuity, it occurs in Iceland, Greenland and Newfoundland. Sometimes preferring the barren heights of the Norwegian fjells, or the elevated plateaux of Newfoundland, at others the seclusion of the pine forest (as with the woodland cariboo of America), its haunts and boundaries are always determined by the distribution of those mosses and lichens which almost exclusively constitute its food—the Cladonia rangiferina or reindeer lichen, with two or three species of Cornicularia and Cetraria.

When we consider the great antiquity of the reindeer, and its occurrence as a true fossil mammal coeval with the mammoth and other gigantic animals now extinct, in connection with its singular adaptation to feed on lichens—those representatives of a primitive vegetation which are still engaged in preparing a soil for higher forms in northern latitudes—we cannot fail in recognising its mission as an animal of the utmost importance in affording food and clothing to the primitive races of mankind of the stone age. With its remains discovered in the bone caves and drift beds of that period are associated stone arrow-heads and bone implements; whilst a resemblance of the animal, fairly wrought upon its own horn, leaves no room to doubt its uses as a beast of the chase, though probably not (in those savage times) of domestication.

Even in Cæsar's day ancient Gaul was a country of gloomy fir forests and extensive morasses, and its climate more like that of Canada at present. The reindeer also was still abundant throughout central Europe (though probably it had long since disappeared from Great

Britain and the south of France), and was in a state of gradual migration to its present northern haunts. A more essentially arctic deer than the elk, the reindeer, in its southern extension, is found with the latter animal co-occupant of the wooded regions which succeed the desert plains on the shores of the Polar ocean, termed "barren grounds" on the American continent, and "Tundras" in Europe and Asia. Its most southern limit in the Old World is reached in Chinese Tartary in lat. 50°. A fact mentioned in the Natural History Review, in an article on the Mammalia of Amoor land, may be here quoted as showing a singular meeting of northern and southern types of animal life. It is stated that the Bengal tiger, ranging northwards occasion-ally to lat. 52°, there chiefly subsists on the flesh of the reindeer, whilst the tail-less hare (pika) a polar resident, sometimes wanders south to lat. 48° where the tiger abounds.*

Following an ascending isotherm through Siberia and Northern Russia, the reindeer comes down on the elevated table-lands of Scandinavia to latitude 60°, "wherever," as Mr. Barnard observes in "Sport in Norway," "the altitude is above the limit of the willow and the birch." From the latter country the animal was successfully in-troduced into Iceland in 1770 (a similar attempt being made at the same time to acclimatize it in Scotland, which ended in failure), and has since so multiplied as to be regarded with disfavour by the inhabitants, who care little for it as a beast of the chase, on account of the

---

* Erman in his Siberian travels, speaking of the fauna of Irkutsk, in the trans-Bakalian districts, says :—" We see the Tunguze, mounted on his reindeer, passing the Buraet with his camel, and discover the tigers of China in the forests where the bear is taking its winter sleep."

damage it does to the **grasses and Iceland** moss on the
**plains.** According to Professor Paijkull, **author of " A**
Summer in Iceland," the desert plains south of Lake
Mývatn are its principal resort.

Crossing the Atlantic to the south of Greenland, which
is inhabited by the variety (or species?) R. Grœnlandicus,
the American reindeer, now termed the cariboo, is first
met with in Newfoundland. It **is** abundant on the
elevated plateaux **and** extensive **savannahs of** this great
island, **and** is sometimes seen on the cliffs even **at Cape**
Race.

The most southerly range attained by the species on
the Atlantic seaboard of North America is determined at
Cape Sable in Nova Scotia, in lat. 43° 30', or about that
of Marseilles. **In** this province the cariboo is becoming
very scarce, and almost altogether restricted to the high
lands of Cape Breton, and the Cobequid range of hills.
**It is** not found **in Prince** Edward's Island **or in**
Anticosti.

Tolerably abundant in New Brunswick and the adjoining portion of Canada south of the St. Lawrence to
the latitude of Quebec, of rarer occurrence in the State of
Maine, **we** find the home of the woodland cariboo
in the great belt of coniferous forest which in Upper
and Lower Canada extends northwards from the basin **of**
the St. Lawrence over an immense wilderness country,
and embraces the southern area **of** the Hudson's Bay
basin. From the western shore of Lake Superior, and
at some distance back from the prairie country, the line
**of** its range across the continent curves to the north-
west, following the rapidly ascending isotherm **into**
the Valley of the Mackenzie, and thence crossing the

Rocky Mountains, passes into the American territory of Alaska.

According to Mr. Lord* it inhabits the high ridges of the Cascade Mountains, the Galton range and western slope of the Rocky Mountains in British Columbia.

In evidence of the transmission of the cariboo into Eastern Asia, it is stated by Dr. Godman that it crosses from Behring's strait to Kamschatka by the Aleutian islands.

Closely associated with man in a state of semi-domestication in Siberia and Lapland, the wild rein-deer also largely contributes to the support of the various nomadic tribes of these countries, by whom it is slaughtered on the paths of its two great annual migrations. In America likewise, though no attempt has been made to convert the cariboo into a beast of burden, its flesh is the mainstay of many wandering Indian tribes who inhabit the subarctic forest region from Labrador to the northern spurs of the Rocky Mountains, and its skin their principal resource for clothing. In its distribution across the American continent, indicated above, it is pursued in the chase by the Montagnais and Nasquapee Indians of Labrador, the Crees and Chipe-wyans of Hudson's Bay, and the Dog-ribs and other tribes of the Mackenzie Valley. To the Micmacs, Malicites and others, south of the St. Lawrence, it is no longer indispensable as a staple of subsistence; they are now intimately associated with the civilisation of the white man, who completely possesses their hunting-grounds, and with whose mode of life they partially comply; but to the wilder races designated above, its gradual dis-

* The Naturalist in British Columbia.

appearance must bring starvation and a corresponding progress towards extinction.

With regard to the barren ground cariboo (R. Grœnlandicus) being distinct from the larger animal of the forests, the separation of the two as species by Professor Baird of the Smithsonian Institution at Washington in the description of North American mammals, which accompanies the War Department Reports of the Pacific Route, joined with the opinion expressed by Sir John Richardson in his "Journal of a Boat Voyage through Rupert's Land and the Arctic Sea," and the further testimony of Dr. King, surgeon to Back's expedition, appears to leave no room for doubt. Mr. Baird says "the animal is much smaller than the woodland reindeer; the does not being larger than a good sized sheep." The average weight of ninety-four deer shot in one season by Captain M'Clintock's men, when cleaned for the table, was sixty pounds. "A full-grown, well-fed buck," says Sir J. Richardson, "seldom weighs more than one hundred and fifty pounds after the intestines are removed. The bucks of the larger kind which were mentioned as frequenting the spurs of the Rocky Mountains, near the Arctic circle, weigh from two hundred pounds to three hundred pounds, also without the intestines." He also states that "this kind does not penetrate far into the forest even in severe seasons, but prefers keeping in the isolated clumps or thin woods that grow on the skirts of the barren grounds, making excursions into the latter in fine weather." Dr. King mentions that the barren-ground species is peculiar not only in the form of its liver, but in not possessing a receptacle for bile. This species ranges along the shores of the Arctic Ocean and of Hudson's Bay, above the northern limit of forest growth; it inhabits Melville and other islands of the Arctic archipelago, and is found in Greenland.

The cariboo of the forests of Lower Canada, Newfoundland and Nova Scotia, which we now proceed to describe, seems to attain in this portion of America, the finest development of which the species is susceptible. It is a strongly-built, thick-set animal, (that is by comparison with the more graceful of the Cervidæ), yet far from being as ungainly and slouching as the Norwegian reindeer is commonly depicted in drawings, though these are probably generally taken from domesticated specimens, which they resemble much more closely than they do the wild deer of the mountains. A very large buck in Newfoundland will exceed four hundred pounds in weight, and measure over four feet in height at the shoulder. I have seen a cariboo in Nova Scotia that must have considerably exceeded four feet six inches in height, and was thought by the Indian at a distance off to have been a moose.

Reindeer of a similar development, and in colour closely resembling the cariboo of Eastern America, were met with by Erman in Eastern Asia, where they are used for the saddle (placed on the shoulder—the only part of the back where the deer can support a load) by the Tunguzes. He states that the Lapland reindeer of menageries and museums appeared to him but dwarfs in comparison with those of Northern Asia, and with their size and strength seemed also to have lost much of their beauty of form.* Certainly the cariboo of Nova

* Speaking of the Tunguzes, Erman says :—" The charm of their look lies in their slim and active figure, as also in their constant connection with

Scotia or New Brunswick, as I have seen them, grace-fully trotting over the plains on light snow, and in Indian file, or, when alarmed, circling round the hunter with neck and head braced up and scut erect, stepping with an astonishing elasticity and spring, is a noble creature in comparison with the specimens of the reindeer of Northern Europe that have appeared in the Society's gardens at Regent's Park: they are, nevertheless, in-dubitably the same species and simply local varia-tions.

The colour of the American cariboo, as described by Audubon and Bachman, is as follows:—

"Tips of hairs light dun gray, whiter on the neck than elsewhere; nose, ears, outer surface of legs and shoulders brownish. Neck and throat dull white; a faint whitish patch on the side of shoulders. Belly and tail white; a band of white around all the legs adjoining the hoofs." From this general description there is, however, consider-able variation. Bucks in their prime are often of a rich, rufous-brown hue on the back and legs, having the neck and pendant mane, tail and rump, snow-white. A patch of dark hair, nearly black, appears on the side of the muzzle and cheek. As the hair grows in length, towards the approach of winter, it lightens considerably in hue: individuals may frequently be seen in a herd with coats of the palest fawn colour, almost white. Young deer are dappled on the side and flank with light sandy spots. The white mane, reaching to over a foot in length in old males, which hangs pendant from the neck with a graceful

one of the handsomest of animals; for when one sees a Tunguze sit, with the proudest deportment, on his reindeer, they both seem made for each other, and it is hard to decide whether the reindeer lends grace to the rider or borrows it from him."—*Travels in Siberia*, by Adolph Erman.

curve to the front, is one of the most noticeable and
ornamental attributes of the species.

The horns of different specimens vary greatly in form
both as regards the development of palmation and the
position of the principal branches. As a general rule,
the horns of the Norwegian reindeer are (according to
my impression) less subject to palmation of the main
shaft, which is longer, and broadens only at the top
where the principal tines are thrown off. I have, however, met with precisely the same form in antlers from
the Labrador. The accompanying figures will illustrate
the forms alluded to. The middle snag of the cariboo's
horn is also more developed than in the case of the
European variety.

In most instances there is but one well-developed
brow antler, the other being a solitary curved prong ;
sometimes, however, as shown in the illustration, very
handsome specimens occur of two perfect brow snags
meeting in front of the forehead, the prongs interweaving
like the fingers of joined hands.

Except in the case of the does and young bucks,
which retain theirs till spring, it is seldom that horns are
seen in a herd of cariboo after Christmas. The reason
to which the retention of the horns by the female reindeer
during winter has been attributed by some speculative
writers—namely, in order to clear away the deep encrusted
snow, and enable her fawns to get at the moss beneath
—is simply wrong. The animal never uses any other
means than its hoofs to scrape for its moss ; whilst the
thin sharp prongs of the doe would prove anything but an
efficient shovel. The latter and true mode of proceeding
I have often watched when worming through the bushes

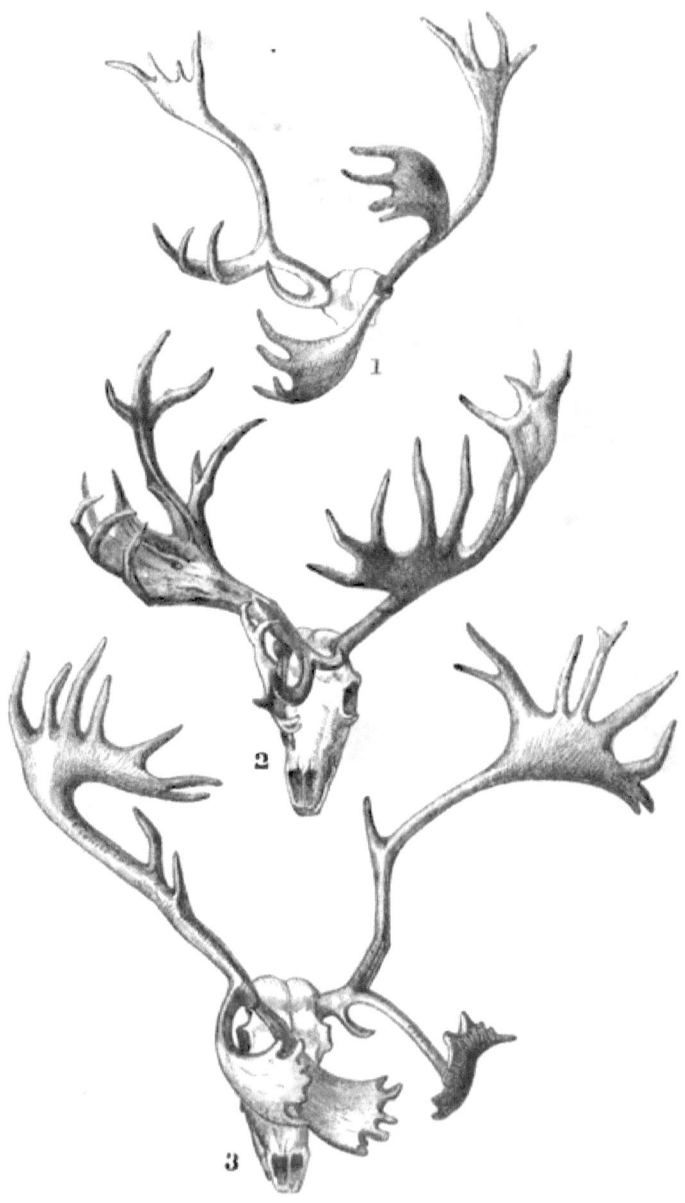

HORNS OF THE CARIBOO.

1. The ordinary Canadian type.
2. Cariboo horns from Newfoundland.
3. Horns from Labrador.

round the edge of a barren to get a shot. Both Mr. Barnard, and the author of "Ten Years in Sweden," allude to the female reindeer using her horns in winter to protect the fawns from the males, thus rightly accounting for this singular provision of nature in the case of a gregarious species in which the males, females, and young herd together at all seasons.

Another misrepresentation has appeared with regard to the reindeer : it has been compared, when obliged to cross a lake on ice, to a cat on walnut-shells! I cannot conceive any variation in a point so intimately connected with its winter habits on the part of the European reindeer, if the two are, as I believe, identical in configuration and subservience to existence under precisely similar circumstances ; but for the cariboo I can aver that its foot is a beautiful adaptation to the snow-covered country in which it resides, and that on ice it has naturally an advantage similar to that obtained artificially by the skater. In winter time the frog is almost entirely absorbed, and the edges of the hoof, now quite concave, grow out in thin sharp ridges ; each division on the under surface presenting the appearance of a huge mussel-shell. According to "The Old Hunter," who has kindly forwarded to me some specimens shot by himself in Newfoundland in the fall of 1867 for comparison with examples of my own shot in winter, the frog is absorbed by the latter end of November, when the lakes are frozen ; the shell grows with great rapidity, and the frog does not fill up again till spring, when the antlers bud out. With this singular conformation of the foot, its great lateral spread, and the additional assistance afforded in maintaining a foot-hold on slippery surfaces

K

by the long stiff bristles which grow downwards at
the fetlock, curving forwards underneath between
the divisions, the cariboo is enabled to proceed over
crusted snow, to cross frozen lakes, or ascend icy precipices with an ease which places him, when in flight,
beyond the reach of all enemies, except perhaps the
nimble and untiring wolf.

The pace of the cariboo when started is like that of
the moose, a long, steady trot, breaking into a brisk walk
at intervals as the point of alarm is left behind. He
sometimes gallops, or rather bounds, for a short distance
at first; this the moose never does. When thoroughly
alarmed, he will travel much further than the moose;
the hunter having disturbed, missed, or slightly wounded
the latter, may, by following him up, very probably get
several chances again the same day. Such is seldom the
case in cariboo hunting, even in districts where the
animals are rarely disturbed. Once off, unless wounded,
you do not see them again.

The cariboo feeds principally on the Cladonia rangiferina, with which barrens and all permanent clearings in
the fir forest are thickly carpeted, and which appears to
grow more luxuriantly in the subarctic regions than in
more temperate latitudes. Mr. Hind, in "Explorations
in Labrador," describes the beauty and luxuriance of this
moss in the Laurentian country, "with admiration for
which," he says, "the traveller is inspired, as well as for
its wonderful adaptation to the climate, and its value as
a source of food to that mainstay of the Indian, and consequently of the fur trade in these regions—the caribou."
The recently-announced discovery by a French chemist
who has succeeded in extracting alcohol in large quanti-

ties from lichens, and especially from **the reindeer** moss (identical in Europe with **that of** America), is interesting, and readily suggests the value of this primitive **vegeta-**tion in supporting animal **life in a** Boreal climate **as a** heat-producing food. Besides **the** above, which appears to be its staple food, the cariboo partakes of the *tripe de roche* (Sticla pulmonaria) **and other** parasitic lichens growing on the bark of trees, and is exceedingly fond of the Usnea, which grows on the boughs (especially affecting the top) of the black spruce, in long, pendant hanks. **In the** forests on the Cumberland **Hills,** in Nova Scotia, I have observed the **snow quite trodden down** during the night by the cariboo, **which had resorted to** feed on the "old man's beards" in the tops of the spruces felled by **the** lumberers on the day previous. **In the** same locality I have observed such frequent scratchings in the first light **snow of the** season at the foot **of the** trees in beech groves, that I am convinced that **the** animal, like **the bear, is partial to** the rich food afforded by the mast.

I am not aware that a favourite item of the diet of the Norwegian reindeer—Ranunculus glacialis—is found in America, and the woodland cariboo has no chance of exhibiting the strange but well-authenticated taste of the former animal by devouring the lemming ; otherwise the habits of the two varieties are perfectly similar as regards food.

The woodland cariboo, like the Laplander's reindeer, is essentially a migratory animal. There are two well-defined periods of migration—in the spring and autumn—whilst throughout the winter it appears constantly seized with an unconquerable desire to change its residence.

The great periodic movements seem to result from an instinctive impulse of the reindeer throughout its whole circumpolar range. Sir J. Richardson, in America, Erman and Von Wrangell, in Northern Europe and Asia—the three distinguished *savants* who have contributed so largely to the natural history of the northern regions—all affirm the regularity of its migrations to the open steppes, barren grounds, and bare mountains, and point to the chief cause—a desire to escape the insupportable torments of the flies which swarm in the forest. In Newfoundland the cariboo acts in a manner precisely similar to that described by Wrangell, in speaking of the reindeer of the Aniui. They leave the lake country and broad savannahs of the interior for the mountain range which covers the long promontory terminating at the Straits of Belleisle, at the commencement of summer, and return when warned by the frosts of September to seek the lowlands. At this time the deer passes, and valleys at the head of the Bay of Exploits may be seen thick with deer moving in long strings; and here the Red Indians of a past age, like the hunters of the Aniui, would congregate to kill their winter's supply of venison.

With regard to the restlessness of this animal at intervals in the forest country in winter time, I have frequently observed a sudden and contemporary shift of all the cariboo throughout a large area of country. One day quietly feeding through the forest in little bands, the next, perhaps, all tracks would show a general move in a certain direction; the deer joining their parties after a while, and entirely leaving the district, travelling in large herds towards new feeding-grounds, almost invariably down the wind. The little Arctic reindeer of North

America is far less migratory in its habits than the larger species, and with the musk-sheep (ovibos) remains in the same localities throughout the year.

In forest districts, in many parts of its range over the Northern American continent, the cariboo is found together with the moose in the same woodlands. They appear, however, to avoid each other's company; and I have observed in following the tracks of a travelling band of cariboo, that, on passing a fresh moose-yard, they have broken into a trot—a sure sign of alarm. In many districts, especially those in which the existing southern limits of the cariboo are marked, this animal is gradually disappearing, whilst the moose is taking its place. To a great extent this is the result of an increasing settlement of the country by man. The moose is a much more domestic animal in its habits, and will remain and multiply in any small forest district, however the latter may be surrounded by roads or settlements; whereas the cariboo is a great wanderer, and requires long and unbroken ranges of wild country in which he can uninterruptedly indulge his vagrant habits. Being moreover more jealous of the advance of civilisation than the moose, he is surely disappearing as his old lines of periodic migration are encroached upon and broken by new settlements and their connecting roads.

In winters of great severity the cariboo always travel to the southernmost limits of their haunts, which they occasionally exceed and enter the settlements. Some years ago, during an unusually cold winter, the deer crossed in large bands from Labrador into Newfoundland over the frozen straits. As assumed by Dr. Gray, a variety appears to be established in the case of the Newfoundland cariboo. These deer certainly attain a greater development than the generality of the specimens shot on the continent: I have heard of bucks weighing six hundred pounds, and even over. The general colour of the former animals is lighter—to be accounted for, perhaps, by the fact that Newfoundland is a far more open country than the eastern parts of Canada and the Lower Provinces. The herds are moreover comparatively undisturbed, and the moss grows in the greatest profusion. I have seen the fat taken off the loins of a Newfoundland deer o the depth of two inches. Further particulars concerning the cariboo on this island and its migrations will be found in a chapter on Newfoundland.

# CHAPTER VI.

## CARIBOO HUNTING.

THE cariboo of the British provinces is only to be approached by the sportsman with the assistance of a regular Indian hunter. In old times the Indians possessed and practised the art of calling the buck in September, as they now do the bull moose, the call-note being a short hoarse bellow; this art however is lost, and at the present day the animal is shot by stalking or "creeping" as it is locally termed, that is, advancing stealthily and in the footsteps of the Indian, bearing in mind the hopelessness of success should sound, sight or scent give warning of approaching danger. As with the moose, the latter faculty seems to impress the cariboo most with a feeling of alarm, which is evinced at an almost incredible distance from the object, and fully accounted for, as a general fact, by the size of the nasal cavity, and the development of the cartilage of the septum. As the cariboo generally travels and feeds down wind, the wonderful tact of the Indian is indispensable in a forest country, where the game cannot be sighted from a distance as on the fjelds of Scandinavia, or Scottish hills. Of course, however, on the plateaux of Newfoundland and Labrador, and on the large cariboo-plains of Nova Scotia and New Brunswick, less Indian craft is brought

into play, and the sport becomes assimilated to that of
deer-stalking.

It is almost hopeless to attempt an explanation of the
Indian's art of hunting in the woods — stalking an
invisible quarry ever on the watch and constantly on the
move, through an ever-varying succession of swamps,
burnt country, or thick forest.    A review of all the
shifts and expedients practised in creeping, from the first
finding of recent tracks to the exciting moment when the
Indian whispers " Quite fresh; put on cap," would be impracticable.    I confess that like many other young hunters
or like the conceited blundering settlers, who are for
ever cruising through the woods, and doing little else
(save by a chance shot) than scaring the country, I once
fondly hoped to be able to master the art, and to hunt on
my own account.    Fifteen years' experience has unde-
ceived me, and compels me to acknowledge the superiority
of the red man in all matters relating to the art of
" venerie " in the American woodlands.

When brought up to the game in the forest, there is
also some difficulty in realising the presence of the
cariboo.    At all times of the year its colour is so similar
to the pervading hues of the woods, that the animal,
when in repose, is exceedingly difficult of detection : in
winter, especially, when standing amongst the snow-
dappled stems of mixed spruce and birch woods, they are
so hard to see, and their light gray hue renders the judging of distance and aim so uncertain, that many escape
the hunter's bullet at distances, and under circumstances,
which should otherwise admit of no excuse for a miss.

And now let us proceed to our hunting ground.

The first light snow had just fallen after two or three

piercingly cold and frosty days towards the close of
November, when our party, consisting of us two and our
attendant Indian, the faithful John Williams, (than
whom a more artful hunter or more agreeable companion
in camp never stepped in mocassin) arrived at the little
town of Windsor, at the head of the basin of Minas,
whence embarking in a small schooner, we were to cross
to the opposite side to hunt the cariboo in the neighbourhood of Parsboro'. The distance across was but a matter
of thirty miles or so, and with light hearts we stepped on
board, and stowed our camping apparatus, bags of provisions, blankets and rifles in the hold of the "Jack
Easy," when presently the rapidly ebbing tide bore us
swiftly down the course of the Avon into the dark-
coloured waters of the arm of the Bay of Fundy.

The first part of the voyage was pleasant enough ; a
light though freshening breeze from the eastward filled
the sails ; and we swept on with the surging tide of red
mud and water past the great dark headland of Blomidon
with its snow-streaked furrows and crown of evergreen
forest, enjoying both our pipes and the prospect, and
recalling the various interesting traditions of this famed
location of the old Acadians whose memory has been so
beautifully perpetuated by Longfellow. But on leaving
the cape and standing across the open bay, we soon
encountered a rougher state of affairs. The dark murky
clouds now commenced discharging a heavy fall of damp
snow, which froze upon everything as soon as it fell,
rendering the process of reefing, which had become necessary from the increasing breeze, very difficult of accom-
plishment. The sheets were coated with a film of ice,
and frozen stiffly in the blocks, and the deck became so

wet and slippery that we were glad to retire below into
the close little cabin. We had embarked at sunset, as
the tide did not suit until then, and not even a small
schooner of the dimensions of the "Jack Easy" can leave
the Windsor river until the impetuous tide of this curious
bay sweeps up, and, rising to the height of forty feet,
bears up all the craft around the wharves from their soft
repose in the red mud. It was now dark, and the storm
increased ; the wind, being against tide, raised a tumultuous sea. Presently there were two or three vivid flashes
of lightning, followed by increased violence of the wind
and dense driving hail, and the little schooner lay heavily
over. We, the passengers, were huddled together in a
cabin so small that it was with difficulty we could keep
our knees from touching the stove round which we
crowded. Everyone smoked, of course, and the strong
black tobacco of the settlers vied with the rushes of
smoke, driven by the wind down the stove-pipe, in producing in the den a state of atmosphere threatening
speedy suffocation, and we were glad to grope our way
into the dark hold and seek an asylum amongst the tubs,
barrels, and potato sacks which were rolling about in
great uneasiness. At last it was over : a quieter state of
affairs, a great deal of stamping and slipping on deck,
and, finally, the long rattle of the cable, told us we were
anchored off Parsboro'—a fact which was corroborated
by the captain opening the hatch and lowering himself amongst us, one mass of ice and snow ; his clothes
rattled and grated as he moved as though they were
constructed of board. There was no shore bed for our
aching bones that night ; the tide did not suit to reach
the wharf, the village was a mile and a half away, and

the night was still stormy, so we again sought soft spots on the inexorable benches around the stove in our den.

" Hurrah, John !" said I, as we followed the Indian up the ladder, and emerged into the cold morning air ; " here's snow enough in all conscience—just the thing for our hunting—step out now for the village, and let's try and scare up a breakfast somewhere."

It was still snowing heavily, and the country looked as wintry as it could do even in North America. In the distance appeared the little white wooden houses and church of the village, and behind them rose up the great grey form of the Cobequid Hills. The brisk walk through the snow soon recalled warmth to our benumbed frames, and, the village inn once reached, it was not long ere the ample breakfast of ham and eggs and potatoes, pickles and cheese, cold squash-pie, and strong black tea, was arranged before us.

" Will the Indian make out with you, gents ?" asked the exceedingly pretty innkeeper's daughter. We all glanced at John, who laughed as he anticipated our reply.

" Oh, of course, yes ; we are all on the same footing this morning, we guess. Come on, John, sit up and give us some ham."

The landlord—who affected to be a bit of a sportsman, of course—told us there were lots of cariboo back in the hills, and some moose, which he reckoned would be the great object of our hunting ; for, in this part of Nova Scotia, the moose has only recently made his appearance, and the settlers look upon him as far nobler game than the common cariboo. Presently a sleigh with a stout pony appeared for us at the door, and, loading it with our baggage, we left to the tune of a peal of merry bells which the pony carried attached to different parts of the harness.

Our road lay through a valley, skirted by the lofty wooded slopes of the Cobequids. These hills are the great stronghold of the cariboo, and his last resort in Nova Scotia; they extend through the isthmus which connects the province with that of New Brunswick, and are covered with large hard-wood forests of sugar and white maple, birch, and beech. On their broad tops and sides the cariboo has an unbroken range of more than a hundred miles, and their eastern spurs, descending into a flat district of dense fir forests, with numerous chains of lakes, offer secure retreats in the breeding season.

The country was new to us, and its features novel: the evergreen forest, so characteristic of the greater portion of the province, here almost entirely gave way to hard-woods, narrow lines of hemlock or spruce springing up from some deep gorge on the mountain side, here and there showing their dark summits, and coursing like veins through the great rolling sea of maples. The latter part of the storm had been unaccompanied by wind, and the snow lay in heavy masses on the trees, giving the forest a most beautiful aspect; it covered every branch and every twig, and was thickly spattered against the stems, and all the complicated tracery of the denuded branches was brought to notice, even in the deepest recesses, by the white pencil of the snow-storm. In the fir forest the effect of newly-fallen snow is very fine also, but the very masses which cover the broad and retentive branches of the evergreens and clog the younger trees until they seem like solid cones of snow, hinder and

choke the view ; whereas in these lofty hard-woods,
under which grows nothing but slender saplings, a most
extensive glimpse of their furthest depths is obtained,
and thousands of delicate little ramifications, before unnoticed, now stand out in bold relief in the grey gloom
of the distance. And then, when the storm has passed
by, and that beautiful blue tint of a wintry sky, coursed
by light fleecy scud, succeeds the heavily laden cloud,
how exquisitely the scene lights up! what a soft warm
tint is thrown upon the light-coloured bark of the maples
and birches, and upon the prominent dottings and lines
of snow which mark their forms, and how lovely is that
light purple shade which continually crosses the road,
marking the shadows! As the sun increases in warmth,
or a passing gust of wind courses through the trees,
avalanches of snow fall in sparkling spray, and the new
snow glitters in myriads of little scintillations, so that
the eye becomes pained by the intensity of brilliancy
pervading the face of nature.

We stopped the sleigh opposite a group of Indian bark
wigwams, which stood a short distance from the road ;
the noise of voices and curling wreaths of smoke from
their tops proved them to be occupied, and, as we required a second Indian hunter, particularly one who was
well acquainted with the neighbourhood, we followed the
track which led up to them, and entered the largest.
The head of the family, who sat upon a spread cariboo-
skin of gigantic proportions, was one of the finest old
Indians I ever saw—one of the last living models of a
race now so changed in physical and moral development
that it may be fairly said to be extinct. An old man of
nearly eighty winters was this aged chief, yet erect, and

with little to mark his age save the grizzly hue pervading
the long hair which streamed over his broad shoulders,
and half concealed the faded epaulettes of red scalloped
cloth and bead-work. A necklace of beads hung round
his neck, and, suspended from it, a silver crucifix lay on
his bare expansive chest. His voice, as he welcomed us,
and beckoned us to the post of honour opposite to the
fire and furthest from the door, though soft and melodious, was deep-toned and most impressive. Williams,
our Indian, greeted and was greeted enthusiastically ; he
had found an old friend, the protector of his youth,
in whose hunting camps he had learnt all his science ;
the old squaw, too, was his aunt, whom he had not seen
for many years.

The chief was engaged in dressing fox-skins : he had
shot no less than twenty-three within the week or two
preceding, and whilst we were in the camp a couple of
traders arrived, and treated with him for the purchase of
the whole, offering two dollars a-piece for the red foxes,
and five or six for the silver or cross-fox, of which there
were three very good specimens in the camp. The skin
of the fox is used for sleigh robes, caps, and trimmings.
The valuable black fox is occasionally shot or trapped by
the Indians, and the skin sold, according to condition
and season, from ten, even as high as twenty pounds.
The coat of a good specimen of the black fox in winter
is of a beautiful jet black colour, the hair very long, soft,
and glossy ; and, as the animal runs past you in the sunshine on the pure snow, and a puff of wind ruffles the
long hair, it gleams like burnished silver. It appears that
the whole of the black fox-skins are exported to Russia,
and are there worn by the nobility round the neck, or as

collars for their cloaks ; the nose is fastened by a clasp to the top of the tail, the rest of which hangs down in front.

The old man told us of the curious method he used in obtaining his fox-skins. He would go off alone into the moonlit forest, to the edge of some little barren, which the foxes often cross, or hunt round its edges at night. Here he would lie down and wait patiently until the dark form of a fox appeared in the open. A little shrill squeak, produced by the lips applied to the thumbs of the closed hands, and the fox would at once gallop up with the utmost boldness, and meet his fate through the Indian's gun.

He regretted that he was too old to accompany us himself, but advised us to take a young Indian who was at that time encamped on the ground to which we were proceeding ; and we left the old man's camp, and resumed our trudge on the main road, after seeing him make a successful bargain for his fox-skins.

That afternoon we had reached our destination ; the last few miles of the road had been more and more wild and uneven, and at last we drew up before a tenement and its outbuildings which stood on the brow of a hill and overlooked a wide extent of country. It was the house of the last settler, and those great undulating forests before us were to be the arena of our sport. Buckling on the loads, we dismissed the sleigh, and turned at once into their depths.

We had not far to carry our loads, for the Indian camp was erected on a hard-wood hill, within reach of the sounds of the last settler's clearing. This we found afterwards to be a great comfort, as we often called on

him for the loan of his sleigh and trusty yoke of oxen,
and drew large supplies of fine mealy potatoes from his
cellar ; great luxuries they are, too, and valuable additions to the camp fare, though they often have to be
omitted, when the distance of the hunting country from
the settler's house precludes any extra weight in the
apportioned loads.

Noel Bonus, the owner of the camp, was at home, just
returned from his hunting, for an early dinner, and to
him we applied direct to act as our landlord and hunter.
I never saw a dirtier or more starved-looking Indian ;
selfishness and cunning were plainly stamped on his
tawny face, which was topped by the shaggiest mass of
long black hair conceivable ; he seemed irresolute for
some moments as to whether he should admit us, and
take the dollar per diem and his share of the meat, or
whether he should continue to hunt on his own account,
and leave us to shift for ourselves.

We did not urge the point, for we had a first-rate
hunter, John Williams, with us, and though he did not
know the country, he would soon master that difficulty ;
and, as to a camp, we had all the requisite appliances for
quickly setting up on our own account.  This became
gradually evident to Master Noel, who at last motioned
us to take off our loads and come in—a proceeding
which we politely declined doing until a thorough reno-
vation and cleansing had taken place, and the dirty
bedding of dried shrivelled fir-boughs, strewed with
bones and bits of hide and hoof, had been swept out
and replaced by fresh.  It was a capital camp, strongly
built, and quite rain-proof, standing on a well-timbered
hard-wood hill, the stems of the smaller trees affording

an unlimited supply of fuel; a small spring trickled down the hill-side close by.

As we unpacked our bundles to get at the ammunition (for we were determined to have a cruise around before dark), Noel told us that he had, early that same morning, missed a cariboo not more than a mile from camp. We started in different directions, I with Noel, and my comrade with the older hunter. It was a bright, frosty afternoon, very calm, and the beautiful woods still retained their oppressive loads of heavy snow, rendering it very difficult to see game between the thickly-growing evergreens. Noel first followed a line of marten traps of his own setting—little dead-falls occurring every fifty yards or so in a line through the woods for nearly a mile. There was nothing in them, though I saw several tracks of marten on the snow. Fox-tracks, and those of the little American hare, commonly called the rabbit, on which the fox preys, were exceedingly numerous, and there was a fair sprinkling of the other tracks which are usually found on the snow in the forest, such as lucifee or wild cat, porcupine, partridge, and squirrel. Presently Noel gave a satisfactory grunt, and pointed to the surface of the snow ahead, which was evidently broken by the track of some large animal.

"Fresh track, caliboo,* thees mornin'," whispered he, as we came up to the trail of two cariboo, which had gone down wind, and in the direction of some large barrens which Noel said lay about a mile away. We might yet have a chance by daylight, so on we went pretty briskly, though cautiously. Noel pointed out several times small pieces which had been bitten off the

* The Indians pronounce the letter r as l.

I.

lichens growing on the stems of the hard-wood trees, of
which they had taken a passing mouthful.  Who but an
Indian could have detected such minute evidences of their
actions ?  There was no doubt but that they were making
for the barrens, or they would have stopped at these
tempting morsels longer, and here and there perhaps
deviated from the line of march.  Probably they knew
of companions, and were going to a rendezvous, or
preferred the reindeer moss amongst the rocks on the
barren.

The tall forest of maples and birches was presently
succeeded by a dense growth of evergreens, which became more and more stunted as we approached the
barren, and here and there opened out into moist swampy
bogs, into which we sank ankle-deep at every step :
finally, we brushed through the thick shrubbery, drenched
with the snow dislodged plentifully over us *en passant*,
and stood on the edge of a most extensive barren.

Such a scene of desolation is seldom witnessed, except
in these great burnt and denuded wastes of the North
American forest.  As far as the eye could reach was a
wild undulating wilderness of rocks and stumps ; a deep
indigo-coloured hill showed the limits of the barren, and
where the heavy fir forest again resumed its sway.  It
appeared to be some ten miles or so in length, and to
slope from us in a gentle declivity towards the westward.  The average breadth might be four or five miles.
Little thickets and groves of wood dotted it in all directions ; sometimes a clump of spruce, against which the
white stem of the birch stood out in bold relief ; or, at
others, a patch of ghost-like rampikes ; whilst the brooks
in the valleys were marked by fringing thickets of alder.

Boulders of rock and fallen trees were strewed over the whole surface of the country in the wildest confusion; and the dark, **snow-laden sky** cast a shade over the scene, investing it with the most forbidding and gloomy appearance imaginable.

Carefully scanning the surrounding country, and not perceiving any signs of the game, we proceeded on their tracks, which were soon increased in number by those of three other cariboo, joining in from the southward. They led **us through** some dense thickets, where we had to proceed with the greatest caution, there being no **wind**, and on account of the uncertainty of the moment or place where we might come upon them. I was getting tired of the whole proceeding, when, **as we were crossing** an open spot amongst rocks **and** sparsely-growing spruce clumps of about our own height, I **saw Noel**, who was ahead, suddenly stop, with his hand held **back**, and slowly subside in the snow, which proceedings of course I followed, without question as to **the** cause or necessity.

" What is it, Noel ?" said I, gaining his side by slowly worming along in the snow, with difficulty keeping the muzzle of my rifle above the surface.

" Caliboo lying down," he replied. " You no see **them now** ? Better fire, I think."

I could not for my life see the cariboo, although I looked along the barrel of his gun, which he pointed for me in the right direction. They are most difficult animals to recognise unless moving, being so exceedingly similar in colour to the rocks and general features of the barren, that only the eye of the Indian can readily detect them when lying down. Noel had at once seen the herd ; and here was I, unable **to** perceive them amongst the rocks and bushes, though pointed to the exact spot, and knowing that they were little more than one hundred yards distant. At last I saw the flapping of one of their ears, and gradually the whole contour of the recumbent animal nearest to me became evident.

I now did a very foolish thing, and was determined to have my shot at the nearest cariboo, lying down. The animal was in a hollow, deeply bedded in the snow, so that very little of the back could be seen, and I aimed at the lowest part visible above the snow. I pulled—a spirt of snow showed that the dazzling surface had deceived me, and the bullet ricochetted harmlessly over the back of the cariboo.

Up they jumped, five of them, apparently rising from all directions around us, and, after a brief stare, made off in long graceful bounds. I at once seized the old musket which the Indian carried, but the hammer descended on harmless copper—the cap was useless. "This is bad," thought I; for I hate missing the first shot on a hunting excursion, particularly with game to which one is not accustomed, as there is still more fear of becoming unsteady, and missing, on the next chance presenting itself; and I watched the cariboo with longing eyes, and a feeling of great disappointment, as they settled down into a long, swinging trot, and wound in file over the barren, towards the line of forest on the north side. As for the hungry-looking Indian, I did not know whether to have at him on the score of his excessive ugliness, or for not carrying better caps for his gun.

"Get back to camp, Noel, as quick as you can," said I; "it will be dark in half an hour. Why didn't you put up the cariboo on their legs for me before I fired?"

"Gentleman just please himself," replied the Indian. "You did very foolish ; nice lot of caliboo, them. Maybe other gentleman get shot, though."

"Oh, it's the fresh steak for supper you are thinking of," thought I to myself, feeling as discontented and generally uncharitable as possible. "I hope sincerely they have not, though ;" and I trudged after the Indian homewards in an unenviable mood. Fortunately there was an old road leading across the barren towards the settlements, and, presently striking it, we obtained easy walking. A couple of hours, the latter part by moonlight, brought us to our camp. No smoke issued from the top, and everything was as we left it. The others had not returned, and we made up a fire and cooked the meal we so much needed.

"I was almost afraid you were lost, John," said I, as the blanket which covered the entrance was withdrawn by the returning hunter and my companion, very late in the evening ; "any sport ?"

"Never fear," replied Williams, laughing, as he lugged in a great sack of potatoes, and produced a bottle of new milk, and some loaves of home-made bread ; "here's our game. We just had first-rate dinner at settler's ; good old man, that old Harrison."

They, too, had fired at cariboo, and wounded a young one slightly. It had led them a race of some miles, and finally, having joined a fresh herd, had escaped through the confusion of tracks. However, we retired to our repose on the soft bed of fir-boughs that night, quite satisfied and hopeful. We were in a fine country, evidently full of game, and we looked forward to our future shots with confidence, satisfied, from what we had seen, that the cariboo was one of the finest deer, for sport, in the wide world.

What a hearty meal is breakfast in the winter camp of a party of hunters in the American backwoods! The pure air which enters freely and circulates round the camp, heated by the great log fire in the centre, round which we range ourselves for sleep, regardless of the cold without (except, perhaps, on some especially severe passage of cold, when actual roasting on one side will scarcely keep the opposite from freezing), conduce to sound and healthy repose, and a feeling of wonderful freshness and activity on awakening and throwing off the blanket or buffalo robe early in the morning.

The Indians are already up, one cleaning the guns, or "fixing" a moccasin, whilst the other is holding the long-handled frying-pan, filled with spluttering slices of bacon, over the glowing embers. Their toilet amounts to nil; when well they always look clean, though they seldom wash; though they never use a comb their long, shining, raven-black hair is always smooth and unruffled. We, with our combs, brushes and towels, step out into the cold morning air and betake ourselves to the little brook for ten minutes or so, and then return with appetites whetted either for venison or the flesh of pig, washed down by potations of strong black tea, which has simmered by the embers, perhaps, for the last half-hour.

"John," said I, as we reclined on our blankets at breakfast the morning after our unsuccessful cariboo hunt, "did you hear the wild geese passing over to the southward last night? I heard their loud 'honk! honk!' several times, and the whistling of their wings as they flew over the camp. It froze pretty sharp, too; the trees cracked loudly in the forest."

"I hear 'um, sure enough," replied the Indian. "Guess winter set in pretty hard up to nor'rerd. I got notion some of us have luck to-day, capten. I dreamin' very hard last night. When I dream so always sure sign we have luck next day. I think it will be you; me and the other gentleman must go back and try to get the wounded caliboo calf."

"Very well, then: Noel hunts with me again to-day," said I, looking at the younger Indian, who nodded assent and drew on his moccasins. "Come on, Noel; put a biscuit in your pocket, and let us be off for the barrens."

It was a lovely morning when we left the camp; not a breath of wind, and the sun shone through the trees, lighting with extraordinary brilliancy the sparkling snow which had been sprinkled during the night with rime frost. All nature seemed to rejoice at the warming influence of the sun's rays. The squirrel raced up the stems with more than usual activity, and the little chickadee birds darted about amongst the spruce boughs in merry troops, dislodging showers of snow, and continuously uttering the cheerful cry which has given them their local *sobriquet*. The tapping of the woodpecker resounded through the calm forest, and the harsh warning note of the blue jay gave notice of our approach to his comrades and the forest denizens in general. Here and there a ruffed grouse started with boisterous flight from our path, as we disturbed his meditations on some sunlit stump; and, soon after entering the barren, a red fox jumped from the warm side of a clump of bushes where he had been basking, and made off at racing speed—a far handsomer animal than our English Reynard, whose fur is quite dingy compared with the bright orange-red coat of the American.

"Ah! I don't like to see this," said Noel, pointing out some large tracks in the snow; "these brutes been huntin' about here some time. You see that track?— that wolf-track—two of them; them tracks we seen yesterday, when we thought dogs were chasing moose, them was wolf-tracks."

The day before we had noticed the tracks of what we then thought had been dogs chasing a young calf-moose. At one place—a very deep, swampy bog—they had nearly run into him, for, on the snow, we saw hair which they had pulled from his flanks. It seems that about ten years ago wolves made their appearance in this province in considerable numbers from New Brunswick, and their nightly howlings caused the farmers to look closely after the safety of their stock and folds for some time in certain settlements. They are, however, now rarely heard of.

We had not been long on the barren ere we came on last night's tracks of five cariboo, and we at once commenced creeping in earnest. Presently we found their beds, deeply sunk in the snow, the surface quite soft, and evidently just quitted. Their tracks showed that they had, on rising, commenced feeding along very leisurely on the mosses of the barren; to get at which they had scraped away the snow with their broad hoofs. It was now a capital morning for creeping, as the surface of the snow on the barren was quite soft, loosened by the power of the sun. Now we enter a little bog, with scattering clumps of spruce growing from its wet, mossy surface; at every step we sink ankle deep into the yielding moss,

and the chilling snow-water soaks into our feet. We
look anxiously ahead for the game, but they have crossed
the bog ; nor are they on the next, which we can scan
from our present position. They must be in that dark
patch of woods just beyond, which skirts the barren,
for we have followed them up to its northern edge.
What a pity! for the snow under the shade of the
forest is still hard and crusted, and its crunching
sound, under the pressure of our moccasins, step we
ever so lightly, cannot escape the ear of the cariboo.
Yes, they have entered the wood, and just as we
prepare to follow them, and gently open our way
through the outlying thickets, I hear a light snap
of a bough within, which sends my heart nearly to
my mouth. Another step, and Noel at once points to
game, and I see some shadowy forms moving among the
trees, at about fifty yards' distance. Now is the time ; an
instant more and we should be discovered, and the
cariboo bound off scatheless, with electric speed. The
quick crack of my rifle is followed by the roar of the
Indian's gun (which I afterwards ascertained contained
two balls, and about four drachms of powder), and the
branches loudly crash in front as the herd starts in
headlong flight.

There was blood on the snow, as we came up to the
spot whence they had fled : a broad trail of it led from
the spot where the animal I had fired at had been standing. Presently I saw the cariboo ahead, going very
slowly, and making round for the barren again, having
left the herd. The poor creature's doom was sealed ; for,
as we emerged from the woods, we saw it lying down,
and a fawn, which had accompanied it, made quickly off

on seeing us approach. I would have spared the latter, but the Indian brought it down at once by a good shot at eighty yards. Mine proved to be a very fine doe, with a dark glossy skin, and in excellent condition.

"Plenty fresh meat in camp now," says Noel, who really looked as if he could have eaten the whole cariboo then and there. He did roast a good junk of it as soon as he could get a fire alight, and the fellow had brought out some salt in a piece of paper in case of an emergency like the present. Whilst Noel was making up the meat with the assistance of the little axe and hunting-knife which are invariably suspended from the hunter's belt, I lighted my pipe and heaped on the dead logs, which lay everywhere under the surface of the snow, until we had a roaring fire that would have roasted a cariboo whole with great ease and dispatch. I never saw fatter meat than that of the largest cariboo when the hide was removed ; the whole saddle was snow-white with fat, which covered the meat to the depth of an inch and a half. Having stacked the quarters in a compact pile, and deeply covered them with a coating of snow, we started for home, leaving the offal for the Canada jays and crows; the former were exceedingly impudent, hopping about within a few yards of us, and screaming most impatiently for our departure. Noel of course carried a goodly load of the meat, including many delicate morsels for our camp frying-pan.

Numerous droves of cariboo had crossed the barren since the morning, and, as we were on our way, we saw a small drove of four passing across at a distance of about 500 yards from us. They appeared scared, walking very

ON THE BARRENS.

briskly, and occasionally breaking into a trot. **Most** probably they had been started by the rest of the party in the woods to the southward. One of them was of a very light colour—the lightest, I think, I ever **saw**— being of a pale, tawny hue all over ; the others were, as usual, dull grey, variegated with dingy white. Sport must have fallen to the lot of **anyone** who had remained concealed **in** some central thicket on the barren this **afternoon, from** the number that **must have** passed at **different times, as** appeared by their tracks. Though it was still **early in** December we had **only as yet seen one** buck who retained his horns ; the does still **wore theirs.** The one I had just killed had **an** exceedingly neat little pair, which, but for her untimely end, would have **graced** her until the ensuing March.

On return to camp, I found that my friend had not been so fortunate ; they had not been able to discover the wounded **cariboo,** and had **started two** herds without getting a shot. This was owing **to the** frozen state of the snow in the woods. We had determined to exchange Indians **next** morning ; but, in consequence **of** his not yet having had success, I agreed to start again with the second hunter, Noel, and **leave** to my friend the undis- turbed possession of the **barrens, my direction** being the Buctégun plains, which were distant some eight miles or so to the westward. Noel, of course, ate until he could eat no **more that** night—in fact, I never saw such gluttony as was displayed by this Indian whenever he **got a** chance. The settler's wife had told me, a few days since, that he made a common practice of going into one house after another along the road, and at each represent- ing **himself as starving.** His appearance not generally belying his assertion, he has succeeded in getting a dinner at each of four different places on the same day. "But," she said, "they found him out; and he finds it rather hard to get asked out, or rather in, to dinner now-a-days." On one occasion, on returning with me to camp, after an unsuccessful morning, a good deal before the usual time for dining, he complained of a severe attack of indigestion, and adopted, as an unfailing remedy, a hearty meal of fried pork—the fattest he could pick out of the bag. He expressed himself to the effect that lubrication was the best remedy for such complaints.

The owls hooted most dismally in the forest that night —a sure sign, as Williams said, of an approaching storm; and, as the sky looked threatening all the latter part of the day, we retired to sleep, trusting to see a fall of fresh snow in the morning, which was much wanted, to obliterate the old tracks, and soften the surface of the crust.

Fresh falls of snow are necessary to continue and ensure sport in the winter hunting-camp, especially in the earlier part of the season. A few bright days thaw the surface so that the night-frost produces a disagreeable crust, which crunches and roars under the moccasin most unmusically; and then, unless the forest trees are shaken by little short of a gale, you may give up all idea of getting within shot of game. Day after day is often thus spent listlessly in camp; the same calm, frosty weather continuing to prevent sport, and the evil of the crust on the snow gradually becoming worse; the Indians shaking their heads at the proposition to hunt and uselessly disturb the country, and betaking themselves to cutting axe-handles, mending their moccasins, or constructing a hand-sled perhaps, whilst you lazily fall back amongst the blankets, and snooze away far into the bright morning, till the noon-day sun strikes down on your face through the aperture in the top of the camp. Then you are told by the dusky cook and steward of the camp that the "pork's giving out," or the "sweetening is getting short," and all things remind you that "it's hard times," and no fresh meat, and all for want of a nice little fall of snow. However, there lies a great ball of a thing, all covered with quills, like a hedgehog, in the cook's corner, and the cook recommends that a "bilin" of soup should be instituted ; so Master Porcupine is scraped, and skinned, and chopped, and, with an odd bone or two which turns up from the larder, a little rice, and lots of sliced onions, he is converted into a broth, and another day in the woods is cleared by the pork thereby saved. At last, when the bitter reflection of having to return from the woods empty-handed presents itself to you some morning on awakening, the joyous flakes are seen gently falling through the top of the camp, and hissing as they meet the embers of the fire. " Now's your time," says the party all round, and the camp is all bustle and animation—such tying on of moccasins, and buckling on of ammunition-belts, and knives, and axes ; not forgetting to provide for the mid-day refreshment, by filling of flasks, and stowing away of biscuits and lumps of cheese. Presently the wind rises, and the storm thickens ; the new covering of snow seems to draw out the frost from the old crusted surface, and the moccasin now steps noiselessly in the tracks of the game. That day, or on the next, there is no need of porcupine soup, for huge steaks hang from the camp-poles, and a rich and savoury odour pervades the camp, whilst the hissing frying-pan tops the logs.

The want of a fresh fall of snow had thus interrupted our sports in the Parsboro' country for some days, when the welcome flakes at last came down one wild stormy night, and covered the forest and barren with a clean mantle of three or four inches, obliterating the old tracks, and softening the crust so that it again became practicable to stalk the wary cariboo. Many times had we started small herds on the barren, and in the greenwoods, without sighting them; the first token of their proximity, and of their having taken alarm, being the crashing of the branches which they breasted in flight.

It was a beautiful hunting morning on which, after the new fall of the previous night, we trudged along the forest-path leading from our camp to the barrens, and made sure of shots during the day, for the change of wind, and the storm, would cause a movement among the deer. A mile or so from camp the snow was ploughed up by a multitude of fresh tracks; a herd of cariboo had just crossed it; there could not have been less than thirty of them, all going south from the barrens. We at once struck into the woods after them, and followed for about an hour, when the herd divided into two streams. One of these we followed, the tracks every moment becoming fresher, until, on passing through a dense alder thicket which grew over water, treacherously covered with raised ice, the ice gave way with a crash, and we at the same moment heard the game start. We rushed on as fast as possible, for they had not seen or winded us, and might possibly think the noise proceeded merely from the ice falling in, as it often does when suspended

over water and laden with snow. Presently the tracks
showed they were walking, and on entering a thick
covert of young spruces, whose lower branches, thickly
covered with snow, prevented our seeing far ahead, the
Indian said, "There—fire!" and a bounding form or two
flashed through an opening in the bush with such
rapidity that we could scarcely say that we had seen
them. Our barrels were levelled and discharged, but, as
might be expected, without effect. The deer had been
lying down, and had seen our legs under the lower
branches before the Indian was aware of their presence.

Williams said, "I 'most afraid we couldn't get shot.
Caliboo very hard to creep when shiftin' their ground :
don't stop and feed much, and when they lie down they
watchin' all the time, and then up agen 'most directly.
I know them caliboo makin' for some big barrens, five or
six mile away." .

We then turned back to the northward, and, recrossing
the road, made for the barrens where my dead cariboo
were lying. The place was marked by the great pile of
snow which we had shovelled over them, and by the
skins suspended on a rampike hard by ; no wild animals
had disturbed the meat, though great numbers of moose-
birds and jays were screaming around, apparently dis-
tressed that the fresh snow had covered up their little
pickings in the shape of offal, which had been left around.
Here we sat down on a log, after clearing off the snow,
to eat our biscuit and broach the flasks (for we had
trudged many miles since breakfast, and the sun was
past the south)—the Indian, always restless, and perhaps
anxious to take a survey of the country unimpeded by

followers, going off towards the greenwoods, distant a few hundred yards, munching as he went.

"A capital fellow is old John," said I to my comrade. "I'll bet you what you like he comes back with some news. I've often seen him go off in this manner whilst you are eating, or resting, or smoking, and uncertain what to do, and come back in half an hour or so, apparently having learnt more of the whereabouts of the game than he had when in your company during the whole morning's hunt."

We were not detained very long, however—indeed, had hardly finished the biscuit—when, on looking towards the edge of the forest, which he had entered a few minutes previously, we saw John emerge, and make his way back to us with unusual celerity ; and, seeing there was game afoot, we picked up the guns and advanced to meet him.

"Come on," says John, "just see three or four of 'em walking quietly along inside the woods—didn't start 'em, I guess. Be easy, now ; lots of time." And off we go after John, as quietly as he would have us, and soon find the track of the cariboo. John leads rapidly forward, bending almost double to get a glimpse of them through the branches ahead ; but no, they have left the woods, and taken to the open again, and we follow into a swamp thickly sprinkled with little fir trees of about our own height. The bog is very wet, having never frozen, and we sink up to our knees in the swamp, through the wet surface-snow, withdrawing our feet and legs at each step, with a noise like drawing a cork. It is hard work getting along, and already we are rather out of breath ; but we must keep on, for cariboo are smart walkers, and

until they come to a place where they have an inclination
to loiter and browse, are apt to lead one a dance for many
hours, particularly when they have taken a notion to
shift their country. Ha! there goes one of them ; his
black muzzle and dusky back just showing above the
bushes at the further end of the swamp—and another,
and another. "Bang" goes a barrel a-piece from each
of us (we are in échelon), and the nearest one falters,
either wounded or confused, as they sometimes become
by the firing. He is again making off, and passing an
opening ; the other guns floundering forward in hopes of
getting nearer, when, steadying myself, and taking good
aim, he falls instantaneously to my second barrel. John,
with a yell, rushes up, and getting astride of the
struggling beast, quickly terminates his existence with
his long hunting-knife. It was a fine doe cariboo, with
a very dark hide, and in fair condition. The others
having never been fairly within shot, we were satisfied,
and after the usual process returned to camp, our path
being enlivened by the bright rays of a lovely moon.
We all agreed that no finer sport could be obtained
amongst the larger game than cariboo-shooting. This
deer is so wary, such a constant and fast traveller, and
so quick in getting up and bounding out of range when
started in the woods, that an aim as rapid and true as in
cock-shooting is required ; and, when he is down, every
pound of the meat repays for backing it out of the woods,
being, in my opinion, far finer wild meat than any other
venison I have tasted.

The next day I walked with the other Indian (Noel)
to the Buctouktéegun plains, some ten miles distant from
our camp—great plains of miles and miles in extent,

covered with little islands of dwarf spruces of a few feet
in height.  This is a great place of resort for cariboo ;
they come out from the forest on to the plains on fine
sunny mornings, and scrape up the snow to get at the
moss.  Having passed a night in a lumberer's camp, we
proceeded next morning to the plains, which the Indian
would scan from a tall spruce, to see if there were game
on them ; and having bagged my cariboo, and given
part of it to the lumberers, who seemed very thankful,
we made up the hind quarters and hide into two loads,
and arrived in camp the same evening.  My companion,
whose shots I had heard the day previous, had had
excellent sport on the barrens, having killed four cariboo;
and the following day I killed a magnificent buck, which
weighed nearly four hundred-weight, after a long chase
of six miles through the green woods from the spot
where I had first wounded him, the Indian (it was
Williams) keeping on his track, though it had passed
through multitudes of others, with unerring perseverance.
Then comes the hauling out the meat.  Old H——, the
last settler, whose house is not far from our camp, is sent
for, and contracts for the job, and one fine morning his
voice, as he urges on his patient bullocks towards the
camp, and the grating of the sled upon the snow, are
heard as we sit at breakfast.  Leaving his team munching an armful of hay in the path, he comes to the camp
door, and, pushing aside the blanket which covers the
entrance, accosts us,—

   " Morning, gents.   Ah ! Ingines, how d'ye make out—
most ready to start ?  We've got a tidy spell to go for
the cariboo by all accounts, and my team aint noways
what you may call strong.   However, I suppose we must

manage it somehow, and accommodate a gentleman like you appear to be."

"All right, my good man, we are ready; and John and Noel will go ahead and haul out the cariboo from the barren to the road;" and off we go, a merry party, following the ox sled, whilst the old settler shouts unceasingly to his cattle, "Haw! Bright—Gee! Diamond; what are ye 'bout there, ye lazy beasts?" and the great strong animals go steadily forward, occasionally bringing their broad foreheads in violent contact with a tree; but proceeding, on being set right, with perfect unconcern, till we come to the edge of the barren. Here the Indians had already hauled out two of the cariboo by straps fastened to the horns, drawing the carcases easily over the surface of the snow, and in a couple of hours we were again *en route* for home, with everything packed up, guns in case, and nine cariboo as trophies.

The frozen carcases were pitched down into the hold of the little schooner, the same one which had brought us across before; and in a few hours, with a fresh breeze following us, we grated safely through the floating field of ice which nearly blocked up the basin of Minas, and landed at Windsor, Nova Scotia, and so to Halifax.

# CHAPTER VII.

---

## THE BEAVER.

THE number and extent of its lakes, scattered throughout the extent of this picturesque province, invariably surprise the visitor to Nova Scotia. Of every variety of size and form, and generally containing groups of little wooded islands, they occupy almost every hollow, and, often connected, stretch away in long chains through the interior, presenting the most charming scenery to those who seek sport or the picturesque through the back country. Lake Rossignol, in the western portion of the province, is the largest; the waters which pass through it rise near Annapolis on the Bay of Fundy, and, accumulating in a long series of lakes, issue from Rossignol as a large river which falls into the Atlantic at the town of Liverpool. By this line of water communication, almost crossing the province, the most secluded recesses of the wild country can be reached by means of the Indian canoe, an easy and delightful mode of progression on the smooth lake, though it involves some danger among the rocks and rapids of the river, which, if insurmountable, entail the "portage," and a weary tramp, perhaps, through a long stretch of forest with canoe, commissariat, and luggage.

To the eye of the naturalist one of the most interesting points in connection with the chain of lakes referred to is, that on their banks are the houses of the few families of beaver left in the province ; for though their works and the fruit of their labours attest their presence formerly in every direction, not a beaver exists from the Port Medway River — a few miles eastward of the Rossignol waters—and the eastern end of Cape Breton. This animal was formerly abundant throughout the British Provinces, and a large portion of the United States, from the Atlantic to the Pacific coast, and would ere this have totally disappeared from the maritime provinces, but for the caprice of fashion in hats which, substituting silk for the beaver-nap, arrested its destruction, and thereby, as Mr. Marsh suggests, in " Man and Nature," involved possible alterations in the physical features of a continent. Nova Scotia abounds in all the conditions necessary to its existence—rivers, brooks and swampy lakes—and its former abundance is attested by the prevalence of such names as " Beaverbank," " Beaver Harbour," and the numerous " Beaver Lakes " and " Beaver Rivers " scattered round the Province. The market being so near, and its haunts so accessible and easy of observation, it is surprising that its extermination in this part of America has not been long since effected. Indeed, the animal now appears to be on the increase.

In past times, undoubtedly, the beaver has had much to do with the formation of the " wild meadows," as they are locally termed, which are of frequent occurrence in the backwoods, and from which the settler draws plentiful supplies for feeding his stock in winter, and the following was evidently the process. Wherever a brook trickled through a valley, the beaver would bar its course by its strong compact dam, thus securing sufficient back-water to form a pond, on the edge of which to build its dome-shaped house. Large spaces in the woods thus became inundated, the drowned trees fell and decayed, and freshets brought accessions of soil from the hills. At length the pond filled up, and the colony migrated, or were exterminated. The water drained through the unrepaired dam ; and on the fine alluvial soil exposed, sprang up those rich waving fields of wild grass, monu-ments of the former industry of the beaver, and now a source of profit to its thankless destroyers.

To return, however, to Lake Rossignol and its beavers. Attracted thither by the charms of a canoe voyage on the lakes at the commencement of the glorious fall, and anxious to inspect the houses and dams of these curious animals, we hired our two frail barks and the services of three Indians at the town of Liverpool, Nova Scotia, and, avoiding the ascent of the rapid river as too arduous a mode of access, sent canoes and luggage by a cross road to a line of waters which flowed evenly into the great lake, and where we embarked for our explorations. The following notes from my Camp Journal will give a nar-ration of our observations and progress :—

" August 28.

" Encamped comfortably in a cove of the second lake of the Rossignol Chain, which was reached late in the evening, *viâ* the Sixteen-Mile Lakes, where the canoes were embarked. The unwonted exercise of the first long day's paddling has somewhat unsteadied the hand for writing up the notes. The scenery on the above-named lakes very pretty, and the water in good order for canoeing, a light breeze following us and cooling the air. Lunched on an island, and, leaving the lakes, entered a small rapid stream. Here the shade of the maples, which completely overhung the brook, was most grateful, and the light green of the sunlit foliage reflected in the water, with masses of king-fern, and a variety of herbaceous plants growing luxuriously on the banks, grey rock boulders with waving crowns of polypodium rising from the stream, and reflected on its smooth though swiftly-gliding surface, and the moss-covered stems of fallen trees which continually bridged it over, formed an ever-changing panorama, which evoked many expressions of delight as we quietly glided down the brook—a beautiful realisation of Tennyson's idyll. The water was clear as crystal, and covered golden gravel, and there were frequent 'silvery water-breaks,' caused by trout jumping at the multitudes of small blue and green ephemerae which danced above. Here we first saw the works of beaver. Pointing towards the bank, on suddenly rounding a turn in the brook, our head Indian Glode whispered, 'There beaver-house ;' and we held by a projecting rock to examine the structure for a few moments. I confess I was disappointed. Instead of the regular mud-plastered dome I had expected and seen depicted in all works of natural history, the house appeared merely as an irregular pile of barked sticks, very broad at the base compared with its height, and looking much like a gigantic crow's nest inverted, and formed without any apparent design. It was in present occupation, for the tall surrounding fern was beaten down all around. 'All pretty much same,' said Glode in answer to our question, as we again dropped down the stream. Presently the rippling of water ahead showed a slight fall, and on arriving at the spot the bow of the canoe grated on submerged bushes. It was the dam—always placed below—belonging to the house, and was evidently in course of construction, a process which we were unavoidably compelled to defer, by standing on a flat rock, and, hauling out bushes by the armful, to open a passage for the canoes. Several other houses were passed, at intervals, of about a quarter of a mile, all similar in appearance, and some of great size. Our anxiety to get to the big lake prevented us, however, from examining the structure closely. On this brook I first saw the blossoms and tendrils of a beautiful climbing plant which grew up luxuriantly amongst the bushes, and encircled small stems to a considerable height—the Indian potato-plant (Apios tuberosa)—one of the sources of food used by the old Indians before they left the woods and their forest fare for the neighbourhood of civilization, and adopted its food, clothing, and depraving associations. The flowers are like those of the sweet pea, and arranged in a whorl, possessing a pleasant though rather faint smell. The cluster of bulbs at its root, called potatoes, are of about the average size of small new potatoes, and have a flavour like a chestnut."

Two or three miles further, through an open country covered with the bleached stems of a burnt forest, brought us to the middle lake of the Rossignol Chain, which we quickly crossed to camp.

On the following afternoon we entered Rossignol after some rather stiff paddling. Two large lakes, affording

no shelter of rocks or islands, were crossed in the teeth
of a strong breeze, and the bows of our canoes were frequently overtopped by the waves. For security the
paddlers crouched in the bottom instead of sitting, as is
usual, on the thin strips of ash which constitute the
thwarts in the bow and stern. Perfect in symmetry,
and capable of conveying four persons, the canoes were
of the smallest construction compatible with safety on
the rapid river or its broad lakes. They were eighteen feet
in length, and weighed but sixty pounds each. From an
end-on point of view, the paddlers seemed supported by
almost nothing—the bark sides projecting but a few
inches beyond the breadth of their bodies, and the gunwale nearly flush with the water. But we were "old
hands," and were determined to camp that night on the
big lake ; and the light barks, impelled by strokes which
made the handles of the paddles bend like reeds, forged
ahead through chopping seas till we reached the shelter
of the rocky islands at the foot of Lake Rossignol. Here
the lakes were connected by a rapid run, where, beaching
the canoes, we enjoyed capital trouting for a couple of
hours—killing over five dozen fish averaging one pound
—and dined on shore, picking a profuse dessert of blue
and huckle berries. A glorious view was unfolded as we
left the run and entered the still water of the lake. The
breeze fell rapidly with the sun, and enabled us to steer
towards the centre, from which alone the size of the lake
could be appreciated, owing to the number of its islands.
These were of every imaginable shape and size—from the
grizzly rock bearing a solitary stunted pine, shaggy with
Usnea, to those of a mile in length, thickly wooded with
maple, beech, and birches, now wearing the first pure

tints of autumnal colour. From near its centre was unfolded a view of the greatest expanse of water. The
distant shores were enveloped in haze, but appeared
fringed with a dark fir forest to the water's edge. Here
and there a bright spot of white sand formed a beach
tempting for a disembarkation; and frequent sylvan
scenes of an almost fairy-land character opened up as
we coasted along the shores—little harbours almost
closed-in from the lake, overgrown with water-lilies,
arrow-heads, and other aquatic plants, with mossy banks
backed by bosky groves of hemlocks ; cool retreats which
the soft moss covering the soil, and the perfect shade of
the dense foliage overhead, indicated as most desirable
spots for camping. The wild cry of the loon resounded
all over the lake, and mergansers and black ducks
wheeled overhead as they left their feeding-grounds for
their accustomed resting-places. Only one sight reminded us of civilization. On the crest of a distant
hill, the rays of the setting sun lighted on a little patch of
cleared ground and glanced on the window of a solitary
dwelling. Our Indians said it was a settler's house in New
Caledonia, on the forest road from Liverpool to Annapolis.

Warned at length by the mellowing light which
seemed to blend lake and sky into one, we steered the
canoes into a sheltered cove, and lighted our first camp
fire on the shores of Lake Rossignol. This was our head-
quarters ; and here for a week we gave ourselves up to
the dreamy pleasures of a life in the woods. Our easy
mode of travel enabling us to take every desirable luxury,
we ate our trout with Worcester sauce, and baked our
bread in an Indian oven ; we fished in the runs, bathed
in the sandy coves, visited and were visited by the lum-

berers, **who** were rafting their logs down **to the sea, and** made **frequent excursions up the** affluent **waters of the** lake in search of beavers **and their** works. **With regard to** the latter, **I will here** again introduce a **few pages of** my journal :—

"AUGUST 30TH.

"A bright morning, **very hot.** After breakfast ascended **the** Tobiaduc **stream** at **the** north-west end of the lake. **Here the** scenery becomes very beautiful. The **river is broad and still ;** the **woods** on **either side** much **inundated ; and** the maple brightly **coloured with** orange and scarlet—probably more from unhealthiness **produced** by the high water than by early frosts. Pass **some** exquisite island **scenery ; the** reflections perfect. A **snake swims across under the bows of my canoe,** its head carried an inch above the surface. Passing a steep bank, a beaver rushes out of **a** dense patch of king-fern, and takes to the water with a plunge ; and **we follow his** track, faintly indicated on the surface, towards an old beaver-house a few rods up stream. 'I heard him dove,' **observed** Glode, on arriving : the animal had mistrusted **the strength** of his fortress ; and pursuit was hopeless.

" **Five** or six miles from the **lake,** we come to the carrying **place or portage, whence a woodland path** leads by a short cut **to** Tobiaduc lake, and saves many a mile of heavy poleing against the **rapids of** the river. The road **lay** through **a** dark mossy forest of hemlocks, soft and pleasant walking when unencumbered by loads, but very fatiguing under the weight **of** canoes and all the **paraphernalia of a** camp. 'Indian mile, long **and narrer,'** drily observed old Glode, on our casual inquiry as to how much further we had to trudge. The forest gloom

at length lightens, and the gleam of water ahead brings
us to the Tobiaduc lakes, where a couple of ruffed grouse,
shot *en route*, were cooked *à la* spatch-cock, and we
dined on a service of birch-bark dishes.

" Late in the afternoon, our canoes, leaving the lakes,
entered the Tobiaduc brook, a picturesque stream similar
to the sixteen-mile brook before mentioned. The lovely
scenery of these forest streams must be seen to be fully
appreciated. The foliage in spots is almost tropical ;
wild vines and creepers crowd the water's edge, with
towering clumps of royal fern (Osmunda regalis) ; airy
groves of birches with stems of purest white are succeeded by fir-woods, under which the graceful moose-
wood and swamp maple brighten the gloom as their
broad leaves catch the sunlight ; the pigeon berry
(Cornus canadensis) bedizens the moss with its well-
contrasting clumps of scarlet berries ; and great boulders
of grey rock, circled over with concentric lichens, moss
covered, and their crannies filled with pollypods and
oak-fern, overhang the water in stern and solitary grandeur. Every rock projecting from the stream is seized
upon by moss, whence grow a few ferns or seedling
maples ; and the play of the sunlight as it breaks
through the arched foliage above and lights up these
little groups produces most exquisite effects. This is the
home of the beaver and the kingfisher. The ferns and
grasses on the banks are trodden down by the former
in its paths, and the latter flits from bush to bush with
loud rattling screams as the canoe invades its piscatorial
domains.

" At length there was an obstruction in the stream over
which the waters fell evenly. It was a beaver-dam—a

BEAVER-DAM ON THE TOBIADUC.

solid construction of interwoven bushes and poles, damming up the water behind to a height of between three
and four feet, and completely altering the features of the
brook, which from this point was all still water. We
landed on the top to open out a portion, and thereby
facilitate the canoes being lifted over. Some of the
work was quite fresh, and green leaves tipped the ends
of projecting branches; whilst on the shore lay a pile of
water-rotted material that had been removed, and evidently considered unserviceable. Stones and mud were
plentifully intermixed with the bushes, which were
mostly cut into lengths of twelve to eighteen feet, and
woven together across the stream. The top, which
would support us all without yielding, was about two
feet broad, and the dam thickened below the surface.
Some stout bushes leaned against the construction in
front. They were planted in the bed of the stream;
and, as Glode said, were used as supports in making the
dam. Above was a long meadow of wild grass to which
the white gaunt stems of dead pines, drowned ages since
by the heightened level of the stream, imparted a desolate appearance, and near the head of which the beavers
had their habitations."

This dam, and one or two others which I had an
opportunity of observing, was built straight across the
stream, but it is a well authenticated fact that in larger
works, where the channel is broader, and liable to heavy
waters, the dam is made convex to the current. Sometimes a small island in the centre is taken advantage of,
and the dam built out to it from either bank, as in-
stanced by a very large one noticed on the Sable river, a
few miles west of Rossignol, where the sticks used in its

construction were often three inches in diameter, and the
country above, on either side, flooded to the extent of
nearly two feet, covering about one thousand acres of
meadow land.  These dams possess great strength and
durability.  In old and deserted works trees spring from
the soil, which is plentifully mixed with the brushwood
and grass covers the embankment.*  Many such monu-
ments of the former labours of the beaver are to be seen
in Nova Scotia, in districts long since untenanted.

As the beaver residing on the lakes does not build a
dam in the vicinity of his dwelling, the reason of the
strong instinct implanted in this animal to produce these
marvellous constructions under other circumstances becomes apparent.†  Whenever, from the situation or nature
of the water, there is a probability of the supply becoming shortened by drought, and to ensure sufficient water
to enter his dwelling from beneath the ice in winter, the
beaver constructs a dam below to maintain the supply of
water necessary to meet either of these contingencies.
In former years, when beaver abounded in all parts of

---

* Mr. Thompson, whose writings are preserved in Canada as most valuable
and authentic, speaking of a beaver-dam which he saw, states : "On a fine
afternoon in October, 1794, the leaves beginning to fall with every breeze,
my guide informed me that we should have to pass over a long beaver-dam.
I naturally expected that we should have to lead our horses carefully over it.
When we came to it, we found it a stripe of apparently old solid ground,
covered with short grass, and wide enough for two horses to walk abreast.
The lower side showed a descent of seven feet, and steep, with a rill of
water from beneath it ; the side of the dam next the water was a gentle
slope.   To the southward was a sheet of water of about one mile and a half
square, surrounded by low grassy banks.  The forests were mostly of poplar
and aspen, with numerous stumps of the trees cut down, and partly carried
away by the beavers.  In two places of this pond were a cluster of beaver-
houses like miniature villages."

† I have, however, seen the outlet of very small lakes dammed up,
evidently to raise the level of the surface to some eligible site near the
margin, which has offered some advantage or other.

the Province, it is evident from the **numerous beaver**
meadows now left dry, that they **took advantage not**
only of valleys traversed by small brooks, **but even of**
swampy lands occasionally inundated by heavy rains.

The beaver-house is constructed of the same materials
as the dam. Branches of trees and bushes, partially
trimmed and closely interwoven, are mixed with stones,
gravel or **mud,** according to the nature of the soil ; and
on the outside are strewed the barked sticks of willow,
poplar, or birch, on which the animal feeds. As before
stated, **it looks like a** huge bird's **nest, turned upside**
down, and is generally located in the grassy **coves of**
lakes, by **the edge of** still-water runs or of artificial
ponds, and, less frequently, **by a** river side, **where a bend**
or jutting rocks afford a **deep** eddying pool **near the**
bank. The house rests **on the bank, but** always overlaps
the water, into which the front part is immersed ; **and,**
**as** a general **rule, the bottom of** the stream or lake is
deepened in the channel **approaching the entrance by**
dredging, thereby ensuring a free passage below the ice.
**In** these channels or canals, easily found **by** probing
with **the paddle,** the hunter sets **his iron** spring-traps.
The following passages from my **camp notes describe the**
**construction of** the beaver-house, **as shown in all the**
habitations **which we examined in these waters :—**

"**Foot of Rossignol,** September 4.

"Camped on **a** beautiful **spot,** the effluence **of the**
river from the lake, in Indian parlance, the 'segedwick,'
always a favourite camping **ground.** It was a decided
**oak** opening, an open grove of white oaks, **with a** soft
sward underneath ; the trees were grouped as in a park.

A few low islands covered with ferns partially broke the
breadth of the river, which here left the smooth expanses
of the lake on its race to the Atlantic, about twenty
miles below; and here our rods bent incessantly over
the struggles of trout, frequently two at a time. We
intend staying here several days to rest after the long
weary journey up and down the Tobiadue stream; and
as it is now September, a brace or two of ruffed grouse, or
even a moose steak, may add to our hitherto scanty forest
fare of porcupine and trout. Beneath these white oaks
repose the sires of the Micmacs of this district; it was
once a populous village, of which the only remaining
tokens are the swelling mounds covered with fern, and
the plentiful bones, the produce of the chase, scattered
over the ground. Our canoe-men seemed quite subdued,
perhaps a little overcome by superstitious awe on pitch-
ing our camp here on the site of their ancestors' most
favoured residence. With a road through to the town
of Liverpool, this lovely spot will one day, ere long,
become a thriving settlement. I would desire no more
romantic retreat were I to become a settler; but always
bear in mind the lesson inculcated for all intending military settlers who may be carried away by their enthu-
siasm for the picturesque scenery of the summer and fall
in Nova Scotia, to try their luck away back from civilization, in the well-told and pathetic story of ' Cucumber
Lake,' by Judge Haliburton. To-day Glode and I walked
back from the lake about three miles, through thick
woods, to see a beaver-house on a brook of which he
knew. We found it without difficulty, as the grass and
fern for some distance below was much trodden down,
and proceeded to make a careful investigation of its

structure. Its site was a dismal one. The surrounding forest had been burnt ages since, for there was no charcoal left on the stems, which were bleached and hard as adamant. A few alders, swamp maples, and briers fringed the brook, the banks of which were overgrown with tall grass, flags, and royal fern. Moose had recently passed through, browsing on the juicy stems of the red maples. It was a large house ; its diameter at the water line nearly eighteen feet, and it was nearly five feet in height. On the outside the sticks were thrown somewhat loosely, but, as we unpiled them and examined the structure more closely, the work appeared better, the boughs laid more horizontally, and firmly bound in with mud and grass. About two feet from the top we unroofed the chamber, and presently disclosed the interior arrangements.

"The chamber—there was but one—was very low, scarcely two feet in height, though about nine feet in diameter. It had a gentle slope upwards from the water, the margin of which could be just seen at the edge. There were two levels inside, one, which we will term the hall, a sloping mudbank on which the animal emerges from the subaqueous tunnel and shakes himself, and the other an elevated bed of boughs ranged round the back of the chamber, and much in the style of a guard-bed— i.e., the sloping wooden trestle usually found in a military guard-room. The couch was comfortably covered with lengths of dried grass and rasped fibres of wood, similar to the shavings of a toy-broom. The ends of the timbers and brushwood, which projected inwards, were smoothly gnawed off all round. There were two entrances—the one led into the water at the edge of the chamber and

let in the light, the other went down at a deeper angle
into black water. The former was evidently the summer
entrance, the latter being used in winter to avoid the
ice. The interior was perfectly clean, no barked sticks
(the refuse of the food) being left about. These were all
distributed on the exterior, a fact which accounts for the
bleached appearance of many houses we have seen. In
turning over the materials of the house, I picked up
several pieces of wood of but two or three inches in
length, which from their shortness puzzled me as to the
wherefore of so much trouble being taken by the beaver
for so (apparently) small a purpose. My Indian, however, enlightened me. The side on which a young tree
is intended to fall is cut through, say two-thirds, the
other side one-third, and a little above. The tree slips
off the stem, but will not fall prostrate, owing to the
intervention of branches of adjacent trees. So the beaver
has to gnaw a little above to start it again, exactly on
the plan adopted by the lumberer in case of a catch
amongst the upper branches, when the impetus of another
slip disengages the whole tree. The occupants of the
house were out for the day, as they generally are
throughout the summer, being engaged in travelling up
and down the brooks, and cutting provisions for the
winter's consumption. Returning to camp by another
route through the woods, we had to cross a large wild
meadow now inundated — a most disagreeable walk
through long grass, the water reaching above the knees.
At the foot, where Glode said a little sluggish brook ran
out, we found a beaver-dam in process of construction—
the work quite fresh, and accounting for the inundation
of the meadow above."

" SEPTEMBER 5.

" Glode and I tried creeping moose, back in the woods, this morning, but without success. No wind and an execrable country ; all windfalls and thick woods, or else burnt barrens. Follow fresh tracks of an enormous bull, but are obliged to leave them for want of a breeze to cloak our somewhat noisy advance amongst the tall huckleberry bushes. Indians are particularly averse to starting game when there is no chance of killing. It scares the country unnecessarily. Disturb a bear revelling amongst the berries, and hear him rush off in a thick swamp. Lots of bear signs everywhere in these woods. In the evening proceed up the lake with one of the canoes. The water calm, and a most lovely sunset. Passing a dark grove of hemlocks, we hear two young bears calling to one another with a sort of plaintive moan. The old ones seldom cry out, being too knowing and ever on the watch. At the head of a grassy cove stood a large beaver-house ; and, as it was now the time of day for the animals to swim round and feed amongst the yellow water-lilies, we concealed ourselves and canoe amongst the tall grass for the purpose of watching. But for the mosquitoes, which attacked us fiercely, it was a most enjoyable evening. The gorgeous sunset reflected in the lake vied with the shadows of the crimson · maples ; and every bank of woods opposed to the sun was suffused with a rich orange hue. The still air bore to our ears the sound of a fall into the lake, some three miles away, as if it were close by, and the cry of the loon resounded in every direction. Wood-ducks and black ducks flew past in abundance, and within easy range of our hidden guns ; and long diverging trails in the

mirror-like surface showed the passage of otter or musk-
rats over the lake. Presently the water broke some sixty
yards from us, and the head and back of a beaver
showed above the surface, whilst another appeared almost
simultaneously farther off. After a cautious glance
around, the animal dived again with a roll like that
of a porpoise, reappearing in a few minutes. He was
feeding on the roots of the yellow lilies (Nuphar advena).
Probably three minutes elapsed during each visit to the
bottom. Taking advantage of one of these intervals,
the Indians pushed the canoe from the concealment
of the grass, and with a few noiseless yet vigorous
strokes of the paddle made towards the spot where we
supposed the animal would rise. As the head reappeared,
we let fly with the rifle, but missed the game, the report
echoing from island to island, and evoking most discordant
yells from the loons far and near. Of course we had
seen all that was to be seen of the animals for the
night ; 'and so,' as Mr. Pepys would say, 'disconsolate
back to camp.'"

During the excursion we had opportunities of examining
many beaver-houses, placed in every variety of situation
—by the lake shore, by the edge of sluggish " still
waters," on the little forest brook, or on the brink of
the rapid river. They all presented a similar appearance—equally rough externally, and all similarly constructed inside. Neither could we observe anything
like a colony of beavers, their houses grouped in close
proximity, as so frequently noticed by travellers. The
beaver of Eastern America appears, indeed, quite un-
sociable in comparison with his brethren of the West.
We saw none but isolated dwellings either on lake or

river-shore, and these placed at several hundred yards apart from each other.

With respect to the number of animals living together in the same house, our Indians, who had lived in this neighbourhood and hunted beaver from their youth, corroborated the fact, often stated by naturalists, of three generations living together—the old pair, the last progeny, and the next eldest (they generally have two at a birth); the latter leaving every summer to set up for themselves.

At the time of our visit the beavers were returning from the summer excursions up and down the rivers, and setting to work to repair damages both to houses and dams. This work is invariably carried on during the night; and the following is the *modus operandi:*—Repairing to the thickets and groves skirting the lake, the beaver, squatting on his hams, rapidly gnaws through the stems of trees of six or even twelve inches diameter, with its powerful incisors. These are again divided, and dragged away to the house or dam. The beaver now plunges into the water, and brings up the mud and small stones from the bottom to the work in progress, carrying them closely under the chin in its fore paws. The vulgar opinion that the broad tail of the beaver was used to plaster down the mud in its work, has long since been pronounced as erroneous. Its real use is evidently to counterpoise, by an action against the water in an upward direction, the tendency to sink head foremost (which the animal would otherwise have) when propelling itself through the water by its powerful and webbed hind feet, and at the same time supporting the load of mud or stones in its fore paws under the chin. Our Indians laughed at the idea

of the trowel story. That, and the assertion that the
tail is likewise used as a vehicle for materials, may be
considered as exploded notions.

The food of the beaver consists of the bark of several
varieties of willow, of poplar, and birch ; they also feed
constantly during summer on the roots and tendrils of
the yellow pond lily (Nuphar advena). They feed in the
evening and throughout the night. For winter supplies
the saplings of the above-mentioned trees are cut into
lengths of two or three feet, and planted in the mud
outside the house. Lengths are brought in and the bark
devoured in the hall, never on the couch, and when
peeled, the sticks are towed outside and used in the spring
to repair the house.

The house is approached from the water by long
trenches, hollowed out to a considerable depth in the
bottom of the lake or brook. In these are piled their
winter stock of food, short lengths of willow and poplar,
which, if left sticking in the mud at the ordinary level of
the bottom below the surface, would become impacted in
the ice. The beaver travels a long distance from his
house in search of materials, both for building and food.
I saw the stumps of small trees, which had been felled at
least three-quarters of a mile from the house. Their
towing power in the water, and that of traction on dry
land, is astonishing. The following is rather a good
story of their coolness and enterprise, told me by a friend,
who was a witness to the fact. It occurred at a little
lake near the head waters of Roseway river. Having
constructed a raft for the purpose of poling round the
edge of the lake, to get at the houses of the beaver, which
were built in a swampy savannah otherwise inaccessible,

it had been left in the evening moored at the edge of the lake nearest the camps, and about a quarter of a mile from the nearest beaver house, the poles lying on it. Next morning, on going down to the raft the poles were missing, so, cutting fresh ones, he started with the Indians towards the houses. There, to his astonishment, was one of the poles, coolly deposited on the top of a house.

Besides the house, the beaver has another place of residence in the summer, and of retreat in the winter, should his house be broken into. In the neighbourhood of the house long burrows, broad enough for the beaver to turn in with ease, extend from ten to twenty feet in the bank, and have their entrance at a considerable depth below the surface of the water. To these they invariably fly when surprised in their houses.

One of the principal causes which have so nearly led to the extermination of the beaver, was the former demand for the castoreum, and the discovery that it could be used as an unfailing bait for the animal itself. This substance is contained in two small sacs near the root of the tail, and is of an orange colour. Now seldom employed in pharmacology for its medicinal properties (stimulant and anti-spasmodic), being superseded by more modern discoveries, it is still used in trapping the animal, as the most certain bait in existence.* It is said

* Erman thus notices it in his Siberian travels :—"There is hardly any drug which recommends itself to man so powerfully by its impression on the external senses as this. The Ostyaks were acquainted with its virtues from the earliest times ; and it was related here (Obdorsk) that they keep a supply of it in every yurt, that the women may recover their strength more quickly after child-birth. In like manner the Kosaks and Russian traders have exalted the beaver-stone into a panacea.

"To the sentence 'God arose, and our enemies were scattered,' the Siberians add, very characteristically, the apocryphal interpolation, 'and we are free from head-ache.' To ensure this most desirable condition, every one to be likewise efficacious in trapping the wild cat, which is excessively fond of the odour. Mr. Thompson, a Canadian writer, thus speaks of it :—"A few years ago the Indians of Canada and New Brunswick, on seeing the steel trap so successful in catching foxes and other animals, thought of applying it to the beaver, instead of the awkward wooden traps they made, which often failed. At first they were set in the landing paths of the beaver, with about four inches of water over them, and a piece of green aspen for a bait, that would allure it to the trap. Various things and mixtures of ingredients were tried without success ; but chance made some try if the male could not be caught by adding the castoreum, beat up with the green buds of the aspen. A piece of willow about eight inches in length, beat and bruised fine, was dipped in this mixture. It was placed at the water edge about a foot from the steel trap, so that the beaver should pass direct over it and be caught. This trap proved successful ; but, to the surprise of the Indians, the females were caught as well as the males. The secret of this bait was soon spread ; every Indian procured from the trader four to six steel traps ; all labour was now at an end, and the hunter moved about with pleasure, with his traps and infallible bait of castoreum. Of the infatuation of this animal for castoreum I saw several instances. A trap was negligently fastened by its small chain to the stake, to prevent the beaver taking away the trap when caught ; it slipped, and the beaver swam away with the trap, and it was looked upon as lost. Two nights after

has recourse, at home or on his travels, and with the firmest faith, to two medicines, and only two, viz., beaver-stone, or beaver efflux as it is here called, and sal-ammoniac."

he was taken in a trap, with the other trap fast on his thigh. Another time a beaver, passing over a trap to get the castoreum, had his hind leg broken ; with his teeth he cut the broken leg off, and went away. We concluded that he would not come again ; but two nights afterwards he was found fast in a trap, in every case tempted by the castoreum. The stick was always licked or sucked clean, and it seemed to act as a soporific, as they always remained more than a day without coming out of their houses."

And yet the beaver is an exceedingly wary animal, possessing the keenest sense of smell. In setting the large iron traps, without teeth, which are generally used in Nova Scotia, and placed in the paths leading from the house to the grove where he feeds, so careful must be the hunter not to leave his scent on the spot, that he generally cuts down a tree and walks on its branches towards the edge of the path, afterwards withdrawing it, and plentifully sprinkling water around.

The presence of the beaver in his snow-covered house is readily detected by the hunter in winter by the appearance (if the dwelling is tenanted) of what is called the " smoke hole," a funnel-shaped passage formed by the warm vapour ascending from the animals beneath.

With regard to specific distinction of the beavers of America, Europe, and Asia, the remarks of Professor Baird, of the Smithsonian Institute, in his report of the mammals of the Pacific railroad routes, summing up the evidence of naturalists on the comparative anatomy of the Castors of the Old and New Worlds, appear worthy of note as establishing a satisfactory result.

The question has been elaborately discussed, and the

results of many comparisons show considerable difference
of arrangement of bones of the skull, a slight difference
as regards size and colour, and an important one as
regards both the form of the castoreum glands, and the
composition of the castoreum itself, Professor Owen,
Bach, and others agreeing on a separation of species.[*]
Hence, instead of being termed Castor Fiber (Var. Americanus), the American Beaver now, (and but recently),
is designated as Castor Canadensis, so termed rather than
C. Americanus, from the prior nomenclature of Kuhl.

THE MUSK RAT (Fiber Zibethicus of Cuvier) is so
like a miniature beaver, both in conformation and habit,
that Linnæus was induced to class it amongst the Castors.
Like that of the latter animal its tail is flattened, though
vertically and to a much less extent, and is proportionally
longer. It is oar-shaped, whilst the form of the beaver's
tail has been aptly compared to the tongue of a mammal.
Both animals have the same long and lustrous brown-red
hair, with a thick undercoat of soft, downy fur, which, in
the musk rat, is of a blueish gray or ashes colour, in the
beaver ferruginous. The little sedge-built water hut of
the rat is similarly constructed to the beaver's dome
of barked sticks and brushwood, and both have burrows
in the banks of the river side as summer resorts.

The range of the musk rat throughout North America
is co-extensive with the distribution of the beaver, and it

---

[*] Dr. Brandt, who has written a most elaborate exposition on the differences of the beavers of the Old and New Worlds, states the castoreum-bag
of the American to be more elongated and thinner skinned than that of the
European ; and that in the secretion of the latter species there is a much
larger proportion of etherial oil, castorine, and castoreum-resinoid.—*Vide
Baird's Mammals of Pacific Route.*

still continues plentiful in Eastern America in **spite of** the immense numbers of skins exported every year. The Indians are ever on the look-out for them on the banks of the alluvial rivers entering the Bay of Fundy, in which they especially abound, and in every settler's barn may **be** seen their jackets expanded to dry.

Their little flattened oval nests, composed **of** bents and sedges, are of frequent occurrence by lake margins ; and **very shallow grassy ponds** are sometimes seen dotted **with them quite** thickly. On the muddy banks of rivers their holes **are as numerous as those of the** European water-rat, the entrance just under the surface of the water, and generally marked by a profusion of **the shells of** the fresh-water mussel. They are vegetable feeders, with, I believe, this solitary exception, though I am sorry to have to record, from **my** own experience, that cannibalism **is a** not unfrequent **trait** when in confinement.

To the canoe-voyageur, or the fisherman on the forest-lakes, the appearance of the musk rat, sailing round **in the** calm **water on** the approach of sunset, when in fine summer weather **the** balmy west wind almost invariably dies away and leaves the surface with faithful reflections of the beautiful marginal foliage of the woods, is one of **the most** familiar and pleasing sights of nature. Coming forth **from their** home in some shady, lily-bearing cove, they gambol **round** in the open lake in widening circles, apparently **fearless of** the passing canoe, now and then diving below **the** surface **for a** few seconds, and reappearing with that grace and freedom from splash, on leaving and regaining the **surface,** which characterise the movements both of this animal **and of the** beaver.

**Travelling** down **the** Shubenacadie and other gently-

running forest-streams in day-time, I have often seen
them crossing and re-crossing the surface in the quiet
reaches through dark overhanging woods, carrying in
their mouths pieces of bracken, probably to feed on the
stem, though it seemed as if to shade themselves from
the sunbeams glancing through the foliage.

The Micmac calls this little animal " Kewesoo," and is
not impartial to its flesh, which is delicate, and not unlike
that of rabbit.

I have heard of a worthy Catholic priest who most
conveniently adopted the belief that both beaver and
musk rat were more of a fishy than a fleshy nature, and
thus mitigated the rigours of a fast-day in the backwoods
by a roasted beaver-tail or savoury stew.  By the Indians
of Nova Scotia or New Brunswick the flesh of the former
animal is rarely tasted, but to the wilder hunters of Newfoundland it is the primest of forest meats.   The musk
rat will readily swim up to the call of the hunter—a sort
of plaintive squeak made by chirping with the lips applied
to the hollow of closed hands.

The acclimatisation of both these rodents in England
has been frequently advocated of late.   In the case of
the beaver, which in historic times was an inhabitant of
Wales and Scotland, according to Giraldus, its introduction must be at the expense of modern cultivation, from
its tendency to destroy surrounding growths of young
forest trees, and to make ponds and swamps of lands
already drained.   The musk rat, I am inclined to think,
in concurrence with Mr. Crichton's opinion, would prove
a valuable addition to the bank fauna of sluggish English
streams.

I have thus classed together as true lake dwellers these

two first-cousins, as they appear to be, the beaver and
the musk rat,* yet, as the heading is somewhat fanciful,
and my object is to notice the water-frequenting mammalia of the woods, I will proceed to mention other
animals which prowl round the margins of lakes or
brooks, more or less taking to the water, under the sub-
divisional title of "dwellers by lake shores."

THE OTTER of Eastern America (Lutra Canadensis),
(there is a distinct species found on the Pacific slope,)
differs from the European animal in colour, size, and conformation. The former is much the darkest coloured, a
peculiarity attached to many North American mammals
when compared with their Old-World congeners. It is
also the largest. Taken *per se*, but slight importance
would attach to such variations ; and it is on the grounds
of well-ascertained osteological differences only that the
separation of species in the case of both the beaver and
the otter of America has been agreed on.

The Canadian otter measures from nose to tip of tail,
in a large specimen, between four and a-half and five feet;
its colour is a dark chestnut brown or liver, and its fur is
very close and lustrous. Under the throat and belly it is
lighter, approaching to tawny. The breeding season is in
February and early March (of wild cat and fox, ibid), and
the she otter brings forth in May a litter of three or four
pups. The clear whistle of the otter is a very common
sound to the ear of the occupant of a fishing camp, and
the Indians frequently call them up by successful imitation of their note. The skin is valuable and much sought

---

* The musk-rat is often found as an occupant of an old beaver-house
deserted by the latter animal.

after in the manufacture of muffs, trimmings, and especially of the tall ornamental fur caps generally worn as
part of the winter costume in Canada. The price of the
skin varies according to season, good ones bringing from
four to six dollars each.

They are most frequently taken in winter by traps—
dead-falls placed over little forest brooks trickling between lakes, and steel-traps submerged at a hand's
depth close to the bank, where they come out from
under the ice to their paths and "rubs." These resorts are readily detected by the tracks and stains on
the snow, and the smooth, shining appearance of the
frozen bank where they indulge in their curious amusement of sliding down, after the manner of the pas-
time termed in Canada "trebogining." Even in confinement the animal is full of sport, and gambols
like a kitten. The term "otter-rub" is applied to the
place where they enter and leave the water, from
their habit of rubbing themselves, like a dog, against a
stump or root on emerging from the water. The
otter is a very wary animal, and I have rarely come
upon and shot them unawares, though in cruising up and
down runs in a canoe in spring I have often seen their
victims, generally a goodly trout, deserted on hearing the
dip of our paddles, and still floundering on the ice. Fresh-
water fish, including trout, perch, eels and suckers, form
their usual food; they will also eat frogs. They have
paths through the woods from lake to lake, often extending over a very considerable distance, and the
shortest cuts that could be adopted—a regular bee-line.
Their track on the snow is most singular. After a yard
or two of foot impressions there comes a long, broad trail,

as if made by a cart-wheel, where the animal must have thrown itself on its belly and slid along the surface for several yards.

THE FISHER, Black Cat, or Pecan (Mustela Pennantii), the largest of the tree martens, a somewhat fox-like weasel, which lives almost constantly in trees, is another dweller by lake shores, though not in the least aquatic in its habits, and, not being piscivorous, quite unentitled to the name first given. Its general colour is dark brown with uncertain shades, a dorsal line of black, shining hair reaching from the neck to the extremity of the tail. The hair underneath is lighter, with several patches of white. The eye is very large, full and expressive.

The skin possesses about the same value as that of the otter. Squirrels, birds and their eggs, rabbits and grouse, contribute to its support. The Indians all agree as to its alleged habit of attacking and killing the porcupine. "The Old Hunter" informs me that "it is a well-known fact that the fisher has been often—very often—trapped with its skin and flesh so filled with quills of this animal that it has been next to an impossibility to remove the felt from the carcass. In my wanderings in the woods in winter time, I have three times seen, where they have killed porcupine, nothing but blood, mess, and quills, denoting that Mr. F. had partaken of his victim's flesh. I searched, but could not find any place where portions of the animal might have been hidden ; this would have been a circumstance of course easy to ascertain on the snow. Now what could have become of that formidable fighting tail and the bones ? I know that a small dog can neither crack the latter, nor those of the beaver."

Mr. Andrew Downs, the well-known Nova Scotian practical naturalist, says he has often found porcu-pine-quills in the fisher's stomach on skinning the animal.

The fisher is becoming rare in the forests of Acadie. According to Dr. Gilpin, a hundred and fifty to two hundred is the usual annual yield of skins in Nova Scotia, and these chiefly come from the Cobequid range of hills in Cumberland.

The length of the animal, tail included, is from forty to fifty inches, of which the tail would be about eighteen.

THE MINK (Putorius vison, Aud. and Bach.) is much more a water-side frequenter than the last described animal, and indeed is quite aquatic in its habits, being constantly seen swimming in lakes like the otter, which it somewhat resembles in its taste for fish and frogs. The mink has, moreover, a strong propensity to maraud poultry yards, and is trapped by the settler, not only in self-defence, but also on account of the two, three, or even five dollars obtainable for a good skin. The general colour is dark, reddish-brown, and the fur is much used for caps, boas and muffs. It is a rich and beautiful fur, finer though shorter than that of the marten.

The droppings of the mink may be seen on almost every flat rock in the forest brook, and where their runs approach the water's edge, perhaps leading through a gap between thickly-growing fir stems, are placed the nume-rous traps devised to secure the prize by settlers and

Indians. Fish, flesh, or fowl alike may form the bait; a piece of gaspereau, or the liver of a rabbit or porcupine, is very enticing. With its half-webbed feet and aquatic habits, the American mink appears to have a well-marked European representative in the lutreola of Finland.

# CHAPTER VIII.

## CAVE LODGERS.

## THE BLACK BEAR.

*(Ursus Americanus, Pallas.)*

THIS species has a most extensive range in North America, is common in all wooded districts from the mouths of the Mississippi to the shores of Hudson's Bay, from the Labrador, Newfoundland, and the islands of the Gulf, to Vancouver, and is found wherever northern fir-thickets or the tangled cane-brakes of more southern regions offer him a retreat.

In the Eastern woodlands the black bear (here the sole representative of his genus) is the only large wild animal that becomes offensive when numerous, as he is still in all the Lower Provinces. He is a continual source of anxious dread to the settler, whose cattle, obliged to wander into the woods to seek provender, often meet their fate at the hands of this lawless freebooter, who will also burglariously break into the settler's barn, and, abstracting sheep and small cattle, drag them off into the neighbouring woods. And he is such an exceedingly cunning, wide-awake beast that it is very seldom he can be pursued and destroyed by the bullet, or deluded into the trap or snare ; and hence he is not so often killed as his numbers and bad character might warrant.

Compared with the U. Arctos—the common brown bear of Europe—the black bear shows many well-marked distinctions, the grizzly (U. horribilis) claiming a much closer relationship with the former. Professor Baird points, however, to important dental differences between them; and considers the invariably broader skulls of the brown bear conclusive as to identity. Perhaps the greater size of the grizzly might be merely regarded as owing to geographical variation; but, taken in conjunction with the above and other osteological differences, and the longer claws and shorter ears of the American, we can only regard them as representative species.

The black bear grows to some six feet in length from the muzzle to the tail (about two inches long), and stands from three to three and a half feet in height at the shoulder. The general colour is a glossy black, the sides of the muzzle pale brown; there is no wool at the base of the hair. In many specimens observed in Nova Scotia I have seen great differences both as regards colour of the skin and length of leg—even in breadth of the skulls. Some animals are brown all over, others glossy black, and wanting the cinnamon patch at the muzzle. There are long and low bears, whereas others have short bodies and great length of limb. The settlers, of course, as they do in the case of other animals, insist upon two species: my own conclusion is that the species is very susceptible of variation. They have a mythical bear called "the ranger," which does not hybernate, and is known by length of limb, and a white spot on the breast. This latter peculiarity I have seen in several skins, but

have only noticed tracks of bears on the snow in winter,
when a sudden and violent rainstorm, or a prolonged
thaw has flooded their den, and sent them forth to look
for fresh shelter, as they cannot endure a wet bed during
hybernation.

The bear is very particular in choosing a comfortable
dormitory for his long winter's nap.  In walking through
the woods, you will find plenty of caves—likely looking
places for a bear's den—but " Bruin," or rather " Mooin,"
as the Indians call him (a name singularly like his European sobriquet in sound) would not condescend to use
one in a hundred, perhaps.  He must have a nice dry
place, so arranged that the snow will not drift in on his
back, or water trickle through; for he grumbles terribly,
when aroused from his lair in mid-winter, either by the
hunter's summons or unseasonable weather.  And then
he is so cautious—the Indians say " he think all the same
as a man "—that he will not go into it if there are any
sticks cut in the vicinity by the hands of man, or
any recent axe-blazings on the neighbouring trees.
Another thing he cannot endure, is the presence of the
porcupine.  The porcupine (Erethizon dorsatus) lives in
rocky places, full of caves, and often takes possession of
large roomy dens, which poor Mooin, coming up rather
in a hurry, having stopped out blueberry picking rather
later than usual, and till all was blue, might envy, but
would not share on any account.  The porcupine is not
over-cleanly in his habits, besides not being a very
pleasant bedfellow *apropos* of his quills; but to which
of these traits the bear takes objection I cannot say—
perhaps both.  The quills are very disagreeable weapons,
and armed with a little barbed head; when they pierce

the skin they are very difficult of extraction, and a portion, breaking off in the wound, will traverse under the surface, reappearing at some very distant point.

Having determined on his winter's residence, and cleaned it out before the commencement of winter (the extra leaves and rubbish scraped out around the entrance being a sure sign to the hunter that the den will afford him one skin at least, when the winter's snow shall have well covered the ground), Mooin, finding it very difficult to procure a further supply of food, and being, moreover, in a very sleepy frame of mind and body—fat as a prize pig from recent excessive gorging on the numerous berries of the barren, or mast under the beechwoods—turns in for the winter; if he has a partner, so much the better and the warmer. He lies with his fore-arms curled around his head and nose, which is poked in underneath the chest. Here he will sleep uninterruptedly till the warm suns late in March influence his somniferous feelings, unless his sweet mid-winter repose be cut short by a sharp poke in the ribs with a pole, when he has nothing for it but to collect his almost lost power of reflection, and crawl out of his den— saluted, as he appears, by a heavy crushing blow over the temples with the back of an axe, and a volley of musket balls into his body as he reels forward, which translates him into a longer and far different state of sleep.

There has been great uncertainty as to what time the female brings forth her young; some say that it is not until she leaves her winter quarters in the early spring, and that though the she-bear has been started from her den in winter, and two little shapeless things found left

behind, these are so absurdly small as to appear pre-
mature.   And then comes the old story of the little ones
being produced without form, and afterwards licked into
shape in the den.   Even the Indians possess many different ideas on this subject, often affirming that the old
bear has never been shot and discovered to be with
young.   Now all this is great nonsense, and as I know of
an instance in which a bear was shot, a few years since,
on the 14th of February, suckling two very little ones in
an open primitive den, formed merely by a sheltering
windfall, and also have consulted the testimony of travellers on the habits of hybernating bears of other
descriptions, capping all by the reliable evidence of my
old Indian hunter, John Williams, I am convinced that
the following is the true state of the case :—The she-
bear gives birth to two cubs, of very small dimensions
—not much larger than good-sized rats—about the
middle of February, in the den; and here she subsists
them, without herself obtaining any nourishment, until
the thaws in March.   A few years ago a cub was brought
to me in May by a settler, who had shot the mother and
kidnapped one of her offspring; it was a curious little
animal, not much larger than a retriever pup of a few
weeks old, and a strange mixture of fun and ferocity.
The settler, as I handed him the purchase money—one
dollar—informed me that it was as playful as a kitten ;
and, having placed it on the floor, and given it a basin of
bread and milk, which it immediately upset—biting the
saucer with its teeth as though it suspected it of trying
to withhold or participate in the enjoyment of its contents—it commenced to evince its playful disposition by
gambolling about the room, climbing the legs of tables,

hauling off the covers with superincumbent ornaments, and tearing sofa covers, until I was fain to end the scene by securing the young urchin. But I got such a bite through my trowsers that I never again admitted him indoors. I never saw such a little demon; when fed with a bowl of Indian meal porridge, he would bite the rim of the bowl in his rage, growling frantically, and then plunge his head into the mixture, the groans and growls still coming up in bubbles to the surface, whilst he swallowed it like a starved pig. I afterwards gave him to a brother officer going to England, and whether (as is the usual fate of bears in captivity) he afterwards killed a child, and met a felon's death, I never heard.

The growth of bears is very slow; they do not reach their full size for four years from their birth.

On entering his den for hybernation the bear is in prime order; the fat pervades his carcase in exactly the same manner as in the case of the pig, the great bulk of it lying, as in the flitch, along the back and on either side; this generally attains a thickness of four inches, though in domesticated specimens, fed purposely by North American hairdressers, it has reached a thickness of eight inches. It is by the absorption of this fat throughout the long fast of four months that the bear is enabled to exist. Of course evaporation is almost at a stand-still, and a plug, called by the Norwegians the "tappen," is formed in the rectum, and retained until the spring. Should this be lost prematurely, it is said that the animal immediately becomes emaciated.

A large bear at the end of the fall will weigh five and even six hundred pounds; this has been increased in domesticated specimens by oatmeal feeding to over seven hundred.

Having awoke at last, the genial warmth of a spring day tempts him forth to try and find something to appease the growing cravings of appetite. What is the bill of fare? meagre enough generally, for the snow still covers the dead timber (where he might find colonies of ants), the roots, and young shoots and buds; but he bethinks himself of the cranberries in the open bogs from which, unshaded by the branches of the dark fir-forest, the snow has disappeared, disclosing the bright crimson berries still clinging to their tendrils on the moss-clumps and rendered tender and luscious by the winter's frost. Even the rank marsh-grass forms part of his diet; and, as the snow disappears, he turns over the fallen timber to look for such insects as ants or wood-lice, which might be sheltered beneath. Although so large an animal, he will seek his food patiently; and the prehensile nature of his lips enables him to pick up the smallest insect or forest berry with great dexterity. The runs between the forest lakes also afford him early and profitable spring fishing; and he may be seen lying on the edge of the ice, fishing for smelts (Osmerus), which delicate little fish abound in the lakes, near their junction with harbours, throughout the winter, tipping them out of the water on to the ice behind him in a most dexterous manner with his paws. Later in the spring he continues his fishing propensities, and makes capital hauls when the *gaspereaux*, or alewives (Alosa vernalis),—a description of herring— rush up the forest brooks in countless multitudes, carrying an ample source of food to the doors of settlers living by the banks in the remotest wilds. Works on natural history supply abundant evidence of his general conformation as a member of the plantigrade family, of the adaptation of the broad, callous soles of his feet for walking, sitting on his haunches, or standing erect, and of the long but not retractile claws fitted for digging, by which he can easily ascend a tree, or split the fallen rampike—like a Samson as he is—striking them into its surface, and rending it in twain, in search of ants ; and what a fearful weapon the fore-hand becomes, armed with these terrible claws, when they are sent home into the flesh of an enemy or intended victim, whenever the rascal takes a notion of laying aside his frugivorous propensities to satisfy a thirst for stronger meat !

Having noticed his tastes as a herbivorous and piscivorous animal, we have yet to mention this, in which, though it has been but slightly implanted in him by nature, he sometimes indulges, and which, once indulged in, becomes a strong habit, and stamps him as being also carnivorous.  Poor Mooin ! still unsatisfied, and half-starved—perhaps unsuccessful in his spring-fishing, or in berrying—hears the distant tinkling of cattle-bells as the animals wander through the woods from some neighbouring settlement.  Nearer and nearer they come ; and he advances cautiously to meet them, keeping a sharp look-out in case they might be attended by a human being, of whom he has a most wholesome dread. By a little careful manœuvring he drives them into a deep, boggy swamp where he can at leisure single out his victim, and, jumping on its back, deals it a few such terrific blows across the back and shoulders, that the poor animal soon succumbs, and falls an easy prey. Stunned, torn, and bemired, it is then dragged back to

the dry slopes of the woods and devoured. The settlers
say that the bear, while killing his victim (which moans
and bellows piteously all the while he is beating it to
death in the swamp), will every now and then retire
to the woods behind and listen for any approaching
signs of rescue, prior to returning and finishing his
work. This wicked appetite of his often leads to his
destruction; for a search being entailed for the missing
beast, and the remains found, the avenger, on the following evening, armed with a gun, goes out to waylay the
bear, who is sure to revisit the carcase. It would never
do to remain in ambush near the spot, for the villain
always comes back on the watch, planting his feet
as cautiously as an Indian creeping on moose, with all
his senses on the *qui vive*. So the man, finding by his
track in which direction he had retreated from the carcase, goes back into the woods some quarter of a mile or
so, and then secretes himself; and Mooin, not suspecting
any ambuscade at this distance from the scene of his
recent feasting, comes along towards sundown, hand over
hand, and probably meets his just fate. Young moose,
too, often fall victims to the bear, though he would
never succeed in an attempt on the life of a full-grown
animal.

The bear is conscious of being a villain, and will never
look a man in the face. This I have observed in the
case of tame animals, and marked the change of expression in their little treacherous black eye) about the size
of a small marble) just before they were about to do
something mischievous. In their quickness of temper, and
in the suddenness with which the usually perfectly dull
and unmeaning eye is lighted up with the most wicked

expression imaginable, immediately followed by action, they put me much in mind of some of the monkey tribe.

The strength of the bear is really prodigious, fully equal to that of ten men, as was once proved by a tame bear in this province hauling a barrel which had been smeared with molasses, and contained a little oatmeal, away from the united efforts of the number of men mentioned, who held on to a rope passed round the barrel. The bear walked away with it as easily as possible. The same bear, having nearly killed a horse, and scalped a boy, was afterwards destroyed by his owner. The way he tried to do for the animal was curious enough; he approached the horse, which was loose in the road, from behind; on its attempting to kick, the bear caught hold of its hind legs, just above the fetlocks, with the quickness of lightning; the horse tried to kick again, and the bear, with the greatest apparent ease, shoved its hind legs under till the horse was fairly brought on its haunches, when the rascal at once jumped on its back, and, with one tremendous blow, buried its powerful claws into the muscle of the shoulder, and the horse, trembling and in a profuse perspiration, rolled over and would have been killed if the affair had not been witnessed and the bear at this juncture driven away.

I have been told by an Indian of a scene he once witnessed in the woods when resting on the shore of a lake before proceeding across a *portage* with his canoe. A crashing of branches proclaimed the rapid advance of a large animal in flight. In a few moments a fine young moose, about half grown, dashed from the forest into the

lake, carrying a bear on its shoulders, and at once struck
out into deep water.  The two were soon separated, and
the Indian at the same time launching his canoe, succeeded
in wounding the bear, which, seeing the man, had turned
back for the shore.  The moose escaped on the opposite
side.

In the spring the old she bear, accompanied by her
brace of little whining cubs, is almost sure to turn on a
human being if suddenly disturbed, though, if made aware
of coming danger in time, she will always conduct them
out of the way.   I have known many instances of settlers,
out trouting by the lakes near home, being chased out of
the woods and nearly run into, by the she bear in spring-
time.

In June, likewise, in the running season, it is not safe
to be back in the woods unarmed or alone.  A whole
gang will go together, making the forest resound with
their hideous snarling and loud moaning cries.  Hearing
the approach of such a procession, the sojourner in camp
piles fuel on the fire, and keeps watch with loaded
gun.  In old times, before they acquired the dread of
fire-arms, the Indians say these animals were much
bolder.

The bear is readily taken in a dead-fall trap with a bait
composed of almost anything : a bundle of birch-bark
tied up, and smeared over with a little honey, molasses,
or tallow, answers very well.

They travel through the woods and along the water-
side in well defined paths, which afford excellent walking
to the hunter.  Bear-traps are placed at intervals in the
vicinity of their roads, and many a rascal loses his jacket
to the settlers in summer time in return for his audacious

raids on the cattle, to obtain which he will sometimes break in the side of a barn.

The skin realises from four to twelve dollars, according to size and condition.

The fall is the best time for bear hunting—" the berry-ing time," as it is designated by the settlers, when he is engaged in laying in a stock of corpulency, the material whereof shall stick to his ribs during the long fast of the coming winter. So intent is he now on his luscious feast on blue and whortle berries, that he does not keep as good a look-out for foes as at other times, and may be easily detected in the early morning by the observant hunter, who knows his habits and meal times, and hunts round the leeward edges of barrens.

Later still, in a good season for beechmast, he may be hunted in hard-wood hills. A little light snow will not send him home to bed, whilst it materially aids the hunter in tracking the animal. Sometimes the bear will go aloft for the mast, and even construct a rough platform amongst the upper branches, where he can rest without holding on. I have seen many such apparent structures, and could in no other way account for their appearance, and to this I may add the testimony of the Indian.

The bear takes a deal of killing, and will run an incredible distance with several mortal wounds. A singular trait, approaching almost to reflective power, is his habit of stopping in his flight to pick up wet moss in a swamp wherewith to plug up the wound.

I but once surprised a bear in the wood in the act of feeding, unconscious of my approach. My Indian saw a portion of his black hair moving just above the side of a large fallen tree, and in a moment we both lay prostrate.

The animal presently rose from his hitherto recumbent position and sat up, munching his mouthful of beech-nuts with great apparent satisfaction—a magnificent specimen, and black as a coal.

We should now have fired, but at this juncture, as luck would have it, a red fox, which our tracks below had probably disturbed, raced up behind and induced us to look round. The bear at once sank quietly down behind the log, and, worming along, bounded over a precipice into a thick spruce swamp before we were aware that we were discovered. This fox must have been his good genius.

Notwithstanding the value of the skin and the standing grievance between the settler of the back-woods and the black bear, the latter is apparently increasing in numbers in many parts of the Lower Provinces. In Nova Scotia there is no bounty on their noses, though the wolf (a rare visitor) is thus placed under a ban. In Anticosti bears are exceedingly numerous, and a well-organised bear hunt on this island would doubtless show a wonderful return of sport; but then—the flies!

---

## THE CANADA PORCUPINE.

### (*Erethizon dorsatus, Cuvier.*)

This species is common in the woodland districts of Eastern North America, from Pennsylvania to the Arctic Circle. West of the Missouri, according to Baird, it is replaced by the yellow-haired porcupine (E. epixanthus).

A cave-dwelling animal, choosing its residence amongst the dark recesses of collocated boulders, or the holes at the roots of large trees, it spends much of its time abroad.

It is sometimes seen sluggishly reposing in tree tops, where it gnaws the bark of the young branches ; and is often (especially in the season of ripe berries) found in the open barren, though never far away from its retreat. A porcupine's den is easily discovered, both by the broad trail or path which leads to it, and by the quantity of ordure by which the entrance is marked. From the den the paths diverge to some favourite feeding ground—perhaps a grove of beech, on the mast of which the animal revels in the fall ; or, if it be winter time, to the shelter of a tall hemlock spruce. The marks of the claws on the bark are a ready indication of its whereabouts ; **and as the Indian** hunter passes in search of larger game, he knows he is sure of roast porcupine if venison is not procurable, and probably **tumbles him** down on return to camp by a bullet through the head.

The spines of the Canadian porcupine are about three inches long, proceeding from a thick coat of dark brownish hair, mixed with sooty-coloured bristles. They are largest **and** most abundant over the loins, where the animal, when brought **to a** stand, sets them up in a fan-like arc, and presents a most formidable array of points always turned towards its opponent. It endeavours at the same time to strike with its thick muscular tail, **leaving, where the** blow falls, a great number of the easily-detached quills firmly sticking in, rooted by their barbed **points.**

A porcupine can gallop or shuffle along at a good pace, and often, when surprised in the open, makes good its retreat to its rocky den, or gains a tree, up which it scrambles rapidly out of reach.

The spines are of a dull white colour, with dusky tips.

To the forest Indians of Acadie the porcupine is an

animal of considerable importance. It is a very common article of food, and its quills are extensively employed by the squaws in ornamentation. Stained most brilliantly by dyes either obtained from the woods or purchased in the settlements, they are worked in fanciful patterns into the birch-bark ware (baskets, screens, or trays), which form their staple of trade with the whites.

All the holes, hollow trees, and rocky precipices in the neighbourhood of an encampment are continually explored by Indian boys in search of a porcupine's den.

The Indians commonly possess little cur dogs, which greatly assist them in discovering the animal's retreat ; they will even draw them forth from their holes without injury to themselves—a feat only to be accomplished by getting hold of them underneath.

It is a curious fact that the settler's dogs in general evince a strong desire to hunt porcupine, notwithstanding the woeful plight, about the head and forelegs, in which they come out of the encounter, and the long period of inflammation to which they are thereby subjected. The Indian's porcupine-dog, however, goes to work in a far more business-like manner—seldom giving his master occasion to extract a single quill. "The Old Hunter" tells me as follows :—" I once knew an instance of an Indian's dog, quite blind, that was particularly *great on porcupines*, so much so, that if they treed, the little animal would sit down beneath, occasionally barking, to inform its master where lodged the 'fretful' one. Another dog belonging to an Indian I knew, was not to be beaten when once on porcupine. If the animal was in den, in he went and, if possible, would haul it out by the tail. If not strong enough, the Indian would fasten his handkerchief round his middle, and attach to it a long twisted withe. The dog would go in, and presently, between the two, out would come the porcupine."

The porcupine becomes loaded with fat in the fall by feasting on the numerous berries found on the barrens. The latter half of September is their running season. The old ones are then very rank, and not fit to eat. Their call is a plaintive whining sound, not very dissimilar to the cry of a calf moose. At this season, when hunting in the woods, I have frequently found old males with bad wounds on the back—the skin extensively abraded by, apparently, a high fall from a tree on the edge of a rock. My Indian says with regard to this, " he make himself sore back, purpose so as to travel light, and get clear of his fat."

The female brings forth two at a birth in the den very early in the spring.

It is a remarkable fact that, though abundant in Nova Scotia, the porcupine is not found in the island of Cape Breton, separated only by the Gut of Canso in places but a few hundred yards across. Frequent attempts have indeed been made by Indians to introduce the animal in Cape Breton by importation from the south side, but have always ended in failure. Though the vegetable features of the island are identical with those of Nova Scotia proper, the porcupine will not live in the woods of the former locality. This is a well-ascertained fact, and no attempt at explanation can be offered.

Again, though it is found on the Labrador, and at the Straits of Belle Isle, the great island of Newfoundland, which is thus separated from the mainland, contains no porcupine.

P

The marmot of the eastern woodlands (Arctomys monax), and the striped ground-squirrel, or " chipmunk " (Tamias striatus, Baird), are more properly burrowing animals than cave-dwellers, under which heading we can class only the bear and the porcupine.

# CHAPTER IX.

## ACADIAN FISH AND FISHING.

## THE BROOK TROUT.

*Salmo Fontinalis* (Mitchell.)

THE following description of this fish—and I believe
the latest—appears in the "Transactions of the Nova
Scotian Institute of Natural Science for 1866," and is
due to Dr. J. Bernard Gilpin, M.D. :—

" The trout, as usually seen in the lakes about Halifax,
are in length from ten to eighteen inches, and weight
from half a pound to two pounds, though these measurements are often exceeded or lessened. The outline of
back, starting from a rather round and blunt nose, rises
gradually to the insertion of the dorsal fin, about two-
thirds of the length of the head from the nose ; it then
gradually declines to the adipose fin, and about a length
and a half from that runs straight to form a strong base
for the tail. The breadth of the tail is about equal to
that of the head. Below, the outline runs nearly straight
from the tail to the anal fin ; from thence it falls rapidly
to form a line more or less convex (as the fish is in or
out of season), and returns to the head. The inter-maxillary very short, the maxillary long with the free end
sharp-pointed, the posterior end of the opercle is more

angular than in the S. Salar, the lower jaw shorter than
upper when closed, appearing longer when open. The
eye large, about two diameters from tip of nose; nostrils
double, nearer the snout than the eye. Of the fins, the
dorsal has ten or eleven rays, not counting the rudimentary ones, in shape irregularly rhomboid, but the free
edge rounded or curved outward : the adipose fin varies,
some sickle-shaped with free end very long, others
having it very straight and short. The caudal fin gently
curved rather than cleft, but differing in individuals. Of
the lower fins they all have the first ray very thick and
flat, and always faced white with a black edge, the other
rays more or less red. The head is blunt, and back
rounded when looked down upon. The teeth are upon
the inter-maxillary bone, maxillary bones, the palatine,
and about nine on the tongue. There are none so-called
vomerine teeth, though now and then we find one tooth
behind the arch of the palate, where they are sometimes
irregularly bunched together. The colour varies ; but
through all the variations there are forms of colour that,
being always persistent, must be regarded as typical.
There are always vermilion spots on the sides ; there
are always other spots, sometimes decided in outline,
in others diffused into dapples, but always present. The
caudal and dorsal fins are always spotted, and of the
prevailing hue of the body. The lower fins have always
broad white edges, lined with black and coloured with
some modification of red. The chin and upper part of
the belly are always white. With these permanent markings, the body colour varies from horn colour to greenish-
grey, blue-grey, running into azure, black, and black
with warm red on the lower parts, dark green with lower

parts bright yellow; and, lastly, in the case of young fish, with vertical bands of dusky black. The spots are very bright and distinct when in high condition or spawning ; faint, diffused, and running into dapples when in poor condition. In the former case all the hues are most vivid, and heightened by profuse nacre. In the other the spots are very pale yellowish-white, running on the back into vermicular lines. The iris in all is dark brown. I have seen the rose or red-coloured ones at all times of the year. The young of the first year are greenish horn colour, with brown vertical stripes and bright scarlet fins and tail, already showing the typical marks and spots, and also the vermilion specs. Fin rays D. 13, P. 13, V. 8, A. 10 ; gill rays 12. Scales very small ; the dorsal has two rudimentary rays, ten or eleven long ones, varying in different fish. Typical marks—axillary plate nearly obsolete, free end of maxillary sharp, bars in young, vermilion specs, both young and adult lower fins red with white and black edge."

To the above description I would add that the numerous yellow spots which prevail in every specimen of S. Fontinalis vary from bright golden to pale primrose, that the colour of the specs inclines more to carmine than vermilion, and that in bright, well-conditioned fish, the latter are surrounded by circlets of pale and purest azure.

It will thus be seen that the American brook trout is one of the most beautiful of fresh-water fishes. Just taken from his element and laid on the moist moss by the edge of the forest stream, a more captivating form can scarcely be imagined. His sides appear as if studded with gems. The brilliant brown eye and bronzy gill-covers reflect golden light; and the gradations of the dark green back, with its fantastic labyrinthine markings, to the soft yellow beneath, are marked by a central roseate tinge inclining to lavender or pale mauve.

This species abounds throughout the Northern States and British provinces, showing a great variety as to form and colour (both external and of the flesh) according to locality. In the swampy bog-hole the trout is black; his flesh of a pale yellowish-white, flabby and insipid. In low-lying forest lakes margined by swamp, where from a rank soft bottom the water-lilies crop up and almost conceal the surface near the shores, he is the same coarse and spiritless fish. Worthless for the camp frying-pan, we leave him to the tender mercies of the mink, the eel, and the leech. The bright, bold trout of the large lakes, is a far different fish. His comparatively small and well-shaped head, followed by an arched, thick shoulder, depth of body, and brilliant colouring; the spirited dash with which he seizes his prey, and, finally, the bright salmon-pink hue of his delicate flesh, make him an object of attraction to both sportsman and epicure. Such fish we find in the clearest water, where the shores of the lake are fringed with granite boulders, with beaches of white sand, or disintegrated granite, where the rush and the water-weeds are only seen in little sheltered coves, where the face of the lake is dotted with rocky, bush-covered islands, and where there are great cool depths to which he can retreat when sickened by the heat of the surface-water at midsummer.

Though more a lacustrine than a river fish, seldom attaining any size if confined to running water between the sea and impassable falls, the American trout is found to most perfection and in greatest number in lakes which communicate with the sea, and allow him to indulge in his well ascertained predilection for salt, or rather brackish tidal-water. A favourite spot is the débouchure of a lake, where the narrowing water gradually acquires velocity of current, and where the trout lie in skulls and give the greatest sport to the fly-fisher.

In a recent notice of S. Fontinalis from the pen of an observant sportsman and naturalist appearing in "Land and Water," this fish is surmised to be a char. Its claim to be a member of the Salveline group is favoured by reference to its similar habits in visiting the tidal portions of rivers on the part of the char of Norway and Sweden, its similar deep red colouring on the belly, and general resemblance. I am quite of "Ubique's" opinion touching this point, and think the common name of the American fish should be char. Indeed, I find the New York char is one of the names it already bears in an American sporting work, though no comparison is made. Besides its sea-going propensities, its preferring dark, still waters, to gravelly shallow streams, and its resplendent colours when in season, a most important point of resemblance to the char would seem to be the minuteness of its scales.

The American trout spawns in October and November in shallow water, and on gravel, sand, or mud, according to the nature of the soil at the bottom of his domains.

In fishing for trout through the ice in winter to add to our camp fare, I have taken them at the "run in" to a large lake, the females full of spawn apparently ready to drop at the end of January, and all in firm condition. This would seem a curious delay of the spawning season : my Indian stated that trout spawn in early spring as well as in the fall.  They congregate at the head of a lake in large numbers in winter, and readily take bait, a piece of pork, or a part of their own white throats, let down on a hook through the ice.  In such localities they get a good livelihood by feeding on the caddis-worms which crawl plentifully over the rocks under water.

## TROUT FISHING.

Before the ice is fairly off the lakes—and then a few days must be allowed for the ice-water to run off— there is no use in attempting to use the fly for trout fishing in rivers or runs, though eager disciples of Walton may succeed in hauling out a few ill-fed, sickly looking fish from spots of open water by diligently tempting with the worm at an earlier date.  Indeed trout may be taken with bait through the ice throughout the winter, but they prove worthless in the eating.  But after the warm rain storms of April have performed their mission, and the soft west wind has coursed over the surface of the water, then may the fisher proceed to the head of the forest lake and cast his flies over the eddying pool where the brook enters, and where the hungry trout, aroused to appetite, are congregated to seek for food.

> "Now, when the first foul torrent of the brooks,
> Swell'd with the vernal rains, is ebbed away,
> And, whitening down their mossy-tinctur'd stream
> Descends the billowy foam   now is the time,
> While yet the dark-brown water aids the guile,
> To tempt the trout."

About the 10th of May in Nova Scotia, when warm hazy weather occurs with westerly wind, the trout in all the lakes and streams (an enumeration of which would be impossible from their extraordinary frequency of occurrence in this province) are in the best mood for taking the fly ; and, moreover, full of the energy of new found life, which appears in these climates to influence such animals as have been dormant during the long winter, equally with the suddenly outbursting vegetation. A few days later, and the great annual feast of the trout commences—the feast of the May-fly. Emerging from their cases all round the shores, rocky shallows, and islands, the May-flies now cover the surface of the lakes in multitudes, and are constantly sucked in by the greedy trout, which leave their haunts, and disperse themselves over the lake in search of the alighting insects. Although the fish thus gorge themselves, and, for some days after the flies have disappeared, are quite apathetic, they derive much benefit in flesh and flavour therefrom. The abun-dance of fish would scarcely be credited till one sees the countless rises over the surface of the water constantly recurring during the prevalence of the May-fly. "It's a steady boil of them," says the ragged urchin with a long "troutin'-pole," as he calls his weapon, in one hand, and a huge cork at the end of a string with a bunch of worms attached, in the other.

There is now no one more likely place than another for a cast. Still sport may be had with the artificial May-fly, especially in sheltered coves, where the fish resort when a strong wind blows the insects off the open water. Some anglers of the more patient type will take fish at this time on the lake by sitting on rocks, and gently flipping out a very fine line with minute hooks, to which the living May-fly is attached by means of a little adhesive fir balsam, as far as they can on the surface of the water, where they float till some passing fish rises and sucks in the bait. However the best sport is to be obtained on the lakes a few days after the " May-fly glut," as it is termed, is over.

The May and stone flies of America, which make their appearance about the same time, much resemble the ephemeral representatives of their order found in the old country. The May-fly of the New World is, however, different to the green drake, being of a glossy black colour.

With the exception of these two insects, we have no representatives of natural flies in our American fly-books. The scale is large and the style gaudy; and, if the bunch of bright feathers, which sometimes falls over the head of Salmo fontinalis, were so presented to the view of a shy English trout, I question whether he would ever rise to the surface again. Artificial flies are sold in most provincial towns in the Lower Provinces, and are much sought for by the rising generation, who, however, often scorn the store-rod, contenting themselves with a good pliable wattle cut in situ. It is surprising to see the bunches of trout the settlers' "sonnies" will bring home from some little lake, perhaps only known to themselves, which they may have discovered back in the woods when hunting up the cows ; and the satisfaction with which the little ragged urchin will show you barefoot the way to your fishing grounds, skipping over the sharp granite rocks strewed in the path, and brushing through fir thickets with the greatest resolution, all to become possessed of a bunch of your flies and a small length of old gut.

The cast of flies best adapted for general use for trout-fishing in Nova Scotia consists of the red hackle or palmer, a bright bushy scarlet fly, with perhaps a bit of gold twist or tinsel further to enhance its charms, a brown palmer, and a yellow-bodied fly of wool with mallard wings. The latter wing on a body of claret wool with gold tinsel is also excellent. Many other and gaudier flies are made and sold to tempt the fish later on in the year : they are quite fanciful, and resemble nothing in nature. I cannot recommend the artificial minnow for use in this part of the world, though trout will take them. They are always catching on submerged rocks, and are very troublesome in many ways. The most successful minnow I ever used was one made on the spot by an Indian who was with me after moose—a common large trout-hook thickly bound round with white worsted, a piece of tinfoil covering the under part, and a good bunch of peacock's herl inserted at the head, bound down along the back, and secured at the end of the shank, leaving a little projection to represent the tail. It was light as a feather, and could be thrown very accurately any-where—a great advantage when you find yourself back in the woods and wish to pull a few trout for the camp frying-pan from out a little pond overhung with bushes. The fish took it most greedily.

The common trout is to be met with in every lake, or even pond, throughout the British Provinces. One cannot walk far through the depths of a forest district before hearing the gurgling of a rill of water amongst stones beneath the moss. Following the stream, one

soon comes on a sparkling forest brook overhung by
waving fern fronds, and little pools with a bottom of
golden gravel.   The trout is sure to be here, and on
your approach darts under the shelter of the projecting
roots of the mossy bank.   A little further, and a winding
lane of still water skirted by graceful maples and birches,
leads to the open expanses of the lake, where the gloom
of the heavy woods is exchanged for the clear daylight.
This is the "run in," in local phraseology, and here the
lake trout resort as a favourite station at all times of the
year.   A basket of two or three dozen of these speckled
beauties is your reward for having found your way to
these wild but enchanting spots.

Though, as has been observed, the trout of America is
more a lake than a river fish, yet the gently running water
at the foot of a lake just before the toss and tumble of a
rapid is reached is a favourite station for trout.   Such
spots are excellent for fly-fishing ; I have frequently taken
five dozen fine fish in an hour, in the Liverpool, Tangier,
and other noble rivers in Nova Scotia, from rapid water,
weighing from one to three pounds.

Towards midsummer the fish begin to refuse fly or
bait, retiring to deep pools under the shade of high rocks,
sickened apparently by the warmth of the lake water.
As, however, the woods, especially in the neighbourhood
of water, are at this season infested with mosquitoes
and black flies, a day's "outing" by the lake or river
side becomes anything but recreative, if not unbearable.
The twinge of the almost invisible sand-fly adds, too,
to our torments.   In Nova Scotia the savage black-
fly (Simulium molestum) disappears at the end of June,
though in New Brunswick the piscator will find these

wretches lively the whole summer. They attack everything of life moving in the woods, being dislodged from
every branch shaken by a passing object. No wonder
the poor moose rush into the lakes, and so bury themselves in the water that their ears and head are alone
seen above the surface. In Labrador the flies are yet
worse, and travelling in the interior becomes all but
impracticable during the summer.

In August the trout recover themselves under the
cooling influence of the frosty atmosphere which now
prevails at night, and will again take the fly readily, continuing to do so until quite late in the fall, and even in
the spawning season.

----

## THE SEA TROUT.

*Salmo Canadensis* (Hamilton Smith).

Closely approximating to the brook trout in shape
and colouring—especially after having been some time
in fresh water—the above named species has been pronounced distinct. They have so near a resemblance that
until separated by the careful comparison of Dr. Gilpin,
I always believed them to be the same fish, especially
as the brook trout as aforesaid is known to frequent
tidal waters at the head of estuaries. The following
description of the sea trout is taken from Dr. Gilpin's
article on the Salmonidæ before alluded to, and is the
result of examination of several fish taken from fresh
water, and in the harbour :—

"Of those from the tide-way, length from twelve to
fourteen inches ; deepest breadth, something more than

one quarter from tip of nose to insertion of tail. The
outline rounds up rather suddenly from a small and
arched head to insertion of dorsal; slopes quickly but
gently to adipose fin; then runs straight to insertion
of caudal; tail gently curved rather than cleft; lower
line straight to anal, then falling rather rapidly to make
a very convex line for belly, and ending at the gills.
The body deeper and more compressed than in the
brook trout. The dorsal is quadrangular; the free edge
convex; the lower fins having the first rays in each
thicker and flatter than the brook trout. The adipose
fin varies, some with very long and arched free end, in
others small and straight. The specimen from the fresh
water was very much longer and thinner, with head
proportionally larger. The colour of those from the
tide-way was more or less dark greenish blue on back
shading to ash blue and white below, lips edged with
dusky. They all had faint cream-coloured spots, both
above and below the lateral line. With one exception,
they all had vermilion specks, but some only on one side,
others two or three. In all, the head was greenish horn
colour. The colour of the fins in pectoral, ventral, and
anal, varied from pale white, bluish-white, to pale
orange, with a dusky streak on different individuals.
Dorsal dusky with faint spots, and caudal with dusky
tips—on some a little orange wash. The lower fins had
the first ray flat, and white edged with dusky. In the
specimen taken on September the 10th from the fresh
water, the blue and silver had disappeared, and dingy
ash colour had spread down below the lateral line; the
greenish horn colour had spread itself over the whole
gills except the chin, which was white. The silvery

reflections were all gone, the cream-coloured dapples were much more decided in colour and shape, and the vermilion specs very numerous. The caudal and all the lower fins had an orange wash, the dorsal dusky yellow with black spots, the lower fins retaining the white flat ray with a dusky edging, and the caudal a few spots. The teeth of all were upon the inter-maxillary, maxillaries, palatine, and the tongue ; none on the vomer except now and then one tooth behind the arch of palate. Fin rays, D. 13, P. 13, V. 8, A. 10 ; gill rays 12. Axillary scale very small. Dorsal, with two rudimentary rays, ten or eleven long ones, free edge convex ; first ray of lower fins flat, scales very small, but rather larger than those of brook trout."

Dr. Gilpin sums up as follows on the question of its identity with brook trout :—

" We must acknowledge it exceedingly closely allied to Fontinalis—that it has the teeth, shape of fins, axillary plate, tail, dapples, vermilion specs, spotted dorsal, alike ; that when it runs to fresh water it changes its colour, and, in doing this, approximates to its red fin and dingy green with more numerous vermilion specs, still more closely. Whilst, on the other hand, we find it living apart from Fontinalis, pursuing its own laws, attaining a greater size, and returning year after year to the sea. The Fontinalis is often found unchanged under the same circumstances. The former fish always preserves its more arched head, deeper and more compressed body, and perhaps shorter fins. In giving it a specific name, therefore, and using the appropriate one given by Colonel Hamilton Smith—so far as I can discover the first describer—I think I will be borne out by all naturalists."

The size attained by this fish along the Atlantic coasts rarely exceeds five pounds : from one to three pounds is the weight of the generality of specimens. The favourite localities for sea trout are the numerous harbours with which the coasts of the maritime provinces (of Nova Scotia in particular) are frequently indented. First seen in the early spring, they affect these harbours throughout the summer, luxuriating on the rich food afforded on the sand flats, or amongst the kelp shoals. On the former localities the sand-hopper (Talitrus) seems to be their principal food; and they pursue the shoals of small fry which haunt the weeds, preying on the smelt (Osmerus) on its way to the brooks, and on the caplin (Mallotus) in the harbours of Newfoundland and Cape Breton. They will take an artificial fly either in the harbour or in fresh water.

When hooked by the fly-fisherman on their first entrance to the fresh water, they afford sport second only to that of salmon-fishing. No more beautiful fish ever reposed in an angler's basket. The gameness with which they prolong the contest—often flinging themselves salmon-like from the water—the flashing lights reflected from their sides as they struggle for life on removal of the fly from their lips, their graceful form, and colouring so exquisitely delicate—sides molten-silver with carmine spangles, and back of light mackerel-green —and, lastly, the delicious flavour of their flesh when brought to table, entitle the sea trout to a high consideration and place amongst the game-fish of the provinces.

In some harbours the trout remains all the summer months feeding on its favourite grounds, but in general it returns to its native fresh water at distinctly marked periods, and in large detachments. In the early spring, before the snow water has left the rivers, a few may be taken at the head of the tide—fresh fish from the salt water mixed with logies, or spent fish that have passed the winter, after spawning in the lakes, under the ice. The best run of fish occurs in June—the midsummer or strawberry run, as it is locally called—the season being indicated by the ripening of the wild strawberry. As with the salmon, there is a final ascent, probably of male fish, late in the fall. The spawning fish remain under the ice all winter in company with the salmon, returning to sea as spent fish with the kelts when the rivers are swelled by freshets from the melting snow.

## SEA TROUT FISHING.

A more delightful season to the sportsman than "strawberry time" on the banks of some fine river entering an Atlantic harbour and well known for its sea trout fishing, can hardly be imagined. With rivers and woods refreshed by recent rains, the former at a perfect state of water for fishing, and the river-side paths through the forest redolent with the aroma of the summer flora, and the delicious perfume of heated fir boughs, the angler's camp is, or should be, a sylvan abode of perfect bliss. Or even better — for then we are free from the persistent attack of mosquito or black fly — is the cabin of a comfortable yacht, in which we shift from harbour to harbour, anchoring near the mouth of the entering river. The flies and sea fog are the only drawbacks to the pleasant holiday

of a trouting cruise along shore.   The former seldom
venture from land (even on the forest lake they leave
the canoe or raft at a few yards' distance from the shore)
and, if the west wind be propitious, the cold damp
fog is driven away to the north-east, following the
coast line, several miles out to sea.

Nothing can exceed the beauty of scenery in some of
the Atlantic harbours of Nova Scotia ; their innumerable islands and heavily-wooded shores fringed with the
golden kelp, the wild undulating hills of maple rising
in the background, the patches of meadow, and the
neat little white shanties of the fishermen's clearings, are
the prettiest and most common details of such pictures,
which never fade from the memory of the lover of
nature.  How easily are recalled to remembrance the
fresh clear summer mornings enjoyed on the water ;
the fir woods of the western shores bathed in the
morning sunbeams, the perfect reflections of the islands
and of the little fishing schooners, the wreaths of blue
smoke rising from their cabin stoves, and rendered
distinct by the dark fir woods behind, and the
roar of the distant rapids, where the river joins the
harbour, borne in cadence on the ear, mingled with the
cheerful sounds of awakening life from the clearings.
The bald-healed eagles (H. leucocephalus) sail majestically through the air, conspicuous when seen against
the line of woods by their snow-white necks and tails.
The graceful little tern (Sterna hirundo) is incessantly
occupied, circling over the harbour, shrilly screaming,
and ever and anon dashing down upon the water to
clutch the small fry ; whilst the common kingfisher, as
abundant by the sea-shore as in the interior, thinking

MUSQUODOBOIT HARBOUR.

all fish, salt or fresh water, that come to his net, equally good, shoots over the harbour with jerking flight, and uttering his wild rattling cry ; now and then he makes an impetuous downward dash, completely burying himself beneath the surface in seizing his prey.

If there is a run of trout, and we wish to fish the river, we go to the sea-pools, which the fish enter with the rising tide, and where we may see their silvery sides flashing as they gambol in the eddies under the apparently delightful influence of the highly-aërated water of a large and rapid stream, or as they rush at the dancing deceit which we agitate over the surface of the pool. Here, in their first resting-place on their way up the river, they will always take the fly most readily; and with good tackle, a propitious day, and the by no means despicable aid of a smart hand with the landing-net, the mossy bank soon glitters with a dozen or two of these delicious fish.

Should they not be running, or shy of rising in the fresh water from some of the many unaccountable humours in which all game fish are apt to indulge, harbour fishing is our resource, and we betake ourselves to the edge of the sand flats where the fish, dispersed in all directions during high water, now congregate and lie under the weeds which fringe the edge of the tide channels. Half-tide is the best time, and the trout rush out from under the kelp at any gaudy fly, temptingly thrown towards the edge, with a wonderful dash, and may be commonly taken two at a time. The trout-beaches in Musquodoboit Harbour, lying off Big Island, of which an engraving is given, may be a pleasant remembrance to many who may read these lines.

A deserted clearing, with soft grassy banks positively reddened with wild strawberries, is a most tempting spot for a picnic, and we go ashore with pots and pans to bivouac on the sward. "Boiled or fried, shall be the trout?" is the question; we try both. Perhaps the former is the best way of cooking the delicate and salmon-flavoured sea trout (especially the larger fish), but in camp we generally patronise a fry, and this is our mode of proceeding. The fire must be bright and low, the logs burning without smoke or steam; the frying-pan is laid on with several thick slices of the best flavoured fat pork, and, when this is sufficiently melted and the pan crackling hot, we put in the trout, split and cleaned, and lay the slices of pork, now sufficiently bereft of their gravy, over them. A little artistic manœuvring, so as to lubricate the rapidly browning sides of the fish, and they are turned so soon as the under surface shows of a light chestnut hue. Just before taking off, add the seasoning and a tablespoonful of Worcester. The tin plates are now held forth to receive the spluttering morsels canted from the pan, and we fall back on the couch of maple boughs to eat in the approved style of the ancients, whilst the fresh mid-day breeze from the Atlantic modifies the heat, and drives away to the shelter of the surrounding bushes the fisherman's most uncompromising foes—the mosquitoes and black flies.

In Nova Scotia the best localities for pursuing this attractive sport are the harbours to the eastward of Halifax—Musquodoboit, Tangier, Ship, Beaver, Liscomb, and Country harbours. In Cape Breton the beautiful Margarie is one of the most noted streams for sea trout,

and its clear water and picturesque scenery, winding
through intervale meadows dotted with groups of witch
elm, and backed by wooded hills over a thousand feet
in height, entitle it to pre-eminence amongst the rivers of
the Gulf.

Prince Edward's Island affords some good sea-trout
fishing, and, further north, the streams of the Bay of
Chaleurs and of both shores of the St. Lawrence are so
thronged with this fish, in its season, near the head of
the tide, as seriously to impede the salmon fisher in his
nobler pursuit, taking the salmon fly with a pertinacity against which it is useless to contend ; nor is he
free from their attacks until a cascade of sufficient
dimensions has intervened between the haunts of the
two fish.

## THE SALMON.

### (Salmo Salar.)

The Salmon of the Atlantic coasts of America not
having been as yet specifically separated from the European fish, a scientific description is unnecessary, and we
pass on to note the habits of this noble game fish of our
provincial rivers.

From the once productive rivers of the United States
—with the exception of an occasional fish taken in the
Penobscot, or the Kennebec in Maine—the salmon has
long since been driven, the last recorded capture in the
Hudson being in the year 1840.  Mr. Roosevelt, a well-
known American sportsman and author, states that
"the rivers flowing into Lake Ontario abounded with
them, even until a recent period, but the persistent

efforts at their extinction have at last prevailed ; and,
except a few stragglers, they have ceased from out our
waters."

Cape Sable being, then, the south-easternmost point
in the salmon's range, we first find him entering the
rivers of the south coast of Nova Scotia very early in
March, long before the snow has left the woods; thus
disproving an assertion that he will not ascend a river
till clear of snow water.   At this time he meets the
spent fish, or kelts, returning from their dreary residence
under the ice in the lakes, and these gaunt, hungry fish
may be taken with most annoying frequency by the
angler for the new comers.

As a broad rule, with, however, some singular excep-
tions, the run of salmon now proceeds with tolerably
progressive regularity along the coast to the eastward
and northward, the bulk of the fish having ascended the
Nova Scotian rivers by the middle of June.   The excep-
tions referred to occur in the case of a large river on the
eastern coast of Nova Scotia—the Saint Mary—and some
of the tributaries of the Bay of Fundy, in which there is
a run of fish in March, as on the south-eastern coast.
This fact militates somewhat against the theory of the
salmon migrating in winter to warmer waters to return
in a body in early spring and ascend their native rivers,
entering them progressively.

In the Bay of Chaleurs the season is somewhat more
delayed ; the fish are not fairly in the fresh water before
the middle of June, which is also the time for their
ascending the rivers of Labrador.

At midsummer in Nova Scotia, and in the middle of
July higher up in the gulf, the grilse make their appear-

ance in fresh water in company with the sea trout. They are locally termed jumpers, and well deserve the title from their liveliness when hooked. With a light rod and fine tackle they afford excellent sport, and take a small bright, yellowish fly with great boldness.

The American salmon spawns very late in the fall, not before November, and for this purpose affects the same localities as his European congener—shallow waters running over beds of sand and gravel. The spawning grounds occur not only in the rivers, but around the large parent lakes, at the entrance of the little brooks that feed them from the forest, and where there are generally deltas formed of sand, gravel, and disintegrated granite washed down from the hills. The spent fish, as a general rule, though some return with the last freshets of the year, remain all winter under the ice (particularly if they have spawned in lakes far removed from the sea), returning in the following spring, when numbers of them are taken by the settlers fishing for trout with worm in pools where the runs enter the lakes. They are then as worthless and slink as if they had but just spawned. In May the young salmon, termed smolts, affect the brackish water at the mouth of rivers, and fall a prey to juvenile anglers in immense numbers—a practice most destructive to the fisheries, as these little fish would return the same season as grilse of three or four pounds weight. The salmon of the Nova Scotian rivers vary in weight from seven to thirty pounds, the latter weight being seldom attained, though a fair proportion of fish brought to market are over twenty pounds. Those taken in the St. Mary are a larger description of fish than the salmon of the southern coast. In the Bay of Chaleurs, in the Restigouche,

salmon of forty and fifty pounds are still taken ; in
former years, sixty pounds and over was not an uncommon weight. The salmon of the Labrador rivers are
not remarkable for size : the average weight of two hundred fish taken with the fly in the river St. John in
July, 1863, was ten pounds, the largest being twenty-
three ; and the largest salmon ever taken by the rod on
this coast weighed forty pounds.

The average weight of the grilse taken in Nova Scotia
and the Gulf appears to be four pounds. Fish of seven
or eight pounds which I have taken in American rivers
are, to my thinking, salmon of another year's growth,
and present an appreciable difference of form to the slim
and graceful grilt. In the latter part of November, the
time when the salmon in the fresh water are in the act
of spawning, a run of fish occurs along the coast of Nova
Scotia. They are taken at sea by nets off the headlands,
and are, as affirmed by the fishermen, proceeding to the
southward. Brought to market, they are found to be
nearly all females, in prime condition, with the ova
very small and in an undeveloped state, similar to that
contained in a fish on its first entrance into fresh water.
Where can these salmon be going at the time when the
rest of their species are busily engaged in reproduction ?
Another of the many mysteries attached to the natural
history of this noble fish ! In fresh running water the
salmon takes the artificial fly or minnow, whether from
hunger or offence it does not clearly appear ; in salt
water he is not unfrequently taken on the coast of Nova
Scotia by bait-fishing at some distance from shore, and
in sixty or seventy fathoms water. The caplin, smelt,
and sand-eel, contribute to his food.

Dr. Gilpin, of Nova Scotia, speaking of many instances of marvellous captures of salmon, tells the following authentic story ; the occurrence happened in his own time and neighbourhood—Annapolis :—

" Mr. Baillie, grandson of the 'Old Frontier Missionary,' was fishing the General's Bridge river up stream for trout, standing above his knees in water, with an old negro named Peter Prince at his elbow. In the very act of casting a trout fly he saw, as is very usual for them, a large salmon lingering in a deep hole a few yards from him. The sun favoured him, throwing his shadow behind. To remain motionless, to pull out a spare hook and penknife, and with a bit of his old hat and some of the grey old negro's wool to make a salmon fly then and there, he and the negro standing in the running stream like statues, and presently to land a fine salmon, was the work of but a few moments. This fly must have been the original of Norris's killing 'silver grey.'"

# THE RIVERS OF NOVA SCOTIA AND THE GULF.

Rivers and streams of varying dimensions, but nearly all accessible to salmon, succeed each other with wonderful frequency throughout the whole Atlantic Sea-board of Nova Scotia. In former years, when they were all open to the ascent of migratory fish, the amount of piscine wealth represented by them was incalculable. The salmon literally swarmed along the coast. Their only enemy was the spear of the native Indian ; and the earlier annals of the province show the prevalence of a

custom with regard to the hiring of labourers similar to
that once existing in some parts of England—a stipulation
that not more than a certain proportion of salmon should
enter into their diet. Now, the salmon having passed the
ordeal of bag-nets, with which the shores of the long
harbours are studded, and arrived in the fresh water,
vainly loiters in the pool below the monstrous wooden
structure called a mill-dam, which effectively debars his
progress to his ancestors' domains in the parent lakes,
and before long falls a prey to the spear or scoop-net of
the miller. From wretchedly inefficient legislation the
salmon of Nova Scotia is on the verge of extinction,
with the gaspereaux and other migratory fish, which
once rendered the immense extent of fresh water of
this country a source of wealth to the province and of
incalculable benefit to the poor settler of the backwoods,
whose barrels of pickled fish were his great stand-by for
winter consumption.

One of the noblest streams of the Nova Scotian
coast is the Liverpool river, in Queen's County, which
connects with the largest sheet of fresh water in the
province, Lake Rossignol, whence streams and brooks
innumerable extend in all directions through the wild
interior, nearly crossing to the Bay of Fundy. All
these once fruitful waters are now a barren waste. The
salmon and gaspereaux are debarred from ascent at the
head of the tide, where a series of utterly impracticable mill-dams oppose their progress to their spawning-
grounds. A pitiful half dozen barrels of salmon taken
at the mouth is now shown against a former yearly
take of two thousand.

A few miles to the eastward we come to the Port

Medway river, nearly as large as the preceding, which, not being so completely closed against the salmon, still affords good sport in the beginning of the season, in April and May. This is the furthest river westwardly from the capital of the province—Halifax—to which the attention of the fly-fisher is directed. There are some excellent pools near the sea, and at its outlet from the lakes, twenty miles above. The fish are large, and have been taken with the fly in the latter part of March. The logs going down the stream are, however, a great hindrance to fishing.

Proceeding to the eastward, the next noticeable salmon river is the La Have, the scenery on which is of the most picturesque description. There are some excellent pools below the first falls. The run of fish is rather later than at Port Medway, or at Gold River, which is further east. On the 4th of May, when excellent sport was being obtained in these waters, I have found no salmon running in the La Have. About the 10th of May appears to be the beginning of its season.

We next come to Mahone Bay, an expansive indentation of the coast, studded with islands, noted for its charms of scenery, and likewise commendable to the visitor in search of salmon-fishing. About six miles west of the little town of Chester, which stands at its head, is the mouth of Gold River. Until very recently this was the favourite resort of sportsmen on the western shore. Its well-defined pools and easy stands for casting added to its inducements; and a throng of fish ascended it from the middle of April to the same time in May. The increase of sporting propensities amongst the rising generation of the neighbouring villages proves of late years a great drawback to the chances of the visitor. The pools are continually occupied by clumsy and undiscerning loafers, who infest the river to the detriment of sport, and do not scruple to come alongside and literally throw across your line. Though dear old Isaac might not possibly object to rival floats a yard apart, another salmon-fly careering in the same pool is not to be endured, and of course spoils sport. Still, however, without such interruptions, fair fishing may be obtained here, and a dozen fish of ten to twenty pounds taken by a rod on a good day. Excessive netting in the salt water is, however, fast destroying all prospects of sport here as elsewhere.

There are two fair sized salmon rivers entering the next harbour, Margaret's Bay, which, being the nearest to the capital of the province, are over-fished. With the exception of a pretty little stream, called the Nine-mile River, which is recovering itself under the protection of the Game and Fish Preservation Society, these conclude the list of the western-shore rivers of Nova Scotia.

The fishing along this shore is quite easy of access by the mail-coach from Halifax, which jolts somewhat roughly three times a week over the rocks and fir-pole bridges of the shore-road through pretty scenery, frequently emerging from the woods, and skirting the bright dancing waters of Margaret's Bay and Chester Basin. The woodland part of a journey in Nova Scotia is dreary enough; the dense thickets of firs on either side being only enlivened by an occasional clearing with its melancholy tenement and crazy wooden out-buildings, and by the tall unbarked spruce-poles stuck in a swamp or held up by piles of rocks at their base, supporting the single wire along which messages are conveyed through the province touching the latest prices afloat of mackerel, cod-fish, or salt, on the magnetic system of Morse.

Indian guides to the pools, who are adepts at camp-keeping, canoeing, and gaffing the fish for you, as well as at doing a little stroke of business for themselves, when opportunities occur, with the forbidden and murderous spear, reside at the mouths of most of these rivers. Their usual charge, as for hunting in the woods, is a dollar per diem.

The flies for the western rivers of Nova Scotia are of a larger make than those used in New Brunswick and Canada, owing to the turbidity of the water at the season when the best fishing is to be obtained. They may be procured in several stores in Halifax, where one Connell ties them in a superior style, and will forward them to order anywhere in the provinces or in Canada. A claret-bodied (pig's wool or mohair) with a dark mixed wing is good for the La Have. Green and grey are good colours for Gold River. With the grey body silver tinsel should be used, and wood-duck introduced into the wing. An olive body is also good. There is no feather that sets off a wing better than wood-duck. It is in my estimation more tempting to fish than the golden pheasant tippet feather. Its broad bars of rich velvety black and purest white give a peculiarly attractive and soft moth-like appearance to the wing.

The harbour of Halifax, nearly twelve miles in length, has but one stream, and that of inconsiderable dimensions, emptying into it. The little Sackville river was, however, once a stream affording capital sport at

Midsummer, its season being announced, as the old
fisherman who lived on it and by it, generally known
as "Old Hopewell," told me, by the arrival of the fire-
flies. He has taken nineteen salmon, of from eight to
eighteen pounds weight, in one morning with the fly.
It offers no sport to speak of now ; the saw mills and
their obstructive dams have quite cut off the fish from
their spawning grounds.

To the eastward, between Halifax and Cape Canseau,
occurs a succession of fine rivers, running through the
most extensive forest district in the province. The
salmon rivers of note are the Musquodoboit, Tangier
river, the Sheet Harbour rivers, and the St. Mary's.
There are no important settlements on the sea-coast,
which is very wild and rugged to the east of Halifax,
and consequently they are less looked after and more
poached. Formerly they teemed with salmon. Besides
the mill-dams, they are netted right across, and the pools
are swept and torched without mercy by settlers and
Indians. The St. Mary's is the noblest and most beautiful river in Nova Scotia, and its salmon are the largest.
The nets overlap one another from either shore throughout the long reaches of intervale and wild meadow,
dotted with groups of elm, which constitute its noted
scenic charms, and the lumbermen vie with the Indians
in skill in their nightly spearing expeditions by the light
of blazing birch-bark torches.

There are many other fine rivers besides those mentioned discharging into the Atlantic, which the salmon
has long ceased to frequent, being completely shut out,
and which would swell the dreary record of the ruin of the
inland fisheries of Nova Scotia. In these waters, at a

distance from the capital, "Halifax law," as the settlers
will tell you, is "no account." The spirit of wanton
extermination is rife ; and, as it has been well remarked,
it really seems as though the man would be loudly
applauded who was discovered to have killed the last
salmon.

Salmon are abundant in the Bay of Fundy, which
washes a large portion of Nova Scotia, but its rivers
are generally ill adapted for sport. Running through
flat alluvial lands, and turbid with the red mud, or
rather, fine sand, of the Bay shores, they are generally
characterised by an absence of good stands and salmon
pools. The Annapolis river was once famous for
salmon fishing. On its tributary, the Nictaux, twenty
or thirty might be taken with the fly in an afternoon ; and the Gaspereau, a very picturesque stream
entering the Basin of Minas at Grand Pré, the once
happy valley of the French Acadians, still affords fair
sport.

We will now turn to the rivers of the Gulf which
enter it from the mainland on the shores of New Brunswick, Lower Canada, and Labrador, commencing with
those of the former province.

Proceeding along the eastern shore of New Brunswick
from its junction with Nova Scotia, we pass several fine
streams with picturesque scenery and strange Indian
names, which, once teeming with fish, now scarcely afford
the resident settler an annual taste of the flesh of salmon.
The Miramichi, however, arrests our attention as being
a noble river ; its yield and exportation of salmon is
still very large. Winding sluggishly through a beautiful
and highly cultivated valley for nearly one hundred

miles from the Atlantic, the first rapids and pools where
fly-fishing may be practised occur in the vicinity of
Boiestown; here the sport afforded, in a good season, is
little inferior to that which may be obtained on the
Nepisiguit. One of its branches, also, the north-west
Miramichi, is worth a visit; and I have known some
excellent sport obtained on it in passing through to the
Nepisiguit, from which river the water communication
for a canoe is interrupted but by a short portage through
the forest.

It is, however, on entering the southern expanses of
the beautiful Bay of Chaleurs that we first find the
paradise of the salmon-fisher; and here still, despite
of many foes—innumerable stake-nets which debar his
entrance, the sweeping seine in the fresh water, the torch
and spear of the Indian tribes, and lastly, and perhaps
the least destructive agent, the tackle of the fly-fisherman—the bright foamy waters of the Nepisiguit, the
Restigouche, the Metapediac, and many others, repay the
visitor and sportsman, whence or how far soever he may
have come, by the sport which they afford, and by the
wild scenery which surrounds their long course through
the forests of New Brunswick.

And, first, of the Nepisiguit. This now famous river,
which of late years has attracted from their homes
many visitors, both English and American, to spend a
few weeks in fishing and pleasantly camping-out on its
banks, discharges its waters into the Baie des Chaleurs
at Bathurst, a small neat town, easily accessible from
either Halifax, St. John, or Quebec, and by various
modes of conveyance—coach, rail, and steamboat. Rising
in the centre of northern New Brunswick, in an elevated

lake region which gives birth to the Tobique and Upsalquitch, rivers of about equal size, the Nepisiguit has an
eastward course of nearly one hundred miles through
a wilderness country, where not even a solitary Indian
camp may be met with. It is one of the wildest of
American rivers ; sometimes contracted between cliffs
to the breadth of a few yards, coursing sullenly and
darkly below overhanging forests, and sometimes, though
rarely, expanding into broad reaches of smoothly-gliding
water—its most common feature is the ever-recurring
cascade and rapid.

The adventurous fisherman will do well to supplement
his sport on the river by embarking on a long journey
through the solitudes of the interior to its parent lakes.
A short portage of a couple of miles, and the canoe
floats on the Tobique lakes, and thence descends the
Tobique through another hundred miles of the wildest
and most beautiful scenery imaginable. At the junction
of this latter river with the broad expanse of the upper
St. John, civilisation reappears ; the traveller changes his
conveyance for the steamer or coach, and the frail canoe
returns, with her hardy and skilful sons of the river, to
battle with the rocks and rapids of the toilsome route.

The whole of this tour is, however, fraught with
interest to the sportsman and lover of wild scenery.
Moose, cariboo, and bear are invariably met with ; the
two former being generally seen bathing in the water
in the evenings, whilst a visit from a bear at night is
by no means an uncommon occurrence at some camp or
another on the way ; or, perchance, Bruin may be surprised when gorging in the early morning, breakfasting
amongst the great thickets of wild raspberries which

R

abound on the banks. A little search up the tributary
brooks will discover the wonderful works of beaver now
in progress; and other frequenters of the river, mink,
otters, and musquash, are plentiful, and frequently to
be seen. In July and August the young flappers of
many species of duck form an agreeable change in the
daily bill of fare; and though salmon do not ascend the
Nepisiguit beyond the Grand Falls, twenty-one miles
from Bathurst, they may be taken at the head waters
of the Tobique; whilst river trout of large size, and
affording excellent sport, will greedily rise at an almost
bare hook throughout the whole extent of water.

Reclining in the bottom of the canoe, the position of
the traveller is most comfortable, and he may make
notes or sketches, as fancy leads him, with ease; indeed,
from the facility with which all necessaries and even
luxuries may be conveyed, but little hardship need be
anticipated in a canoe voyage through the rivers of
northern New Brunswick.

The length of the journey just described much
depends on the state of the water and the number of
the party. With good water a canoe will get through
with two sportsmen, two canoe men, and all their goods
—camps, blankets, and provisions—in ten or twelve
days; but should the rivers be low, two canoes must
be employed by the same number. A few years since I
took a still more northern route to the upper St. John,
viâ the Restigouche and Grand River; the head-waters
were so shallow that we literally had to drag our canoe,
fixed on long protecting slabs of cedar, for some days
over the rocky bed; we were, moreover, nearly starved,
and occupied nearly three weeks in reaching Fredericton

on the St. John, down whose broad, deep stream, however, we paddled at the rate of fifty miles a day.

The scenery on this line of water-communication with
the St. John is grander, but not so wild as on the former
route, which I recommend as possessing many advantages, particularly in the way of sport.

*Mais revenons à nos saumons*—to describe the capabilities of the Nepisiguit to afford sport to the salmon-
fisher, and direct the visitor. The ascent of salmon
in this river is restricted to twenty-one miles of water
by an insuperable barrier—the Grand Falls; but from
the head of the tide, two miles above the town, to this
point, are a succession of beautiful pools with every
variety of water, so stocked with fish, and with such
picturesque surrounding scenery, that the eye of the
sportsman who may happily combine the love of nature
with the lust of sport drinks in constant and ever-
varying delight as he is introduced to these bewitching
spots. And now of the pools *seriatim*.

Two miles above Bathurst we come to the "Rough
Waters," where there is good fishing. No camp is
needed here; for it is so near the accommodation of a
comfortable hotel, that I question whether any one would
care to experiment, except for novelty. It is a pretty
spot, and the dark water here and there breaks into pure
white foam as it passes over a ledge which crosses the
channel from the steep red sandstone cliffs opposite. A
short distance above are the "Round Rocks," with little
falls and intervening pools, where the river begins to
show its true character; and here, as at the last-men-
tioned spot, a good day's fishing may be obtained from
the town. But one is now-a-days liable to interference,

however, for of late years the little ragged urchins from
the Acadian settlement on the south shore have imbibed
a strong love of sport in addition to their hereditary
poaching propensities, and with a rough pole, a few
yards of coarse line, and a bait in appearance anything
but a salmon fly, they will hook some dozen or more
salmon in a day when they are running freely, of
course losing nearly every fish.

Distant eight miles from Bathurst, and accessible by
a fair waggon road, are the Pabineau Falls, one of the
choicest fishing stations on the river. The scenery here
is most beautiful ; the forest has now claimed the banks,
and, as the stranger emerges from its shade, and stands
on the broad, smooth expanses of light grey and pink
rocks which slope from him towards the brink of the
stream, viewing its clear grass-green waters rolling in
such fierce undulations over long descents, and thun-
dering, enveloped in mist, through various contracted
passes into boiling pools, with congregated masses of
foam ever circling over their black depths, he becomes
impressed with the idea of irresistible power, and is
constrained to acknowledge that he stands in the presence of no ordinary stream, but of a mighty river.

I have here stood by the margin of the water, where
hundreds of tons momentarily rushed past my feet in
a compact mass, and watched the bright gleam of the
salmon as they would dart up from below like arrows to
encounter the fall ; a slight pause as they near the head ;
another convulsive effort, and they are safely over ; but
many fall back, at present unequal for the contest, into
the dark pool.

There are several well-built bark shanties on the rocks

THE PABINEAU FALLS, RIVER NEPISIGUIT.

above the falls, for the fine scenery, and the ease with which the numerous pools in the neighbourhood of the Pabineau can be fished, have made this a favourite haunt for anglers.

Two miles above are the Beeterbox Pools, where there is some swift, deep water at a curve in the river, and at the foot of a long reach of rapids. It is a very good station to fish, *en passant*, but not of sufficient extent to induce more than an occasional visit.

" Mid-landing " is the next spot where good sport may be obtained, particularly at the end of July, when the river becomes low. The great depths of water here, shaded by high rocks, induce large fish to remain long in these cool retreats. Very small, dark flies, and the most transparent gut must be used ; and with these precautions, when other pools have been failing in a dry season, I have taken half a dozen salmon a day from the deep waters of Mid-landing, and from the long, rough rapid which runs into the pool.

Three miles above are the " Chains of Rocks," the great and the little. A camp below the last fall of the lower chain will command all the pools. This range of pools contains an abundance of fish. Below the fall is a long expanse of smooth water, at the head of which salmon congregate in great numbers preparatory to ascending the rough water above ; they lie in several deep, eddying pools, where projecting ledges narrow the channel, and may be seen flinging themselves out of water throughout the day. Above this long series of cascades which fall over terraces of dark rocks, for nearly half a mile, there is some evenly-gliding water, in which fish may be taken from stands on the left

bank.    Here, and at the little chain just above, is
my favourite resort at this part of the river; there is
excellent camping-ground in the tall fir-woods on the
north shore, and bold jutting rocks command the pools
admirably.

Between this spot and the Basin, two miles above,
there are but few spots where the fly may be cast profitably; and, taking the bush-path which skirts the river,
we may now shoulder our rods, and trudge up to the
Grand Falls, our canoes following, spurting through the
rapid water in long strides as they are impelled by the
vigorous thrusts of the long iron-shod fir-poles.    The
Basin is a broad and deep expansion of the river, and a
reservoir where the salmon congregate in multitudes,
ultimately spawning at the entrance of numerous gravelly
brooks which flow into it from the surrounding forest,
and daily making sorties to the Falls, a mile above, to
enjoy the cool water which flows thence to the lake
between tall, overhanging cliffs, sometimes completely
shaded from the sunlight save during a very limited
portion of the day.

In this mile of deep swift water, which winds in a
dark thread from the Basin to the foot of the falls
between lofty walls of slate rock, salmon lie during the
day in thousands; there are certain spots which they
prefer, found by experience to be the best pools, where
the splash of the fish and the voice of the angler awaken
echoes from the cliffs throughout the season.    Fine
fishing, and fine tackle for these—aye, and a good
temper, too—for it is the most favoured resort for rods,
and we may often be compelled to cease awhile from our
sport, whilst a canoe (here the only mode of conveyance

from pool to pool) with its scarlet-shirted paddlers, creeps through the water by the opposite shore.

There are but one or two places in the cliffs here where a camp may be pitched, and, if these are occupied, we must drop down-stream again to some less-frequented locality. The best of these is a green sloping bank, over which a cool brook courses between copses of hazel and alder into the river below. It is a charming situation, and from a grassy plateau overhanging the river, where the camps are usually placed, we may look down into a clear pool, some seventy feet below, and watch the salmon which occupy it, dressed in distinct ranks.

The Grand Falls are rather more than 100 feet in height. The river, here greatly contracted, descends into a deep boiling pool, first by a succession of headlong tumbles, and then in a compact and perpendicular fall of forty feet. The first fishing pool is just below the eddying basin at the foot of the fall, which is seldom entered by the canoe men, as currents both of air and water sweep round it towards the pitch; besides, the fish here are so engaged in battling with the heaving water, in their vain attempts to surmount the falls, that they will not regard the fly.

All this portion of the Nepisiguit must be fished from a canoe, excepting a few rocky stands, where almost every cast is made at the risk of the hook snapping against the cliffs behind ; and this leads us to say a few words on the canoe men of the river. They are a hardy and generally intelligent race of Acadian-French, apparently a good deal crossed with Indian blood, exceedingly skilful in managing their bark canoes, and in getting fish for the sportsman; they have great experience in

the requirements of a camp in the woods, and are,
withal, very merry, companionable fellows.     For a
fishing camp anywhere above the Pabineau, a canoe and
three men (one to act as cook and camp-keeper), are
indispensable; and on arriving at Bathurst, the services
of any of the following men of good character should be
secured : The Chamberlains, the Vineaus, David Buchet,
Joe Young, and others; Baldwin, the landlord of the
little hotel, knows them all well.     Their wages are a
dollar a day for the canoe men ; the cook may be hired
for half a dollar, but he will grumble, and most likely
succeed in getting three shillings.     If a voyage through
to the St. John, *via* the Nictaux and Tobique lakes, be
contemplated, selection should be made of those men
who have taken parties through before.     All provisions
necessary for a sojourn on the river—everything, from
an excellent ham to a tin of the best chocolate—are to
be had at the store of Messrs. Ferguson, Rankin, and Co.,
in Bathurst, obliging people, very moderate and liberal;
they will deduct for all the cooking utensils, supplied
by them, which may be returned on coming down the
river.

Notwithstanding the immense destruction of fish in
the Nepisiguit in every possible way—netting and
torching in fresh water, whenever the nature of the
stream allows of such proceedings, wholesale sweeping
and spearing on their spawning beds by tribes of Indians,
even into the month of November, when they are quite
black and slimy, extensive netting at its mouth, and
the number taken by fly-fishers—even yet the river
swarms with salmon ; a favourable condition of the
water and the command of a few pools will insure good

sport. The fish are not very large, as in the more northern rivers of the bay; the average of the weights, of seventy salmon killed by one rod at the **Grand Falls** a few seasons since, was 11lb. 8oz.; and of thirty grilse, 4lb. The fish commence running up in June, but, from the height of the water, there is rarely good fishing before July; the 10th is about the best time, and by that time they have gone up as high as the Grand Falls. The flies for the Nepisiguit should be small and neat, and of three sizes to each pattern, for different states of water. As mistakes are often made from the different mode of numbering by different makers, it will be sufficient to say that the length of the medium fly should be 1⅜in. from the point of the shank to the extreme bend, measuring diagonally across. The patterns should be generally dark, and all mixed wings should be as modest as possible; no gaudy contrasts of colour, as used in Norway or Scotland, will do here. A dark fly, tied as follows, is a great favourite: body of black mohair, ribbed with fine gold thread, black hackle, very dark mallard wing, a narrow tip of orange silk, and a very small feather from the crest of golden pheasant for a tail. Then I like a rich claret body with dark mixed wing and tail, claret hackle, and a few fibres of English jay in the shoulder. Small grey-bodied flies ribbed with silver, grey legs, and wing mixed with wood-duck and golden pheasant, will do well. Many other and brighter flies may be used in the rough water, and a primrose body, with black head and tip, and butterfly wing of golden pheasant, will prove very tempting to grilse, which, late in July, may be taken in any number in many parts of the river, particularly at the Pabineau and Chain of Rocks. These flies will do anywhere in New Brunswick.

At the head of the Bay of Chaleurs, and about fifty miles from Bathurst, we come to the Restigouche, one of the largest rivers of British North America, 220 miles in length, and formerly teeming with salmon from the sea to its upper waters. So abundant were the fish some twenty-five years ago, that Mr. Perley, Her Majesty's Commissioner for the Fisheries, states that 3000 barrels were shipped annually from this river, and in those days salmon of 60lb. weight were not uncommon. Of late years there has been a sad falling-off, and instead of eleven salmon going to a barrel of 200lb., more than twice the number must now be used. Unfortunately for the preservation of the fish, and the prospects of the fly-fisher, the character of this beautiful river is very different to that of the Nepisiguit. For 100 miles the Restigouche runs in a narrow valley between wooded mountains with an almost unvarying rapid current, with but few deep pools and no falls. Hence the chances of rod-fishing are greatly diminished, whilst settlers and Indians torch and spear everywhere. The channel is much used by the lumberers for the water-conveyance of provisions to the gangs employed in the woods at its head-waters—scows (*i.e.*, large flat-bottomed barges) being employed, drawn by teams of horses which find a natural tow-path in its shingly beaches by the edge of the forest. High up the river there are many rifts and sand-beaches, partly exposed in a dry season, through which the channel winds ; and the scow is often dragged through shallow places, thus ploughing up the spawning grounds of the salmon.

A few years since, after a fortnight's fishing on the Nepisiguit, during which my companion and myself took eighty salmon, notwithstanding an unprecedented drought, we visited the Restigouche, more for the sake of enjoying its fine scenery than expecting sport. Staying for a day, however, at the house of a hospitable farmer who dwelt by the river-side, at the junction of the Matapediac with the main stream, I had the pleasure of hooking the first salmon ever taken with a fly in the Restigouche water, a fine clean fish of twelve pounds. In an hour's fishing I had taken three salmon, each differently shaped, and at once pronounced by my host to be frequenters of three separate rivers which here unite—the two already mentioned and the Upsalquitch.

The Matapediac has a course of sixty miles from a large lake in Rimouski, Lower Canada, and the Upsalquitch runs in on the New Brunswick side. They are both fine rivers, and ascended by salmon in large numbers ; the latter is stated to be very like the Nepisiguit in character—full of falls and rapids, and I believe it would afford equal sport. It looked most tempting as we passed its mouth on our long canoe voyage up the main river, but we had not time to stay and test its capabilities. About sixty miles from the sea we discovered a salmon pool in the Restigouche, and took eight small fish from it in an afternoon ; but such pools are few and far between, and I would not recommend any one to ascend this river for sport above the Upsalquitch. The flies we used here were dark clarets and reds ; I believe any fly will take, recommending, however, larger sizes than the Nepisiguit flies, as the

Restigouche salmon run much larger, and even in these days commonly weigh thirty pounds.

Campbelltown, a neat little village at the head of the tide, twenty miles from the sea, is to be reached from Bathurst by coach; and here the traveller or sportsman intending to ascend the Restigouche or its before-mentioned tributaries, will find a large settlement of Indians of the Micmac tribe. They all have canoes, and many of them are good guides, and trustworthy. There is a good store at which to purchase provisions, and a very comfortable little hotel kept by a Mr. M'Leod.

We now leave the rivers of New Brunswick: the Restigouche being the dividing line between the two provinces, the rivers of the north shore of Chaleurs Bay are Canadian. About thirty miles from the head of the bay we come to the Cascapediac, a large river running in a deep chasm through the mountains of Bonaventure. It is frequented by salmon of large size, and I have been told by Mr. R. H. Montgomery, who resides near its mouth, that the average weight is between thirty and forty pounds. He offered to procure me good Indians and canoes for ascending to the first rapids, which are some distance up the river. The whole district of Gaspé is intersected by numerous and splendid rivers, abounding in salmon and sea trout, the latter of four pounds to seven pounds in weight. The mountain scenery through which they flow is magnificent, and many of them have never been thrown over with a fly rod. Amongst the largest may be noticed the Bonaventure, the Malbaie, and the Magdeleine.

On the south shore of the St. Lawrence, from Gaspé to Quebec, there are several streams which formerly

abounded in salmon, but of late years have been so un-
productive that attention need not be directed to them.
From the Jacques Cartier, a few miles above Quebec, to
the Labrador, the north shore of the St. Lawrence is
intersected by innumerable rivers ; in many of these the
salmon fishery has been nearly destroyed, but the energy
of the Canadian Government is fast remedying the evil.
The process of reproduction by artificial propagation
under an able superintendent, and the preservation of
the rivers, are bringing back the salmon to comparative
plenty in many a worn-out stream ; and the visitor to
Quebec will soon be enabled to obtain sport on the beautiful Jacques Cartier and other rivers in the neighbourhood, without having to seek the distant fishing stations
of the Labrador. The Saguenay, too, with its thirty
tributaries, is improving ; for many years past this
noble river has scarcely proved worth a visit, except
for its wonderful scenery. In fact, the legislature, aided
by an excellently constituted club for the protection
of fish and game, have taken the matter up in earnest;
fish-ways are placed on those rivers which have dams or
slides upon them ; netting and spearing in the fresh
water is prevented ; an able superintendent of fisheries,
and several overseers, have been appointed ; and, finally,
an excellent measure has been adopted—the annual
leasing of salmon rivers to gentlemen for fly-fishing, for
small rents—on condition of their aiding and carrying
out the proper preservation of the fisheries.

Amongst the largest and most notable salmon rivers
which are passed in proceeding from the Saguenay along
the northern shore are the Escoumins, Portneuf, Bersia-
mits, Outardes, Manacouagan, Godbout, Trinity, St. Mar-

garet, Moisie, St. John, Mingan, Natashquan, and Esquimaux. Salmon ascend all these rivers, and take the fly
readily. Whether they will rise in the rivers of the
north-eastern coast, past the straits of Belle-Isle, remains
to be proved. It has been affirmed that they will not
do so in the Labrador rivers of high northern latitude,
thus evincing the same peculiarity which has been
observed on the part of the true sea salmon of Siberian
rivers flowing into the Arctic Ocean. I have heard,
however, that they will rise at a piece of red cloth
trailed on a hook over the water from the stern of
a boat.

In conclusion, the salmon rivers of the Gulf of St.
Lawrence, though they offer no extraordinary sport,
possess the charms of wild and often noble scenery; life
in the woods, in a summer camp, will agreeably surprise those who hold back for fear of hard work, and the
discomforts of "roughing it." Any point, excepting the
extremes of Labrador, may be reached with ease from
either Quebec or Halifax; whilst the economy which
may be practised by a party of two or three, will be found
to be within the means of most sportsmen. At the termination of the fishing season a few weeks may be spent
in tourising through the Canadas or the States; and in
the month of September the glowing forests of Nova
Scotia or New Brunswick may be traversed in search of
moose, cariboo, or bear. Between the Ottawa and the
great lakes there is excellent duck-shooting, and the woods
abound in deer (Cervus Virginianus), whilst the vast expanses of wilderness in Newfoundland teem with cariboo,
ptarmigan, and wild fowl; the former so abundant as
sometimes to tempt the sportsman (?) to kill more than

THE GRAND FALLS, NEPISIGUIT.

he can carry away or dispose of, leaving the meat rotting
in the woods. To all such, Avaunt! say we; wholesale
and thoughtless slaughter, except on the fiercer species
—the natural enemies of man—is always to be depre-
cated; but the true sportsman we confidently invite to
the forests and rivers of British North America, believing that his example in carrying out the fair English
principles of sport, will tend much to the preservation
of game.

## GLOVER'S SALMON.

### *S. Gloverii* (Girard.)

My first acquaintance with this handsome salmonoid
began many years since, when I would take basketsfull
in the month of April in the runs connecting the upper
lakes of the Shubenacadie river in Nova Scotia. At first
I took them to be young salmon, both from their jumping propensities when hooked and the resemblance they
bore to the parr on scraping away the scales from the
sides. Yet their rich olive black backs and beautiful
bronze spots on the head and gill covers made them
appear dissimilar, and I could no longer doubt them
distinct from salmon, when I had succeeded in taking
them of one, two, and three pounds weight, and still
spotted, in the early summer, quite dissimilar in colour
from grilse, and far exceeding the size of smolts, which
the smaller individuals somewhat resembled. Finding out
their haunts, and seasons for changing their abode, we
were content to take them in the spring and late in the
autumn, in the runs and streams lying between their
spawning grounds and the deep waters of large lake

basins (where they spent the hot season and could only
be tempted by bait), under the common local misnomer
of Grayling. And glorious sport we found it; the
dash with which this game fish seizes the fly, its
surprising jumps to the level of one's shoulder, and its
beautiful metallic hues, particularly in the spring, invested it with an interest far exceeding that of fishing
for S. Fontinalis.

At length, however, on referring several specimens
to Dr. Gilpin, they were identified by him in the
" Proceedings of the Nova Scotian Institute " as S.
Gloverii, or Glover's Salmon of Girard, better known
in New Brunswick as the Silvery Salmon Trout of the
Scoodic Lakes, where its abundance in the rapid waters
connecting the upper lakes of the St. Croix river, render
this locality one of the most famed fishing stations of the
Lower Provinces. The following is Dr. Gilpin's description taken from specimens forwarded by myself and
others :—

" Length, about seventeen inches ; breadth of widest
part from first dorsal, two and a half inches ; length of
head nearly two and a half inches ; the shape of the
head fine and small, the back rising rather suddenly,
from posterior to head, sloping very gradually upward
to insertion of dorsal, thence downward to insertion of
tail, lower line corresponding with line of back ; a long
elegant shaped fish with a strong base to a powerful tail ;
eye large, nearly half an inch in diameter and two
diameters from end of nose ; opercles rounded, and with
the pre-opercles marked with numerous concentric
streaks ; the lower line of inter-opercle parallel with
line of the body, labials, both upper and lower, arched,

line of pre-opercle not so rounded as opercle; the
pectoral fins coming out very far forward, almost
touching the gill rays, dorsal commencing about two
lengths of head from tip of nose, sub-quadrangular,
free edge concave; ventral about opposite sixth ray of
dorsal; adipose fin opposite posterior edge of anal;
caudal deeply cleft, and very nearly the length of head
in depth. In one instance the tail was square. Inter-
maxillaries, maxillaries, palatines, vomer and tongue
armed with sharp and recurved teeth, the teeth on the
vomer extending half an inch down the roof of mouth, a
fleshy line extending from them to the gullet, the upper
jaw notched to receive the lower. In two specimens a
prolonged hook in lower jaw advancing beyond the
teeth. Girard says the male fish has adipose fins opposite anterior edge of anal, the female opposite posterior
edge. Whilst in the following description, taken from a
female fish, I have verified his remarks, I have added, that
in the male the adipose fin is very much larger, which is
almost the same thing. Colour black above, shading
down to sepia brown at the lateral line, the brown being
the back ground to numerous black spots, some round,
some lunated extending from opercles to tail. The opercles
partake of the same general colour with yellow reflections
and blue tints, but also marked with spots extending to
the pre-opercles, beautifully round and distinct; sides
yellowish, and belly white with pearly tints, the whole
covered with bright scales larger about the sides than
beneath. The colours vary much by the reflected lights
made in turning the fish. The colour of the fins when fresh
out of water,—caudal brown, dorsal brownish black, and
spotted, lower fins dark brown, edges and tips dark,

8

a very fleeting lavender wash on dorsal.  Sides yellowish.
In one adult specimen I noticed a few red spots on sides,
but in the young fish they are very marked and beautiful.   Some seen by myself in July had vertical bars,
red spots, very silvery on sides, and all, even the
smallest, had the typical opercular spots very distinct.
They were exceedingly beautiful and might have readily
been taken for a different species.   On opening the fish
from gills to tail, the heart with its single auricle and
ventricle first presented, the liver overlapping the
stomach and pale yellow; the stomach descended about
one-half the length of the fish, was then reflected suddenly upon itself where it was covered by numerous
cæca (about thirty); these are the *pyloric cæca* of
authors.   It then turned down again, and soon was lost
in small intestine ending at the vent.   The spawn were
each of the size of currants and bright scarlet, about a
thousand in number, and encased in a very thin bilo-
bular ovary, the left lobe occupying the left side, being
a little over three inches, and only one half the length
of right lobe occupying right side; a second fish gave the
same placing of ovary.   Both these fish were taken on
the 2nd and 4th November at Grand Lake, Halifax, and
evidently near spawning.   Fins, D. 12 or 13, P. 14, V. 9,
A. 9, C. 20.   Axillary scale small.   The first dorsal ray
in some instances contains two, in other three small rays.
Typical marks, spots on opercles."

In its general appearance, markings, and delicate
primrose tint on the belly, the fish is not unlike the
trout of gravelly streams in England.

In former years, before the construction of the Shubenacadie Canal, it was found in that river during the

summer months far below the lakes. A place called
the "Black Rock," just above the head of the tide,
was a famous stand for grayling fishing; and five
and six pound fish were not unfrequent. Now cut
off from salt water by the locks, their migrations
are restricted between the deep basin of the Grand
Lake and the numerous chains of lakes which give
rise to its affluents; and the fish, whilst they seldom
attain a greater weight than three pounds, are not so
silvery in the spring as formerly. The same fish taken
at Loch Lomond, near Saint John's, New Brunswick, are
much smaller, browner, and paler in flesh than the St.
Croix trout, and apparently from the same cause.

In Nova Scotia this trout will take the fly as readily
late in the fall (even to first week in November) as in
the spring, and long after the common brook-trout ceases
to rise. As it is then, however, immediately proceeding to
the spawning grounds, and with fully developed ova, this
sport should be rendered illegal after October.

Two great lake trout inhabit the deep lakes of the
Provinces—Salmo confinis and S. Amethystus—the former
being abundant, and sometimes attaining a weight of
twenty pounds. They may be taken in deep holes with
bait or spoon-hook trolled and well sunk. Their flavour
is insipid, and they are unentitled to more than a passing
notice in a description of the game fish of Acadie.

The yellow perch (Perca flavescens) is exceedingly numerous in lakes and rivers. Though seldom exceeding
half a pound in weight, heavy baskets may be taken in a
day's fishing on some lakes (where they seem to affect
particular localities) by those who care for such sport.
It is a handsome fish, of a bright golden yellow colour,

260 FOREST LIFE IN ACADIE.

striped with dusky perpendicular bands. Its fins are vermilion ; and altogether it is a decided analogue to the English river perch. It may be taken on either a fly or bait. When properly cooked it is very palatable. The so-called white perch, also very abundant in fresh waters, is in reality a bass (Labrax pallidus), and a worthless fish. The common sucker (Catostomus) will sometimes rise at the fly, as also will the cat-fish, whose enormous mouth, surrounded by long fleshy feelers, gives it a hideous appearance. It will seize a trout of half its own size.

# CHAPTER X.

I KNOW of no country so near England which offers the same amount of inducement to the explorer, naturalist, or sportsman as Newfoundland. To one who combines the advantages of a good practical knowledge of geology with the love of sport the interior of this great island, much of which is quite unknown, may indeed prove a field of valuable and remunerative discovery, for its mineral resources, now under the examination of a Government geological survey, are unquestionably of vast importance, and quite undeveloped. Numerous discoveries of copper have been made at various points, particularly on the western side, and coal and petroleum have been found in the interior. So completely, however, is the population devoted to the prosecution of the fisheries, that even agriculture is unheeded, though there is plenty of good land close to the harbours. Between these, with the exception of a few roads in the province of Avalon (the peninsula which contains the capital of the colony, St. John's), there is no communication except by water.

As a field for sport, likewise, Newfoundland is but little known. Some half-dozen or so of regular visitors from the continent, one or two resident sportsmen, and the same number from England, comprise the list of those who have encamped in its vast solitudes in quest of its principal large game—the cariboo—which is scattered more or less abundantly over an area of some twenty-five thousand square miles of unbroken wilderness.

Like Nova Scotia, the face of the country is dotted with lakes innumerable, some of which, as the Grand Lake (fifty miles in length) and the Red Indian Pond, are of much larger dimensions than any found in the former province. These waters all abound with trout; and beaver,* otter, and musk-rats, being subject to less persecution, are much more numerous than on the continent. The willow grouse (Lagopus albus) is the common resident game bird of the country, and is exceedingly abundant; and the migratory fowl pursued for sport include the Canada goose, that excellent bird the black duck (Anas obscura), curlew, and snipe. The black bear and the wolf are of frequent occurrence in the interior, and add a flavour of excitement to the varied catalogue of sport.

The following observations and scraps of information collected on several occasions of visits of inspection to the garrison town of St. John's are here presented with a view to their proving of use to the intending visitor in search of sport, or as interesting to the naturalist.

The route from Halifax to St. John's is traversed fortnightly in summer, and monthly in the winter months, by small screw steamers subsidied for the mail service, and is as uncomfortable a voyage as may well be imagined at times, the direction being that of the northern line of the fog, which sometimes envelopes the steamer throughout,

---

* The beaver is not now found on the peninsula of Avalon.

or, at all events, until the vessel rounds Cape Race—
nearly at the end of the journey. Near the Cape icebergs
are frequent during the summer months, and it is not an
uncommon circumstance to hear the dull roar of the surf
upon their precipitous sides as one passes in uncomfortable
proximity in a dense fog. Field ice, too, is another
drawback in the spring; enormous areas come down
from the Gulf, and more than once the little steamer has
spent a fortnight or so enclosed, drifting into one of the
wild, inhospitable harbours of the southern coast. The
duration of the voyage from Halifax to St. John's is
from three to five days—a little longer when, as is
generally the case, Sydney, Cape Breton, is touched at.
In fine summer weather coasting along the shores of
Nova Scotia and Cape Breton is pleasant enough, particularly in the evenings, when the heated atmosphere,
blown off from the fir woods, is charged with delicious
fragrance. The scenery, viewed from the deck of a
vessel passing at some two or three leagues distance, has
nothing of especial interest, as might be inferred ; the
numerous indentations of the harbours are hardly perceptible, and the wooded country behind rises but a few
hundred feet or so in a continuous undulating line of hills.
A noticeable rock, which may be seen at a considerable
distance out to sea, termed "The Ship," terminates a
headland on the western side of the harbour of that
name. It looks just like a schooner, or rather brigantine,
under full sail.

This part of the North American coast is marked by
the presence of multitudes of sea birds, which, at the
periods of their annual migrations, afford abundant and
exciting sport. Formerly they resorted to the numerous

islands of Nova Scotia and Cape Breton to breed. Now,
driven away by persecution, the bulk of them go much
further to the north-east.

Every fisherman along shore has a fowling-piece, and
shoots "sea-ducks," as he indiscriminately calls a variety
of species—eiders, pintails, mergansers, loons, and coots—
and when we consider the wholesale destruction caused
by the eggers at their breeding-grounds in the Gulf, it is
surprising that the birds have not more quickly followed
the great auk in progress towards extinction. As has
been stated before, there is no record of the latter bird
affecting these shores within the memory of those living,
though the Penguin Islands (the bird had much resemblance to the true penguin of the Southern Ocean)
certainly derived their name from its former abundance.

The Canadian Government have lately terminated the
wholesale destruction of sea-birds' eggs in the Gulf by
stringent enactments, and the egging trade is virtually
abolished. The wanton destruction which accompanied
the arrival of an egging vessel at the breeding-grounds
was most disgraceful. Armed with sticks, the crew first
broke every egg on the island (tens of thousands.) A
partial re-commencement of laying ensued, and the
harvest was immediately gleaned with the assurance
that the cargo on reaching port would consist of none
but fresh eggs. The bulk of the spoil consisted of the
eggs of the guillemots, and were sold at about three
cents apiece. I have frequently eaten them and found
them exceedingly palatable; the white somewhat resembles that of a plover's egg in appearance and
flavour.

The local names of the sea-birds are singular. The

beautiful and quite common harlequin duck (Anas histrionica) is called "a lord :" the long-tailed duck (A. glacialis) rejoices in the name of "cockawee," from its note, and sometimes the "old squaw," "from the ludicrous similarity between the gabbling of a flock of these birds and an animated discussion of a piece of scandal in the Micmac language between a number of antiquated ladies of that interesting tribe."[*] The puffin is termed a parrot, and the little auk, the bull-bird. The name of shell-ducks or shell-drakes, applied to the mergansers (more especially to the goosander), is a misnomer prevalent along the whole coast and in Labrador : no true tadorna is found in North America.

In several of the harbours on the Nova Scotian coast excellent sport may be obtained in winter, shooting wildfowl on the ice, for many of these birds remain all winter. Canada geese and brant are shot only during migration. Scatterie, a desolate island lying off the eastern end of Cape Breton, is a great resort of sea-birds

---

[*] The Rev. J. Ambrose, on " Birds frequenting St. Margaret's Bay, N. S.," from " Proceedings of N. S. Inst. Nat. Science." The writer further observes :—" The shooting of sea-birds is not only a source of profit to our fishermen, and a means of providing them with an agreeable variety at their frugal board, but it also relieves a great deal of the tedium of their winter season of inactivity. It is surprising, however, that accidents do not more frequently happen from their mode of charging their guns. Three fingers of powder and two of shot is the smallest load for their old militia muskets—the approved gun here—and in the hurry of loading in a boat much more powder is frequently poured in. Black eyes and bloody noses are the not uncommon penalties of a morning's sport, and I know one fisherman whose nose has been knocked permanently out of shape by the frequent kicking of his gun. In several instances the gun has gone clean overboard out of the fowler's hands, by the recoil. But nothing can daunt these men, or induce them to load with a lighter hand. There is one living at Nor'-West Cove, who has had his right eye destroyed by his gun, but who is now as great a duck-shooter as ever, firing, however, from the left shoulder."

of all descriptions, as is also Sydney harbour. Prince Edward Island and the Gulf shore of New Brunswick afford wonderful sport during the passage of the geese.

To return, however, to the subject before us—Newfoundland, its characteristic features and wild sports.

A marked difference of outline to those of the shores of Acadie is readily perceived on approaching its southern coast. The cliffs rise from the sea to the height of some five hundred feet, with a precipitous face and comparatively level summits, forming long stretches of table land. Then the tall arrow-headed pines are missed, and on passing quite close, the vegetation with which the country is clothed appears singularly colourless as well as stunted. A chilling melancholy aspect pervades the face of nature; except for the number of little fishing smacks with which the coast is dotted, we might seem to be passing the shores of Greenland. A few hours before, perhaps, we were in the warm atmosphere, blown with us by a balmy west wind from the fir-covered hills of Cape Breton; now we are faced by a biting north-east breeze which at once reminds us of the chills of early spring on the Atlantic coast. Rounding Cape Race, and we are fairly in the great Arctic current, and most probably within view of icebergs—at least up to the end of August. The water in the early summer is strewn through large areas with floating pieces of field ice, detachments from the great fields which float down the coast in spring, sometimes, indeed, entering and blocking up the harbours for miles out to sea. St. John's harbour has thus been blockaded even in the month of June, whilst the sea to the distance of twenty miles from the shore has been frozen so that a traveller might visit on foot any post along shore within seventy miles to the north-east.

The chilling effect of this proximity to the southern passage of ice through so large a portion of the year is readily perceptible on the vegetation in this part of the island. The stunted character of the deciduous trees (of few species compared with their representatives on the eastern shores of the mainland) and of the spruces, the absence of the broad-leaved maple, with which the continental forests are enriched, and the nakedness of the dull grey rocks, give an air of dreariness to the country, which it seems at first to the stranger impossible to shake off.

From comparative observations I should assign a fortnight as the difference in the progress of vegetation between Nova Scotia and the country round St. John's. On July 14th, the common lilac, long since faded in the gardens at Halifax, was here found in full bloom. On the 18th I observed various Vaccineæ, the purple iris, the pigeon-berry, and Smilacina bifolia in flower, and the kalmia just coming out, indicating fully the difference of season already stated.

Although in the interior, and especially on the western side of the island, Newfoundland can boast of forests, but little wood deserving that name appears in the vicinity of St. John's. The wilderness is generally covered with low alder bushes and thickets of white spruce (Abies alba), with a scanty mixture of balsam fir. A few small white birch, willows of several species, and one description of maple (Acer montanum), with the Amelanchier, or Indian pear, and wild cherry, constitute the bulk of the deciduous vegetation. The swamps (of great extent and constant occurrence) are covered with cotton grass, and Indian cups (Sarracenia), and the sphagnum with creeping tendrils of the cranberry. Dry elevated bogs have thick growths of huckle and blueberries (Gaylussacia resinosa and Vaccinium Canadense), with the common partridge berry, Labrador tea (Ledum), and sweet-scented myrica, and open spots are carpeted with reindeer lichen. Empetrum nigrum (locally misnamed heather), on the numerous black berries of which the curlew and wild goose feed, is a very abundant shrub, growing in the open, with patches of ground juniper.

It was probably to the profusion of berries (Vaccineæ) that the original name of Newfoundland, given by its early Norwegian visitors—Winland—was due, a country frequently alluded to in Norwegian and Icelandic historical records. The huckle-berries, especially, are so large and juicy that they might naturally have passed for the wild grapes for which the island was said to be famous, and which, it is almost needless to state, do not therein exist.*

The birches appear to be the only deciduous timber trees in Newfoundland, for, with the exception of the species already mentioned and moose wood (Abies striatum) —both mere shrubs—neither maple nor beech are to be found. On the western side of the island, where the soil and climate approximate to those of the adjacent coasts of the mainland, the hard-wood forests attain a fine development, affording a plentiful supply of fuel, and wood for manufacture. The yellow birch (Betula excelsa)

---

* A tolerably palatable red wine is commonly made in Nova Scotia, by the settlers, from blueberries.

grows here with a diameter of nearly three feet, and pine, spruce, and larch are abundant. The scenery of the western coast differs greatly from that of the southern and eastern. St. George's Bay and the Bay of Islands are surrounded by rolling forest-covered hills, and fine woods skirt the Humber river which enters the latter basin, and the great lakes in the interior whence it flows. With a soil quite capable of yielding abundantly to the agriculturist, the presence of coal-fields, vast mineral wealth, and extensive forests verging on the harbours and rivers, it is surprising that this part of the island is not more thickly settled. The fog, constantly shrouding the southern shores, and often extending for some distance up the eastern, is here of quite unfrequent occurrence, and the easterly winds which chill the soil and retard vegetation round St. John's, are divested of their bitterness on crossing the island.

Much light is thrown upon the interior features of the main island to the southward of the great lakes by the curious narrative of his journey across from Trinity Bay on the east coast to St. George's on the west, published as a pamphlet many years since by Mr. W. E. Cormack. His account is still regarded as the best description of the interior, of which but little more is known at the present day than at the time of his visit. The journey across the island was undertaken on foot, of course; a single Indian accompanied him, and all the necessaries of life were carried in knapsacks. After difficult progress of some days' duration through scanty spruce forests, he thus describes his first view of the interior :—

" We soon found that we were on a great granitic ridge, covered, not as the lower grounds are, with

crowded pines and green moss, but with scattered trees ;
and a variety of beautiful lichens, or reindeer moss,
partridge-berries, and whortle-berries, loaded the ground.
The Xylosteum villosum, a pretty, erect shrub, was in
full fruit by the sides of the rocks ; grouse, Tetrao albus,
the indigenous game-bird of the country, rose in coveys
in every direction, and snipes from every marsh. The
birds of passage, ducks and geese, were flying over us to
and fro from their breeding places in the interior and the
sea coast; tracks of deer, of wolves fearfully large, of
bears, foxes, and martens were seen everywhere.

"On looking back towards the sea coast, the scene was
magnificent. We discovered that under cover of the
forest we had been uniformly ascending ever since we
left the salt water at Random Bar, and then soon arrived
at the summit of what we saw to be a great mountain
ridge that seems to serve as a barrier between the sea
and the interior. The dense black forest, through which
we had pilgrimaged, presented a novel feature, appearing spotted with bright yellow marshes and a few glossy
lakes in its bosom, some of which we had passed close by
without seeing them.

"In the westward, to our inexpressible delight, the interior broke in sublimity before us. What a contrast did
this present to the conjectures entertained of Newfoundland! The hitherto mysterious interior lay unfolded
before us—a boundless scene, emerald surface, a vast
basin. The eye strides again and again over a succession of northerly and southerly ranges of green plains,
marbled with woods and lakes of every form and extent.
The imagination hovers in the distance, and clings invo-
luntarily to the undulating horizon of vapours far into

the west, until it is lost. A new world seemed to invite
us onward, or rather we claimed the dominion, and were
impatient to take possession. Our view extended for
more than forty miles in all directions, and the great
exterior features of the eastern portion of the main body
of the island are seen perfectly from these commanding
heights.

"*September* 11.—We descended into the bosom of the
interior.

"The plains which shone so brilliantly are steppes, or
savannas, composed of fine black compact peat mould,
formed by the growth and decay of mosses (principally
the Sphagnum capillifolium), and covered uniformly with
wiry grass, the Euphrasia officinalis being in some places
intermixed. They are in the form of extensive gently
undulating beds, stretching northwards and southwards,
with running waters and lakes, skirted with woods, lying
between them. Their yellow-green surfaces are sometimes uninterrupted by either tree, shrub, rock, or any
inequality for more than ten miles. They are chequered
everywhere upon the surface by deep-beaten deer paths,
and are in reality magnificent deer-parks, adorned by
woods and water. The trees here sometimes grow to a
considerable size, particularly the larch; birch is also
common. The deer herd upon them to graze. It is
impossible to describe the grandeur and richness of the
scenery, which will probably remain long undefined by
the hand of man, in search of whose associations the
eye vainly wandered.

"Our progress over the savanna country was attended
with great labour, and consequently slow, being only at
a rate of five to seven miles a day to the westward,

whilst the distance walked was equivalent to three or
four times as much.   Always inclining in our course to
the westward, we traversed in every direction, partly
from choice, in order to view and examine the country,
and partly from the necessity to get round the extremities of lakes and woods, and to look for game for
subsistence.

"It was impossible to ascertain the depths of these
savannas, but judging from the great expanse of the
undulations, and the total absence of inequalities on the
surfaces, it must often be many fathoms.   Portions of
some of the marshes, from some cause under the surface,
are broken up and sunk below the level, forming gullies
and pools.   The peat is there exposed sometimes to a
depth of ten feet and more without any rock or soil
underneath ; and the process of its formation is distinctly
exhibited from the dying and dead roots of the green
surface moss descending linearly into gradual decay,
until perfected into a fine black compact peat, in which
the original organic structure of the parent is lost.   The
savanna peat immediately under the roots of the grass
on the surface is very similar to the perfected peat of the
marshes.   The savannas are continually moist or wet on
the surface, even in the middle of summer, but hard
underneath.   Roots of trees, apparently where they grew,
are to be found by digging the surfaces of some of them,
and probably of all.   From what was seen of their edges
at the water-courses, they lie on the solid rock, without
the intervention of any soil.   The rocks exhibited were
transition clay slate, mica slate, and granitic.

"One of the most striking features of the interior is
the innumerable deer paths on the savannas.   They are

narrow, and take directions as various as the winds, giving the whole country a chequered appearance. Of the millions of acres here, there is no one spot exceeding a few superficial yards that is not bounded on all sides by deer paths. We, however, met some small herds only of these animals, the savannas and plains being in the summer season deserted by them for the mountains in the west part of the island. The Newfoundland deer, and there is only one species in the island, is a variety of the reindeer (Cervus tarandus, or cariboo); and, like that animal in every other country, it is migratory, always changing place with the seasons, for sake of its favourite kinds of food. Although they migrate in herds, they travel in files, with their heads in some degree to windward, in order that they may, by the scent, discover their enemies the wolves; their senses of smelling and hearing are very acute, but they do not trust much to their sight. This is the reason of their paths taking so many directions in straight lines; they become in consequence an easy prey to the hunter by stratagem. The paths tend from park to park through the intervening woods, in lines as established and deep beaten as cattlepaths on an old grazing farm."

Occupying nearly a month in toiling through the savanna country, the latter portion of his journey being impeded by deep snow, and living in an uncertain manner on deer's meat, beaver, geese, and ducks, Mr. Cormack further writes on approaching the western coast at the end of October :—

" We met many thousand of the deer, all hastening to the eastward, on their periodical migration. They had been dispersed since the spring, on the mountains and

barren tracks, in the west and north-west division of the
interior, to bring forth and rear their young amidst the
profusion of lichens and mountain herbage, and where
they were, comparatively with the mountain lowlands,
free from the persecution of flies.   When the first frosts,
as now in October, nip vegetation, the deer immediately
turn towards the south and east, and the first fall of
snow quickens their pace in those directions, as we now
met them, towards the low grounds where browse is to
be got, and the snow not so deep over the lichens.   In
travelling, herd follow herd in rapid succession over the
whole surface of the country, all bending their course
the same way in parallel lines.   The herds consist of
from twenty to two hundred each, connected by stragglers
or piquets, the animals following each other in single
files, a few yards or feet apart, as their paths show; were
they to be in close bodies, they could not graze freely.
They continue to travel south-eastward until February
or March, by which time the returning sun has power to
soften the snow, and permit of their scraping it off to
obtain the lichens underneath.   They then turn round
towards the west, and in April are again on the rocky
barrens and mountains where their favourite mossy food
abounds the most, and where in June they bring forth
their young.   In October the frosty warning to travel
returns.  They generally follow the same routes year after
year, but these sometimes vary, owing to irregularities
in the seasons, and interruptions by the Indians.   Such
are, in a general view, the courses and causes of the
migrations of the deer, and these seem to be the chief
design of animated nature in this portion of the earth.
Lakes and mountains intervening, cause the lines of the

migration paths to deviate from the parallel ; and at the necks of land that separate large lakes, at the extremity of lakes, and at the straits and running waters which unite lakes, the deer unavoidably concentrate in travelling. At those passes the Indians encamp in parties, and stay for considerable interval of time, because they can there procure the deer with comparatively little trouble."

The Indians here alluded to, whom Mr. Cormack believed to be still inhabiting the shores of the large lakes to the northward of his course through the island, and the remains of whose fences or pounds for snaring deer may be seen at the present day by the banks of the Exploits river, were the Red Indians, or Bœothics—a tribe long since extinct. The last of her race, a Red Indian woman, named Shanaandithith, called Mary March by her captors, who brought her in to St. John's, died there of consumption in 1829. As far as was known of them, this tribe lived entirely in the wilder portions of the interior, probably from distrust of the whites, who had ruthlessly attacked and slain them whenever met with, as also on account of the harassing invasions of the Micmacs, who frequently crossed from Acadia in fleets of canoes for that purpose. Smallpox has been assigned as the cause of their extinction, and it has been likewise supposed that the remnant of the tribe migrated into the interior of Labrador, where strange Indians are reported to have been seen from time to time, not agreeing in type with any of the known resident tribes.

The Bœothics have been described as a fine athletic race, and, until the latter obtained possession of firearms,

superior in war to the Indians of the mainland. Their
language was quite distinct from that of any of the surrounding tribes.

In a pamphlet published in London in 1622, by one
Richard Whitburne, who had had much experience in the
great bank fisheries, and was sent out to institute a com-
mission to inquire into some abuses which were connected with the latter, are to be found some very
interesting accounts of Newfoundland at that very early
date of its history. Of the Red Indians, he says :—" It
is well known that the natives of those parts have great
stores of red ochre wherewith they use to colour their
bodies, bowes, arrows, and cannows in a painting manner,
which cannows are their boats that they used to go to sea
in, which are built in shape like the wherries on the
River of Thames, with small timbers no thicker nor
broader than hoopes, and instead of boards they use the
barkes of birche trees, which they sew very artificially and
close together, and then overlay the seams with turpen-
tine, as pitch is used on the seames of ships and boats ;
and in like manner they use to sew the barkes of spruce
and firre trees round and deep in proportion like a brasse
kettle to boil their meet in, as it hath been well approved by divers men, but most especially to my certain
knowledge by three mariners of a ship of Tapson, in the
County of Devon, which ship riding there at anchor
neere by me at the Harbor called Hearts Ease on the
North side of Trinity Bay, and being robbed in the
night by the savages of their apparell and divers other
provisions did the next day seeke after them, and happened to come suddenly where they had set up three
tents and were feasting, having three such cannows by

them, and three pots made of such rinds of trees, standing each of them on three stones, boyling, with twelve
fowles in each of them, every fowle as big as a widgeon
and some so big as a ducke; they had also many such
pots so served and fashioned, like leather buckets that
are used for quenching of fire, and those were full of
the yolks of eggs that they had taken and boyled hard
and so dried small as it had been powder sugar, which
the savages used in their broth as sugar is often used in
some meates; they had great store of the skins of deere,
beavers, beares, seals, otters and divers other fine skins
which were excellent well dressed, as also great store of
severall sorts of flesh dryed, and by shooting off a musket
towards them they all ran away, naked, without any
apparall but only some of them had their hats on their
heads, which were made of seale skins, in fashion like
our hats sewed handsomely with narrow bands about
them set round with fine white shels. All their three
cannows, their flesh, skins, yolks of eggs, targets, bows
and arrows, and much fine okar, and divers others things
they tooke and brought away and shared it among those
that tooke it, and they brought to me the best cannow,
bows, and arrows and divers of their skins and many
other artificial things worth the noting which may seeme
much to invite us to endeavour to finde out some other
good trades with them."

The zoology of Newfoundland is of a more Arctic type
than that of the neighbouring Acadian Provinces, being
characterised by the presence of the ptarmigan, and Arctic
hare, and showing a remarkable falling off in the number
of species of the continental fauna. Thus there is not a
squirrel on the island, and neither porcupine, racoon, or

mink.  The presence of the wild cat is uncertain.  Fewer
species of the ordinary migratory birds, visitors of the
Lower Provinces, are found here.  At midsummer, in the
neighbourhood of St. John's, I have noticed the absence
of the night-hawk, so common a bird on the Continent.
Neither were fire-flies, which were scintillating in myriads
over the swamps in Nova Scotia at the time, to be seen.
Many birds, however, passing over, or merely resting for
a week or two on their way, on the eastern shores of
Acadie, visit Newfoundland to breed, such as the
Canada goose, fox-coloured sparrow (F. iliaca), snipe, and
others, whilst migration of American species has a still
further range to the north-east, and American birds form
a large proportion of the avi-fauna of Greenland, according to Dr. Reinhardt.  The woodcock is not indigenous
to Newfoundland ; and, strange to say, the only specimen
shot quite recently near St. John's was a European
bird.

Considering the immense portion of this island which
is claimed by water, bogs, and swamps, the well-ascertained absence of reptilia is singular.  In the peninsula
of Avalon I have plodded frequently along the edges of
ponds and swamps, hoping to see some little croaker take
a header from the bank, or in search of snakes by sunny
woodland slopes—situations where they might be found
at every few paces on the mainland—but all in vain.
Indeed, more than once has the experiment been tried of
turning out some of the large green-headed frogs (R.
clamitans), to end in failure: in a few days they would
all be found stiff on their backs.  Cormack met with
neither frog, snake, nor toad, on his journey across the
main island, and observes that his Indians had never

seen or heard of one.[*] The island of **Anticosti is said to** be similarly deficient in representatives of this class. As has been written of Ireland in an ancient poem, composed by a St. Donatus, and dating as far back as the ninth century :—

> " Nulla venena nocent, nec serpens serpit in herba,
> Nec conquesta canit garrula rana lacu."

From foregoing remarks, it will be readily seen that the interior of Newfoundland is a vast field of discovery, especially interesting to the enterprising sportsman. In August and September, when the berries are ripe, animal life is wonderfully abundant (for America) on the open barrens. The deer begin their descent from the hills ; willow grouse, now well grown, associate in large coveys ; wild geese and curlew are found feeding on the upland barrens, and snipe are plentiful in the marshes. Bears are reported very numerous in the interior, where their well-beaten paths, traversed for ages, afford good walking to the traveller. When discovered at a distance, revelling amongst thickets of berry-bearing bushes, they may be easily approached under cover of ridges or rock boulders. Furs of many sorts would repay the trapper ;

[*] Whitburne appears to have been aware of this circumstance, for he writes : " Neither are there any Snakes, Toads, Serpents, or any other venomous Wormes that ever were knowne to hurt any man in that country, but only a very little nimble fly (the least of all other flies) which is called a Miskieto, those flies seem to have a great power and authority upon all loytering and idle people that come to the Newfoundland : for they have this property that when they finde any such lying lazily, or sleeping in the woods, they will presently bee more nimble to seize on them than any Sargent will be to arrest a man for debt. Neither will they leave stinging or sucking out the blood of such sluggards, until like a Beadel they bring him to his master, where he should labour, in which time of loytering, those flies will so brand such idle persons in their faces, that they may be knowne from others as the Turks do their slaves."

foxes, marten, otter, beaver, or musk-rat.  That of the
Arctic hare (Lepus Arcticus) is a handsome, though not
a very valuable skin ; the ears are tipped with black, the
rest of its winter dress being pure white.  This animal
will attain a weight of fourteen pounds in Newfoundland : it appears to present no appreciable difference to
L. variabilis of Europe.  It is said that there are two
species of ptarmigan on the island.  If so, the other and
less common description is probably the somewhat
smaller and more slenderly-billed bird—Lagopus rupestris,
or rock ptarmigan.  In its summer plumage, the former
species is one of the handsomest game birds the world
can produce.  At this season, the wings only are white,
all the rest being a rich mottled chesnut ; an arch of
scarlet fringe over the eye.  Grouse shooting (these birds
are called grouse on the island, or sometimes by the
fishermen and settlers—"pattermegans") begins in the
neighbourhood of St. John's, where they are protected,
and the law receives the assistance of a game society, on
the 25th August.  The game laws are strictly observed in
the vicinity of the capital ; snipe are included in the Act.

Although the cariboo is generally dispersed through
the interior, it will have been seen that the great bulk
of these animals shift from the low-lying lake and
savanna country to the hills, and vice versa, in the spring
and fall.  To reach the interior from their great stronghold in the high lands which form the extension of the
island towards the Straits of Belle-Isle, they must cross
the two chains of lakes and rivers which, overlapping
each other near the centre of the island, discharge their
waters respectively into the Bay of Islands and Notre
Dame.

Into the latter great basin, and a little to the north of Exploits River, empties a stream called the Hall's Bay River. It flows from a chain of small lakes running nearly east and west at the south-eastern termination of the mountain range before mentioned; and here the great body of the cariboo pass, commencing their southerly migration about the end of August. Hall's Bay is to be reached only by sailing-vessel from St. John's, but the hunting grounds may also be attained by ascending the magnificent river Humber from the Bay of Islands on the western side of the island—a course on which much grand scenery is to be viewed.

The north-eastern extremity of the Grand Pond, some fifty miles in length, with which it communicates, approaches the Hall's Bay chain with easy access. Cariboo hunting may, however, be obtained by entering the interior from the heads of any of the great bays which so deeply indent the coast line of Newfoundland.

Although the Indian race, which once wholly subsisted on their flesh, is long since extinct, and there are but few resident Micmac hunters, the cariboo are much kept down by their bitter persecutors in every part of the globe where the reindeer is found—the wolves. "The Old Hunter," whose camp has been frequently pitched in the proximity of the famous deer passes just mentioned, tells me of the great destruction caused amongst the deer by this fleet and wily brute, which he has often seen and shot in the act of pursuit. The splendid head of a Newfoundland cariboo, figured No. 2 in the engraving of horns, was obtained from an animal shot at Deer Harbour, Trinity Bay, by Mr. F. N. Gisborne (who has kindly allowed me to copy it), when nearly run into

by a wolf.    It would appear singular that these magnificent Newfoundland bucks, which will attain the weight
of five or even six hundred pounds, with ponderous
antlers, should fly from the wolf, considering the tremendous power of a blow from their hoofs.    The specimen
last mentioned weighed 428 pounds after being cleaned.

With regard to the sport which may be expected by
the angler on this island, it may be briefly stated that
every lake abounds with the ordinary trout of Eastern
America—S. fontinalis : sea-trout ascend all the rivers
in July in astonishing abundance, taking anything in the
shape of bait or fly readily and indiscriminately.  Salmon
fishing, however, appears to be uncertain ; and a general
belief obtains that, on the larger rivers of the north-east
coast, they are shy of taking the fly.    I am, however,
informed by my friend Mr. Gisborne,* to whom I am
indebted for much information on the sports of Newfoundland, and who has hunted and explored the country
in every direction, that Gander Bay River, an important
stream affording excellent canoeing on its course to its
large parent lake in the interior, and flowing into the
southern end of Notre Dame Bay, is believed by him to
be as fine a river for salmon-fishing as any in North
America.

* Frederic Newton Gisborne, to whose skill as an electrician, and the
energy which he displayed in exploring and completing a line of telegraph
across the wild southern interior of Newfoundland, from the east coast to
the Gulf of St. Lawrence, and further uniting that island with the continent
by a submarine cable, testimony has been borne not only by the community
of Newfoundland, but by the inhabitants of all the British North American
provinces bordering on the Atlantic.    Whatever praise may be accorded to
another great name in completing and successfully carrying out the gigantic
scheme which followed—the connexion of the two hemispheres by the
Atlantic cable—Mr. Gisborne is rightly accredited in British North America
with being its original projector.    *Palmam qui meruit ferat.*

# CHAPTER XI.

THE necessities and shifts of a life in the woods are described in so many works on North American travel, with exhaustive treatises on *matériel* and outfits, that it becomes unnecessary to dilate on this topic. Indeed there is not much to be said with regard to camping in these eastern woodlands. Our expeditions never extend very far from the base of supply, nor have we to contend with such dangers as those incident on prairie travel.

Everything necessary for the woods is to be got in the stores of all the large provincial towns, and almost every storekeeper will be able to inform the traveller of what he wants in the way of tin ware and provisions, and how the outfit should be packed.

Bringing with him his particular fancies in the way of breechloaders or the old style, he can get fair rods, quite good enough for the rough work on American forest streams, and good tackle and flies in either Halifax or St. John's, where also a first-rate American click reel may be got of German silver or bronzed aluminum.

An elaborate canteen, with all its nicely-fitting arrangements, got up for a Crimean or Abyssinian campaign, is all very well, perhaps, for such purposes; but where tinsmiths' shops are frequent at the starting point, no good

is to be got by bringing such traps across the Atlantic.
To save trouble and room I have frequently purchased
my bunch of tins at the very last settlement where a
store existed, before turning into the woods. It is well
to remember, however, to get the handle of the frying-
pan " fixed " so as to double back, and so pack with the
plates, mugs, &c., into the big outside tin can, which holds
the entire camp service; otherwise the Indian who
carries it through the woods will probably grumble all the
way, as the stem is constantly catching in the bushes.

Except in winter, when opportunities occur of getting
one's traps hauled in on a sled over some logging road,
everything has to be "backed" through the woods, to
the hunting camp, and, consequently, anything pro-
truding from the loads is liable to impede one's progress.
Hence the bundles should be as near as possible the
breadth of the back, all loads being thus carried, with a
strap (the broader the better) encircling the chest and
shoulders.

The Indian, used to the work from infancy, will often
carry a hundred weight by a withy of birch or witherod
bush, which seems as though it would cut to the bone ;
but to the white man, unaccustomed to carrying a load
thus, a well-balanced bundle and broad carrying-strap are
of the first importance, particularly as long journeys are
often thus made, and every true sportsman likes to do a
fair share of the work.

A hint may be inserted here that one of the greatest
drawbacks to progress under such unavoidable circumstances is to lose one's temper, and a firm determination
should be made at starting to avoid doing so. I grant it
is often hard of prevention when two or three consecutive

stumbles over windfalls or painful collision of the shins with sharp stumps are followed by suddenly sinking on one leg up to the knee in a black mud hole, and the load, slewing round, brings you over altogether into wet moss, or still worse, when the unpractised hand nervously attempts the often necessary passage of a deep brook or still-water stream (the latter is a frequent feature in the forest), and the uncertain foot glides from the slippery bridge—a fallen tree—followed by a tremendous splash, and one or two expletives as a matter of course; but depend upon it, the less you fret under such circumstances the better you will come in to camp by a deal. The Indians generally carry 50 lb. to 70 lb. weight, including gun (7 lb. or 8 lb.); yours would be 20 lb. to 30 lb., and this you ought to carry if you are fit to enter the woods at all. To let you know, however, what is often before you, here is a description of a very common feature in the woods—an alder swamp :—

Take a substratum of black mud, into which you will sink at least up to your knees, perhaps up to your hips; cover this over with a treacherous crust of peat, turf, and moss; over this strew windfalls, i.e., dead, fallen trees, with the branches broken off close to the trunks, leaving sharp spikes; form an interlaced network of these, sprinkling in a few granite rocks; and cover all this over with a thick growth of alder bushes about five feet high, so that you cannot possibly see where you are putting your feet; vary the ground with a few boggy streams and " honey pots " or mud holes. Then walk across this with a good load on your back, and your gun under your arm, without losing your temper !

For either winter or summer work the common gray

homespun of the country is the best material for the
woods.  It is very strong, almost impossible to tear by
catching against the trees, and porous, which is also a
great advantage, as it dries so quickly.  Its colour, too, is
in its favour, being so like that of rocks or tree stems.
An almost colourless material is as necessary for moose
hunting as it is for fishing, though I have seen a good
New York sportsman flinging over a clean pool on the
brightest of days with a scarlet flannel shirt and black
continuations, and get fish withal.

The Canadian smock, known in England as the Norfolk
blouse, is a capital style of coat for hunting.  Pockets
according to taste, and a piece of leather on either
shoulder and another on the inside of the right arm to
ease the pressure of the gun.

The camp generally taken into the woods is a spread
of strong cotton cloth soaked with boiled oil and well
dried in the sun.  Its shape is best understood by describing the framework of the camp as follows :—Two
uprights with forks at the end stuck into the ground some
eight or ten feet apart, the crutches about six feet from the
base ; a cross piece between these well lashed on, on
which rest the tops of some half-dozen long slanting poles
—fir or larch saplings.  The canvas is spread over and
tied ; two wings (triangular pieces) form the sides, and
are tied to the uprights.  This is the usual form of open
camp for summer or the fall.  The fire is arranged in
front.  You sleep on an elastic bed of silver-fir boughs
(not spruce, mind, or you would be most uncomfortably
pricked), artistically spread by the Indians underneath ;
they rough it in the open, and coil up under their blankets
at the foot of a tree on the opposite side of the fire.  If

you are on a fishing excursion, encamped by the water-side and it rains, they turn the canoes, bottom up, over themselves.

In winter they make a leaning cover for themselves of boughs and birch bark nearly joining yours (room being left above for the ascent of the smoke), and fill in the sides with the bushes and slabs of split fir, the doorway being covered by a suspended rug. With plenty of firewood at hand, no one who had not been in the woods in winter would credit the comfort and cosiness found in these hunting camps. In fact, the ease with which the wilderness can be made a home with so little labour, and the entire independence of the sojourner in the woods who has set up a good camp well stocked with provision for a fortnight's campaign, and a few changes of flannels and stockings, contribute principally to the charms of forest life. We are seldom storm staid or lose a day by remaining within.

> " The frost might glitter, it would blight no crop,
> The falling rain will spoil no holiday.
> We were made freemen of the forest laws,
> All dressed, like Nature, fit for her own ends,
> Essaying nothing she cannot perform."

writes one of America's poets ;* and when the snow-storm is driving or the rain drops patter on the autumnal leaves strewn on the ground, it is often seasonable weather to the hunter; and the evening closes over many an exciting tale of what has been seen or done in the chase on such days.

As a summer residence I have used a very portable little square camp, opening at one end. The top was

* Ralph Waldo Emerson.

suspended on a ridge pole bound to two uprights, and the sloping sides stretched and fastened to pegs; it had a valence all round about two feet high. The area of the surface it covered was some eight feet by ten. Not being oiled, it weighed only a dozen pounds or so, and when well stretched was quite rain-proof, unless the sides were touched by a gun or anything leaning against them, when it would drip.

Never encamp in a low site at the foot of a hill; for it is not pleasant, however well you may be protected from the falling waters, to find yourself becoming suddenly soaked by the rising flood, in the nice comfortable hollow which your form has made in your bed of boughs. We never expect, and rarely find, any unpleasant results in the way of a severe cold from these little disagreeables of camping out; living constantly in the open air steels the sensibility of the system to catarrhal affections, and the Indians aver that they are more apt to take cold by going into a house than we are by going into the open air. And so we take things very philosophically; so much so, sometimes, that a friend of mine, on being roused from his slumbers, on the plea that he was lying in three inches of water, immediately lay down again in the old spot, averring that "the water there was warmer than anywhere else in the camp." In this country, storms of this description never last very long, twelve to twenty-four hours from the commencement being the general duration, when the wind veering round to the west (our fine-weather quarter), soon clears off the rolling cloud masses from the sky, and a glorious sun and cool zephyr quickly dry the dripping forest.

I like to have the sound of a bubbling brook for a

lullaby when camped in the woods ; one's somniferous tendencies are greatly assisted by the curious chatterings and tinklings of its little falls and rapids. As sleep draws nigh, the multitudinous sounds in turn resemble, almost to reality, those produced by far different causes—now it is men talking in low tones close at hand ; then a distant shout or despairing shriek ; and now the impression is that a herd of cattle are crossing the brook, splashing the water ; the deception being aided by the resemblance to the sound of cattle-bells often made by the miniature cascades.

Such streams are sure to occur not far from one's camp by the lake or river side. They come dancing down from the lakes back in the woods to join the river, shaded by dark firs and hemlocks, full of little falls, eddying round great rocks, which stand out from the stream capped with ferns and lichens, and at whose base are little gravelly pools—the very counterpart in miniature of some of our grander salmon rivers. Had Tennyson ever seen an American forest brook when he wrote his charming little idyll, " The Brook ?" I must insert one verse :—

> " And here and there a foamy flake
>    Upon me, as I travel,
>  With many a silvery water-break
>    Above the golden gravel."

To return, however, to the sober description of practical experience. Never trust to finding a camp, of the existence of which you may have heard, standing, and ready for habitation ; and always allow plenty of daylight to make a new one, in case the old is *non est*, or gone to pieces. I remember one blazing hot summer's afternoon going up the banks of Gold River, Nova Scotia, to try

some salmon pools at the Grand Falls on the next morning—a twelve miles' walk. There was a nice camp (so
reported) all ready to receive us. Feverish from the heat
of the woods, and the severe biting we had received from
the huge moose flies and clouds of mosquitoes on the
way, we reached the spot long after sundown, in hopes
of finding shelter and a good night's repose, for we were
fatigued. An old camp of the meanest construction was
found, after considerable search with birch-bark torches,
and under its very questionable shelter we extended ourselves in front of a meagre fire which had been kindled
with difficulty, there being nothing but fir woods around.
Presently we found that the whole of the ancient bedding
of dry fir boughs was overrun by large black ants. Now,
I had rather be coursed over by rats than by ants at
night, as the former vermin seldom act on the offensive
towards a sleeping human being; and so, sleep was out
of the question till the enemy was exterminated. To
effect this, we arose and parted with our beds—to wit,
the brown spruce boughs, which we committed to the
flames. We then again tried to rest, lying down in the
ashes round the fire, but no—on they came again in
battalion. With one consent we arose, and rushed up
the hill-side into the dark woods, depositing ourselves in
the soft moss under the hemlocks. Presently down came
a new enemy—pattering drops of rain, precursors of a
heavy summer shower. Back to camp; but the ants
had not retired for the night; so, peeling off the sheets
of bark from the poles, we finally sought a hard bed on
the naked rocks by the water's edge, shielding ourselves
from the rain with our birchen waterproofs. Next morning it was discovered that our little packet of tea, care-

lessly pitched into the back part of the camp, had been
burned with the fir boughs ; so our beverage that morning was an infusion of hemlock boughs, a few sprays of
which were boiled in water—one of the many devices
adopted in the woods as substitutes for tea. Morning
disclosed, moreover, a patch of the broad, sickly-looking
green leaves of the poison-ivy (Rhus toxicodendron),
growing hard by where we had reposed, contact with
which would have driven us wild with dangerous irritation. On returning to the sea-pools, however, our miseries
were somewhat compensated by killing five dozen newly
run sea trout at a pretty stand in a wild meadow, where
a cool brook joined the river.

*Apropos* of the flies which have been just alluded to,
none of his relations could have identified my companion
(a novice in the woods) next morning. So swollen was
his whole countenance that features were obliterated, and
for nearly the whole day he was helplessly blind. Many
people suffer similarly ; others enjoy comparative immunity from swelling, though copiously bled. On landing
from a canoe, the only plan is to light a fire, and make
as dense a smoke as possible. Lime juice, petroleum,
pork fat, or tar are used, according to fancy, to smear
the face and hands as preventives, but the flies will
scarcely be denied by such appliances. On salmon-
fishing excursions of extended duration on the Nepisiquit
and elsewhere, I have generally taken mosquito curtains
to cover one's body at night. By day I and the insects
fight it out in a continuous tussle. In a recent number
of *Land and Water*, however, I find a receipt given by
my friend " Ubique," an old hand at " camping out,"
which, though I have not had an opportunity of trying

for myself is worthy of note. " In nearly all timber lands," he says, speaking of this part of North America, " large fungi will be found growing on the sides of semi-decayed trees ; this gather, and dry thoroughly in the sun, when it will smoulder if lighted, like a joss-stick. The smoke is not disagreeable to man, and two or three pieces kept frequently at work will soon drive all the winged pests to other quarters. A piece about the size of a walnut will burn for over a quarter of an hour."

Overtaken by nightfall, one is sometimes compelled to camp in low-lying swampy ground, when it becomes exceedingly hard to light a fire, owing to the steam rising from the damp, peaty soil beneath. In this case we resort to the following expedient—an excellent plan, worth remembering—namely, to cut down two or three small firs and chop them into lengths of four or five feet, placing them side by side ; this forms a platform, and the fire kindles readily upon it, and the platform itself burns with the rest. Another plan for establishing a good fire when there are plenty of rocks to be obtained near the camp, is to make a good broad hearth with flat slabs ; the stones will themselves emit much heat when the fire is established, and it will burn better and clearer, and may always be relighted with very little trouble ; and, moreover, the great hole which the fire soon burns in the ground beneath, and into which it sinks, will thus be avoided.

And now for a few remarks on the interior economy of a camp. A small amount of light literature will while away idle hours spent within—magazines or reviews are the best generally. For a fishing camp there are several excellent American publications on the sport of the British provinces, entertainingly descriptive, and sound in advice, which would prove highly useful. They include "Game Fish of the North," by Roosevelt; Norris's "American Angler," and Frank Forester's "Fish and Fishing." In the former work some excellent receipts will be found for the camp cuisine. I confess to being somewhat of a Spartan as manager of this department, and, before the invention of the really invaluable meat essences, if moose meat, porcupine, or salmon were not in the larder, would fall back upon the staples of a woodman's diet—navy pork and pilot bread, from day to day, unvaryingly. A Sunday dinner, however, would always comprise a boiling of pea-soup—one of the best descriptions of camp messes—made of split peas, pork bones, lots of sliced onions, potatoes, and pounded biscuit, the latter being added with the seasoning at the last. The utmost vigilance is required towards the close of the performance to prevent any solid crust or deposit adhering to the bottom of the pot, as it would then immediately burn, and burnt pea-soup is altogether uneatable. We write and read in the camp, as we lie on our blankets extended over the comfortable bedding of fir-boughs, by the light of a little lamp filled with the American burning-fluid; it is one of the best and most portable means of lighting a camp that can be taken. A wax candle stuck in a noose of birch-bark drawn tightly round, and held in a split stick sharpened at the end, which is planted in the ground under the name of the Indian candlestick, is another and more common means of illumination; and, should candles or fluid have been forgotten, the following will do as a *dernier ressort* :—A common tin box (as a percussion-cap box), with a wick passed through a hole in the lid, and fed with lumps of fat ; the tin, becoming warm, will keep the fat in the proper state of liquefaction for feeding the wick.

The death of a moose or cariboo is of course an event of great importance in the hunter's camp, and is duly celebrated. What gorging, however, on the part of the Indians—they will broil tit bits through half the night. Moose meat is very digestible ; cariboo (of a closer fibre) somewhat less so ; bear most easily assimilated of all, and "grand to travel on" says the Indian, who never knows when to stop. Failing this, or venison, the porcupine is the great resource of the hunting camp throughout the provinces, with the exception of Cape Breton and Newfoundland, where it is not found. Scalded, scraped, and singed, its bare body expanded on a cross to roast, it looks anything but enticing to a novice. But the appetite of the woods prevails, and overcomes all scruples. It has, at the same time, a drawback in the frequent occurrence of large quantities of entozoa (Tænia pectinata)—no drawback to the Indian, however ; sometimes rather the contrary. An Indian told me, " my grandfather, he like 'em ; taste hard though—'most like mustard."

The hare, and the two sorts of tree grouse, locally known as the birch and spruce partridges (T. umbellus and T. canadensis) also contribute to the camp larder. Two or three hanks of brass wire for snaring the former animal should not be omitted in the outfit. Of the two partridges, the birch (the ruffed grouse) is by far the best. It is white-fleshed and delicate eating : the spruce bird has very dark meat, and tastes like an old pine board.

The universal charge made by the Indian hunters or canoe men, is one dollar per diem, though possibly the camp-keeper who stays at home, cooks, cuts firewood, and sets rabbit snares, &c., may be hired for two-thirds of that amount. They also charge so much a day, say half a dollar, for canoe hire, unless you buy the canoe outright for from eight to twenty dollars, according to her age and size. Bark is getting so scarce in many parts that their charge in this respect is not unreasonable, for in taking a party up a river or through lakes with heavy loads there is considerable wear and tear. To see their faces of anxiety on shooting shoal rapids! not from physical fear, but for the canoe ; and the agonised look when a long grating rub proclaims contact with the rocks, and how eagerly on reaching shore they turn her over to inspect the bottom bark and ascertain if the cut is deep or not ! The canoe is their pride ; and to many the loss of their little craft would bring the greatest temporary distress. These beautiful adaptations for water transport in the wilderness are far from being so frail as would be imagined at first sight. Though they can be made scarcely exceeding sixty pounds weight, and at the same time sufficiently capacious to carry four persons and luggage, they are models of strength in the framework. The strips of ash which form the gunwale, and the delicate hooped ribs of fir which almost touch each other throughout the length, are most carefully selected. The thwarts are of thin ash, one is placed at either extremity, on which sit the paddlers (kneeling, however, in the bottom in case of rapid water, or a heavy sea on a lake), the other two crossing amidships as supports. I know of no more delightful life than a canoe expedition through the forest. So many luxuries may be taken; and the position in which one reclines, legs stretched at full length in the bottom, with the back propped up against the blankets and loads, is just the one in which to enjoy the ever changing scenery; and whilst on the water you are blessed by a perfect immunity from the flies.

Though of course each fresh abrasion of the outside bark takes off from the value of the canoe, injuries to the bottom or sides are generally mended with great ease and celerity. The slightest puncture is soon detected by the Indian, on turning her over, by suction, the mouth being applied to doubtful looking spots. Rents or gashes of considerable extent are " fixed " by a piece of rag dipped in melted resin softened somewhat by tallow: the forest remedy is the hard gum which plentifully exudes from the black spruce—" chewing gum," as it is called, being the favourite sweetmeat of the backwoodsman. The bark, however, must be quite dry before the application is made.

In smooth water two vigorous Indians will paddle the canoe, well loaded, about six miles an hour. In a spurt, however, when they strain to pass another canoe, or to avoid some rapid or rock towards which they are drifting, or to overtake wounded game in the water, they can nearly double this speed. It is a charming sight to watch the passing canoe thus powerfully impelled, from the shore. With its exquisitely symmetrical lines and fragile appearance, as it glides noiselessly yet swiftly through the water, one is strongly impressed with the poet's fancy that " the forest's life was in it, all its mystery and its magic." Reclining by the river side in the vicinity of

the fishing camp, to see a handsome Indian youth bring
up his canoe to the shallow landing-place in a graceful
sweep, without the slightest concussion, and, lightly
stepping out, draw her head up into the bushes, is to
recall a just image of a Hiawatha.

> " Then once more Cheemaun he patted,
> To his birch canoe said ' Onward !'
> And it stirred in all its fibres,
> And with one great bound of triumph
> Leaped across the water-lilies,
> Leaped through tangled flags and rushes,
> And upon the beach beyond them
> Dry-shod landed Hiawatha."

As it may be inferred that every sportsman who visits
the woodlands or streams of Acadie would wish to be
acquainted with the existing local regulations for the
protection of game and fish, a summary of the laws
framed for this purpose is here introduced.

In Nova Scotia, with regard to fish, it is enacted that,—

" Any person taking salmon in fresh water westward
of Halifax Harbour between the 31st day of July and
the 1st of March, or in fresh water eastward of Halifax
Harbour between the 15th day of August and the 1st of
March, is liable to a penalty of forty dollars."

" Bag nets shall not be used in any river or harbour
nor within a mile from the mouth of any river under a
penalty of forty dollars."

" No nets shall be set or allowed to remain set between an hour before sunset on Saturday, and an hour
after sunrise on Monday, under a penalty of forty
dollars."

" Any person spearing salmon or sweeping with a net
therefor in fresh water is liable to a penalty of forty
dollars."

"Nets shall only be placed on one side of a river, shall not extend more than one-third across the same, shall not be placed nearer than an eighth of a mile to each other, nor nearer.than an eighth of a mile to any dam."

"Every dam shall have a sufficient fish way, which shall be kept open during the months of March, May, June, and July. The owner or occupier is liable to a penalty of forty dollars for every time he shall close such passage."

"The owner of a mill who, after being duly notified, shall neglect or refuse to construct a sufficient fish way is liable to a penalty of one hundred dollars, and if within ten days after such penalty has been inflicted he does not construct such fish way he is liable to have his dam wholly prostrated."

In respect of the large game, the law stands,—

"No person shall kill, or pursue with intent to kill, any moose, save only during the months of September, October, November, and December, or shall expose for sale, or have in his or her possession, any green moose skin or fresh moose meat, save only in the months aforesaid, and the first five days in the month of January ; and no person shall kill, or pursue with intent to kill, any cariboo between the first days of March and September inclusive in any year."

"No person shall kill more than five moose or cariboo, *during any one year or season*, under a penalty of twenty dollars for each offence — one-half to the informer."

"No person whatever shall set snares or traps, for moose or cariboo, under a penalty of twenty dollars— one half to the informer."

" The export from this Province of moose or cariboo hides is hereby prohibited and unlawful, and the hides attempted to be exported shall be forfeited, and the owner or person attempting to export the same shall, on conviction, be liable to pay a sum not to exceed five dollars on each hide, to be recovered in the name of any prosecutor in a summary manner before two justices of the peace, and, when recovered, to go to the prosecutor."

With regard to smaller game,—

" No snares shall be set for hares between the first days of March and September in any year, under a penalty of two dollars for each offence ; and all snares shall be taken up during the aforesaid close season under a penalty of two dollars for each snare not removed by the parties setting the same, on or before the first day of March, to be recovered in the same manner as in the preceding section."

" Partridges, snipe, and woodcock, are protected from 1st day of March to 1st of September,—penalty, ten shillings for every bird killed out of season."

" No person is permitted to have any of the above in his possession in the close season, under a penalty of ten shillings for each."

Exceptional cases to all the game laws are made on behalf of the Indians, who abuse their privilege, however, most shamefully, and to the detriment of those for whom the preservation of the animals of the forest is yearly becoming of more importance. It is very well to argue that the poor Indian has a right to shoot a moose or spear a salmon for his own use at any time of the year ; but when they shoot moose wholesale in the deep snow

late in the spring, disturbing the cows when they ought
to be at peace, and often leaving piles of meat to decay
in the fast-melting snow of April, it is time that this
wanton mode of proceeding should be put an end to. It
is hardly, however, at their doors that the blame is to
be laid—it is the ready market that tempts them ; and
although a question would be raised if they were to
bring their meat into the larger provincial towns, yet the
residents at the smaller settlements will always purchase
whenever they can procure it, the local magistrates themselves sometimes setting the example. The month of
April is an idle time with the settlers, and they often
accompany the Indians, who may be located in their
neighbourhood, for a "spree" in the woods, chasing and
scaring the moose with long-legged noisy curs, on the
crusted surface of the old snow. Throughout North
America there seems to be a general difficulty and
unwillingness, on the part of the local authorities, to
maintain the dignity of the game laws—the more so as
the locality is further from the seat of government where
the laws are framed. And until the government can
pay overseers who shall be scrupulously independent of
favour or partiality, in the districts to which they are
appointed, and whose whole care shall be to bring to
justice every case in which the law is transgressed, we
can hope for no satisfactory and impartial protection of
game or salmon in those districts in which such protection is most required.

The author, for many years connected with the Council
of the Nova Scotian Inland Fisheries and Game Preservation Society (latterly as Vice-President), under the
continued direction of his esteemed personal friend, fre-

quently mentioned in these pages as "The Old Hunter,"* who has presided over it since its inception, has had much to do with the framing of the present laws relating to large game.

From the almost incredible slaughter of moose in the concluding winter months, consequent, in some seasons, on a continuance of deep encrusted snow in the woods, a restriction of the season in which these animals might formerly be killed (lasting until the last day of February) appeared a most necessary step. Though as true sport moose hunting is seldom pursued in the latter part of the winter, yet the instincts of the Indians, and of the settlers generally, appear so ferocious that they seek the opportunity of the animals' most prostrate and defenceless condition to inflict a slaughter the excitement of which apparently temporarily blinds them to reason. Of the Indians it is the old story, corroborated by every traveller from Labrador to Vancouver, from the Prairies to the Pole. With regard to the latter class, it is enough to say that the time when the crust will bear their yelping curs, racing the plunging, bleeding moose through the forest, is looked forward to with the greatest anticipations of pleasure.

In view of amendment of this lamentable state of affairs, the regulations concerning the hunting of the elk in the Scandinavian peninsula were referred to. Once, the elk, unprotected, and regarded as a noxious animal, was on the point of extinction in Norway. Government thereupon enacted a stringent law forbidding these animals being shot for a long term of years. This was afterwards

* Lieut.-Colonel William Chearnley, commanding Halifax Volunteer Battalion, late Captain H.M. 8th Regt. (King's Own).

modified, and the shooting season as regards elk is now from the 1st of August to the last day of October.

As, however, in Nova Scotia our best hunting season is comprised in the first two winter months—the snow being light, and so giving the moose every chance of escape, whilst it enables the carcass, when shot, to be taken easily out of the woods—it was deemed expedient to terminate moose hunting with the last day of the year; and so the case now stands.

In a country like Nova Scotia, where a gun is kept in almost every homestead bordering on the forest, or where by the river side the barns are constantly occupied by drying nets, whilst the placid pools are nightly enlivened by burning birch bark, that its fish and wild unprotected game of all descriptions should have rapidly declined in abundance within the memory of comparatively young people, is not much to be wondered at. The whole continent of North America, not only within its settled districts but even in the remotest wilds penetrated by the mercenary hunter, has undergone a great change in the relation between the distribution of its animal life and the other features of its physical geography within the last quarter of a century. The Anglo-Saxon transplanted has revelled in his inherent love of sport, which frequently turns into a lust of slaughter, until the game of North America has in many cases altogether disappeared before the cruel tide of wanton destruction which has overtaken it. This decrease is yearly accelerated by increasing demand for the spoils of the chase or the products of the waters, the inevitable result being extinction of species.

And now our neighbours of the Northern States, who have completely lost their salmon long since, and can

scarcely boast of any game in their wild lands east of the
prairies, are calling loudly for restocking their rivers artificially in the one case, and, in the other, have enacted
stringent laws to preserve the scanty remnant of their
deer and grouse.

However inexpedient or impracticable it may have
been in the earlier history of the country to stem the
torrent of wasteful destruction which has swept over this
continent, there is no doubt that here, as in every other
part of the world, increasing civilisation would at length
call for protection of game. Game, both as a luxury and
as a means of recreation, is a necessary adjunct to the
establishment of a country tenanted by Anglo-Saxons.
Witness the anxiety with which our antipodal colonists
are watching their attempts to introduce deer, game
birds, and salmon into Australia, Tasmania, and New
Zealand ; and the eagerness with which the young sportsmen of the great cities of the States disperse themselves
throughout the land in search of recreation from the
prairies to the rivers of Labrador. This demand will
eventually in this country ensure protection. Nature's
great stock-farm, though nearly worn out by the recklessness of the first-comers, will yet repay careful
husbandry ; and where so large a portion, of British
North America especially, is destined for ever to remain
in a state of nature, it is the duty of the people to prevent it from becoming an unprofitable, repulsive wilderness ; and how much better to take vigorous measures to
preserve the remnant of the former stock than at length
be compelled to have recourse to the tedious process of
acclimatisation or of artificial propagation.

It is perhaps within the last fifteen years that the most

startling decrease has taken place, both in the salmon
fisheries and game of British North America, and has
engaged the attention of the various colonial govern-
ments. Laws to protect the wild animals at certain times
called close seasons, and stringent regulations to ensure
fair play to the salmon, have been passed throughout our
Atlantic colonies within this period. As regards legislation, nothing seems neglected, and still the game and fish
are decreasing as heretofore. We, at least in these provinces, never hear of cases of game-law breakers in the
police reports, yet, granted that the law is sufficient to
protect, it must be through its violation that the evil is
not checked. The constant cause of this we all know to
be the defectiveness of administration, and in this part of
the world, where there is no such thing as poaching upon
private property, which in England would lead to prosecution through the injured rights of an individual, we
do not wonder at it. In the old country the game is
private property, to protect which the game-laws are
framed ; whilst in the protection of the salmon there are
mixed interests—the great value of the fisheries to the
country, the netting interests at the mouths, and those
of the proprietors of the inland fisheries on the rivers
passing through their estates or rented. Consequently
any violation of either game or fishery law is there
directly injurious to a proprietor, and so meets with quick
justice.

In Nova Scotia, New Brunswick, or Canada, on the
other hand, the wild denizens of the forests, commonly
called game, are public property, or rather the property
of the country. No private rights are infringed by moose
hunting or partridge shooting in any part of the country

at any season, whilst, **in the** absence **of proprietors of** inland fisheries, the **netting** interests become **so over-** whelming that it is not surprising that the **law should be** boldly challenged to prevent the salmon being **speared** and netted on their beds to the very end of the spawning season. It is **to** assist in carrying out the protection afforded by law that societies have sprung up in various parts of British America within the above-mentioned period of time—public associations of **all members** of the **community who are anxious** to arrest the decline of fish and game, **and** willing to pay a small annual **subscription** to the funds of the society, binding themselves **to bring** to its notice for prosecution all cases of infringement of the law coming under their cognisance. The **Canadian** fish and game clubs radiating through the country **from** the parent society at Quebec, **where the** system **com-** menced in 1857, have met with marked success, from **the** spirit with which they have been **conducted ; and now** the tributaries **of the Saint Lawrence in the vicinity of** Quebec again afford excellent sport, and promise fairly to return to their former importance as salmon rivers, where for years before this fish had all but become **extinct.**

The Nova Scotian Association before alluded to has likewise similarly striven, and succeeded in enlisting a large number **of** sympathising contributors to its support, not only from the sporting community but amongst some **of** the **mill-owners themselves. To the** willingness of this **class in** many instances to **open** up the rivers, which their mills and mill-dams at present obstruct, to the **passage of** salmon and gaspereaux, I gladly bear witness. The one uncompromising form of fish-ladder, however, which it was **first** attempted by government to force upon them,

x

regardless of local peculiarities of their "water privileges," proved a nauseating dose, and no wonder. Every mill-dam has some peculiar features as regards the bed of the river. In many cases a few natural steps by the rocky sides of a fall will answer all the purposes; in others a single slanting board opposing the fall over a small dam will give all the water necessary to the ascent of fish. At all events, local circumstances are so various that no one pattern of fish-ladder can be authorised for any number of streams. A government officer—a thorough engineer, and perfectly acquainted with the habits and necessities of salmon and other migratory fish, is what is wanted in Nova Scotia (in Canada the want is supplied), and to conclude in my own words in framing a report on this subject two years since, "Your committee beg to state their conviction that, although the society has not been idle, *but little can be effected in carrying out a proper supervision of the inland fisheries, unless an independent and salaried officer be appointed* by the Provincial Government.

"The difficulties of prosecution, owing to the local partialities of both witnesses and magistrates, would then be removed, whilst the judgment and advice of such an executive, with regard to the placing of efficient fish-ladders, under the various peculiarities of river banks and mill-dams, would be considered decisive in overcoming all obstructions."

# CHAPTER XII.

THE parting of the icy chains of winter, and the return of spring, is the most acceptable change in the seasons of the year in North America. The latter part of the winter is most tedious, and the strong links with which it binds the face of nature are snapped but slowly—so slowly that one is apt to become very impatient—heartily sick of the sight of snow and the tinkling sleigh-bells. The 17th March, as a general rule, is about the time of the first appreciable change. Warm rains and reeking fogs cause the snow to disappear rapidly ; here and there the roads exhibit patches of bare ground with deep mud, and the settler's sled has to seek the strips of snow which still fringe the edge of the road, or often altogether to turn into the woods. Now may be seen the wild goose winging his way in long wedge-shaped flights to his distant breeding-grounds in Hudson's Bay, alighting on the way in the various large harbours which, from the extent of the flats left uncovered by the receding tide, offer a secure rest and an abundant supply of marine grasses. I know of no more pleasing sight at this season than the passage of a phalanx of wild geese : majestically cleaving the air with slow, measured strokes, they press onwards towards their distant resorts, hundreds of feet above you, now and

x 2

again uttering their wild note of apparent encouragement
—" honk ! hawnk !"—a sure sign of the winter breaking
up for good.

"Hawnk ! honk ! and for'ard to the Nor'ard, is the trumpet-tone,
What goose can lag, or feather flag, or break the goodly cone ?
Hawnk ! onward to the cool blue lakes where lie our safe love-bowers ;
No stop, no drop of ocean brine, near stool or hassock hoary,
Our travelling watchword is "Our mates, our goslings, and our glory ! "
Symsonia and Labrador for us are crown'd with flowers,
And not a breast on wave shall rest until that heaven is ours.
　　　　　　　　Hawnk ! hawnk ! E-e hawnk !
　　　　　　　　　　　　FRANK FORESTER.

Then come a few warm, sunny days, and the expression of Nature's features appears quite altered, and our
welcome guests, the early migratory birds, arrive from
the more genial southern climes, filling the long-silent
woods with animation and melody. And, first, the well-
known robin, or rather red-breasted thrush (Turdus
migratorius), affects warm, sunny banks in open woods,
whence he springs with a sudden note of alarm as the
murderous boy, bent on developing his sporting propensities, creeps with levelled gun over the hill's brow,
and seeks to "fill his gaping tuneful bill with blood."
Then is heard the whistle of the rusty grackle (Q. ferrugineus), and the cheerful notes of the song sparrow
(F. melodia), and before the end of March the woodcock
(M. Americana) may be seen, in the evening, running
through the swamps and warm springs by the road-side,
every now and then stopping to bore for worms, and from
its comparative tameness at this season, becoming an easy
prey to the poacher or our friend (?) the robin-shooter.
But, alas ! all these pleasant appearances of spring are
but transient charms ; back comes the frost, and the
wintry blast, and the snow-storm ; the gentle advances

of spring are rudely repelled, and the rills from the melting snow again arrested, and—

"What will the robin do then, poor thing?"

However, April ushers in some fine days, and the increasing power of the sun tells upon the masses of snow in the fir-woods and the rotting ice in the lakes; and at last comes a fierce storm of wind and rain, with a warm, oppressive atmosphere, as if the genial breath of spring, tired of attempting to coax away the departing chills of winter, had now determined to exert all its force, and with hot gales and heavy rains ease the surface of the country and lakes of their icy garments.   Now a change is indeed evident; the snow, with the exception of a patch or two in hollows, has all disappeared from the face of the earth, and the great monotonous fir-woods themselves lose their dark wintry aspect and blackness, assuming a lively green tint, and emitting, as one wanders through their sunny glades, faint odours of that delicious aroma which pervades the atmosphere in the heat of midsummer. How great a relief this to the resident in these climes, subject so long to the stern rule of winter !   What heart does not feel forgotten memories recalled, when, wandering along sunny banks in the fir-woods, the first blossom of the fragrant May-flower is seen and culled ?   " We bloom amid the snow," is the motto of our province ; and the May-flower (Epigæa repens) is to us what the violet, sought in hedge-rows, is to our friends at home—entailing the same close search for its retiring blossoms, and evoking the same feelings of gladness and hope.   And we cling to these balmy spring days all the more closely as we dread the chill easterly wind, and the dark sea-fog

which may cover us with its gloom on the morrow ; for
we live on the shores of the "mournful and misty Atlantic," and many a spring day must yet be darkened by fog
and chilled by gales from the floating ice-fields drifting
down the coast, before the tardy green leaves of the hard-
woods fully appear.

About the 20th of May the presence of spring is perceptible in the sprouting of little leaves on almost all the
smaller deciduous shrubs, simultaneously with the light
green sprays of the larch. From this time vegetation
progresses with extraordinary rapidity ; a delightful
change in the atmosphere almost invariably occurs ; the
cold easterly winds cease ; balmy airs from the westward
succeed, and assist in developing the tender buds and
blossoms, and in a few days the face of the country,
lately so bare and dreary, glows with warmth and beauty.
All nature rejoices in this pleasant season ; the songs of
the hermit-thrush (T. solitarius), robin, and of a host of
warblers, the cheerful piping of the frogs throughout the
warm night, and the soft west wind, which borrows an
indescribable fragrance from the blossoms of innumerable
shrubs and plants now flowering in the woods and on the
barrens, afford charms which more than repay for the
gloom of the long and trying winter.

The red blossoming maple (Acer rubrum) now exhibits
crimson flower-clusters topping each spray, almost vieing
in colour with the glories of its autumnal foliage : the
Indian pear (Amelanchier) and wild cherry (C. Pennsylvanica), growing in great abundance throughout the
country, seem overburdened with their masses of delicate
white blossoms, and impart a fragrance to the air, in
which are mingled a thousand other scents ; for in this

land nearly every shrub and plant bears sweet-smelling
flowers. The blueberry, huckleberry, and other Vacciniæ
now show their pretty heath-like blossoms in promise of
the abundant harvest of delicious fruit which is so acceptable to birds, bears, and bipeds throughout the fall ;
the rich carpet of mosses in the fir-woods is adorned
with a great variety of flowers, the most frequent being
the common pigeon-berry (Cornus Canadensis), whose
bright scarlet clusters of berries look so pretty in the fall
in contrast with the green moss ; and large tracts of
country are tinted by the rich lilac flower-masses of the
wild azalea (Rhodora Canadensis), which blossoms even
before its leaves have sprouted from their buds. Many
of the young leaves of the poplars, willows, and others
are coated with a canescent down, and, as they tremble
in the sunlight, with waving masses of white blossoms,
give a sparkling and silvery appearance to the country,
which is very beautiful and attractive.

This delightful season is, however, of short duration—
imperceptibly losing itself in the increasing heat and
development of summer. A few days change the aspect
of the country marvellously, and the broadly-expanding
leaves of the maples produce a dense canopy of shade
in the forest, hiding the granite boulders and prostrate
rampikes on the barren by covering the bushes with a
drapery of lovely green. Nothing can be brighter than
American spring verdure, nor does it degenerate into
the dull heavy green of English summer foliage—the
leaves maintaining their vernal hue on the same branch,
side by side with the brilliant orange scarlet of their
dying fellows, at that beautiful season the fall of the
leaf.

The advent of summer is characterized by the waning of the flower-masses of the Rhodora, and the succession of the crimson whorls of the Kalmias (K. angustifolia and K. glauca) as prominent species. The Kalmia, locally termed laurel, enlivens large tracts of forest, as does the last-named shrub earlier, and forms a pleasing contrast to the new green shoots of the young coniferæ. The moss in the greenwoods is now covered with the nodding bells of the twin flower (Linnæa borealis) which, in imparting fragrance to the atmosphere, takes the place of two pretty little spring flowers, the star-shaped Tri-entalis, and the (locally so called) lily of the valley (Smilacina bifolia). The swamp vegetation, headed by the Indian cup (Sarracenia purpurea) and blue flag (Iris versicolor), flowers abundantly in ponds and moist hollows in the woods, the dark-red drooping petals of the former prettily contrasting with the blue of the iris. The large, yellow-throated frog (Rana fontinalis) here rules the world of reptile life ; his solemn ejaculation—" glum ! glumpk ! " is heard in every direction and at regular intervals, mingled with the long trilling love-note of Bufo Americanus—the common toad—and the sharp and ceaseless cries of the little Hylodes (H. Pickeringii). The deciduous foliage attains its full development ; ferns are strong and their spores beginning to ripen. The whip-poor-will (Caprimulgus vociferus), and the night hawk (C. Virginianus) — leading representatives of summer birds—arrive ; and the plaintive song of the former— " Wȳp-ŏ-ĭl "—repeated in fast succession and at frequent intervals, is now heard in the maple-bush copses by lake or river-side throughout the night, with the shrill scream of the night hawk, and the strange booming sound which is produced by the latter bird in rushing perpendicularly downwards on its prey.

The fir forest at this season becomes intensely heated, and emits a strong aromatic odour. Where a tree has fallen its withering branches fill the air for some distance around with a most delightfully fragrant scent of strawberries. To the sojourner or traveller in the woods, the shelter and cool air under deciduous trees, in groves of maple or birches, is an appreciable relief.

Lastly comes the flora of autumn, with its asters and golden-rods; and these, choosing open barrens and fields as their residence, leave the woodlands almost without a flower.

Towards the end of August some of the features of the fall are developed. Maple leaves turn colour in unhealthy situations — as where the trees have been subjected to inundation during the summer, and have consequently lost the vigour necessary to resist the frosty air of the nights.

The plovers arrive, and the wild pigeon is found in large flocks on the ground feeding on the ripe pigeon-berries. The barrens now afford astonishing supplies of berries of many sorts of Ericaceæ, and an unpremeditated meeting not unfrequently occurs between the bear and the biped, both intent on culling a portion of the luscious harvest.

In September the full brightness of the fall colour is brought out on deciduous foliage ; fast fading, however, towards the close of the month, and altogether disappearing by the end of October—the last lingering phases of autumnal glory being the rich golden-yellow hue assumed

by the larch, and the dark Indian-red of the leaves of
the oak and whortleberry.

Then comes the Indian summer—a season of dreamy
delight, when a warm, hazy atmosphere mellows the
rich brown foreground and distant blue hills of the
woodland picture, and all nature seems to bask in a calm
serenity. The hermit thrush now warbles forth his fare-
well from the spruce groves; the robins congregate on
the barrens, busily picking the remains of the berry-har-
vest ere their departure for the south; and the squirrels
and wood-marmots hasten into their granaries their
winter supplies of acorns and beech-mast.

November is not far advanced before cold northerly
winds and black frosts remove all traces of the beautiful
fall. The bear and the marmot hybernate; the moose
select their winter yards; the last detachments of
lingering robins depart, and the retreating columns of
wild geese are soon followed by the fierce driving storm,
which buries the hard-frozen ground under the first snows
of the long American winter. Varying in intensity of cold
and general changeableness of climate, according to distance from the sea and the influence of the gulf stream,
the winter drags on with but little to mark the monotony
of its course. On the sea-board of the maritime provinces snow and rain constantly succeed each other, and
fields and clearings are often buried and as often bared;
but back in the woods even the long January thaw,
which is of regular occurrence in these regions, makes
but little impression on the steadily accumulating snow.

The summer birds have all left, and the frogs are deeply
buried beneath the mud at the bottom of ponds. On
the smooth white surface, which is spread over his former

hiding-places in the forest, the little American hare (**Lepus** Americanus) has assumed his winter coat, assimilated in colour to the face of nature, and affording somewhat of protection from the numerous enemies which hunt him on the snow so unrelentingly—the two lynxes, the foxes, the great fisher-marten, and the tree-marten, and lastly, and most perseveringly of all, the little ermine weasel. But he has feathered enemies besides—the horned and snowy owls, as well as one or two of the larger hawks. Considering the abundance in which the former bird occurs in the forest, and the lengthy list of his foes, it appears marvellous 'that the little rabbit, as he is locally called, is able, with his family increasing only in the summer months, not merely to exist as a species, but to contribute so largely as he does to the winter food of the human population.

Undeniably gloomy as is the general character of the American winter, apart from the vigorous bustle of civilization, there are days when even the forest affords sensations of pleasure to the observer of nature. What can be more beautiful than early morning, after a long-continued snow-storm, when the sun rises in a sky of purest blue, speckled, perhaps, with light fleecy cirrhi, and looking almost as the sky of a summer day? Every branch and bough is covered with radiant crystals of the new snow, and the air holds a delicious freshness.

Rising from his soft bed of silver-fir boughs before the embers of the great logs which have warmed the camp throughout the night, the hunter steps forth into the bright morning with feelings of the highest exhilaration. Not a branch stirs, save where the busy little

titmice or gold-crests, sporting amongst the foliage, dis-
lodge a shower of sparkling crystals—

> "Myriads of gems that in the waving gleam
> Gay-twinkle as they scatter,"

when the disencumbered bough flies back to its original
position.  The faintest sound finds an echo amongst the
stems of the forest trees; the chopping of an axe is
borne through the still rarified air for many a mile.
Bird-life is in full activity.  The Corvidæ, the raven,
crow, blue-jay, and moose-bird are hunting round for
their morning meal of carrion.  The grosbeaks and
crossbills, busily engaged on the fir-cones, frequently
rest to deliver their low but melodious song from the
topmost sprays of the pines.  The taps of the woodpeckers resound from the hard surface of barked trees,
and the sharp, wrathful chirrup of the common red
squirrel (Sciurus Hudsonius) is heard in every direction.
The very flight of birds may be heard at a considerable
distance, as may also the scratching of a squirrel against
the bark as he races up a trunk some two hundred yards
away, or the shuffling of the porcupine in the top
branches of a hemlock, his favourite retreat on a fine
winter's day.

Short-lived, however, are such pleasant breaks in the
winter weather.  The short day, commencing so brilliantly, more frequently closes with a prevailing leaden
gloom portending more snow, or, if near the sea-coast, a
fierce southerly gale and rain.

In a damp atmosphere, or with gentle rain, the stratum
of air nearest the ground being of a temperature below
freezing point, every spray in the forest becomes coated

with ice.  Thus originates the beautiful phenomenon called a silver thaw.  Seen in sunlight, when the mists have dispersed, the forest presents a wonderful and magic appearance under such circumstances.  The network of the smallest bushes is brought out to prominent notice by the sparkling casing of ice, and the surface of the snow gleams like a mirror.  Such a scene as I once beheld it at night by the light of a full moon was most impressively beautiful, and, I would almost say, unreal.

Should a wind arise before the ice has melted, much mischief is caused amongst the heavily-laden branches, which make the wood resound with their snappings.

The close of the winter is the most disagreeable season of the year, and the discoloured snow, assuming a round granular shape, resists the sun with wonderful tenacity. Night frosts consolidate the surface, so that small animals, and man himself, are carried on the snow, and leave no track.  The bulky moose sinks through ; flying from his pursuers with laborious and painful strides, and leaving a trail of blood along his tracks from the sharp edge of the incrustation cutting his legs, he soon succumbs an easy prey to the wanton poacher.  The settlers' sleds and ox-teams are now in full activity, drawing out the logs felled during the winter through the woods and over the lakes to the river-side ; and the farmers hasten their remaining stock of produce to the market and purchase their seeds, striving to return before the final breaking up of the snow leaves the roadway an impassable sea of mud.

## NOTES ON PERIODIC PHENOMENA.

THE following observations of periodic phenomena were made in Halifax, Nova Scotia, an excellent and central station for observing the natural features of the seasons in the lower provinces, being on the line of migration of water birds as well as of such land birds as pass over farther to the north or eastward, to Newfoundland or Labrador. Some allowance must be made with regard to locality in different parts of the provinces —as, for instance, in the case of Montreal, where the advent of winter and of spring phenomena is rather earlier than at Halifax, or of Quebec, where the latter season is more backward, and a lower degree of mean winter temperature prevails — yet, excepting that a larger number of species is comprised in the fauna and flora of the Canadas, and, on the other hand, in Newfoundland, a great reduction occurs in the representation of both kingdoms with an entire absence of the class Reptilia, it may be said that the phenomena of the seasons in Nova Scotia afford a fair index to such occurrences throughout the British provinces of North America bordering on the Atlantic.*

* Mean temperature and atmospheric pressure for four years, from 1863 to 1866 inclusive :—

|         | Thermometer. | Barometer. |
|---------|--------------|------------|
| Winter      | 24°  | 29·66° |
| Spring.     | 39°  | 29·62° |
| Summer      | 61°  | 29·68° |
| Autumn      | 48°  | 29·67° |
| Mean        | 43°  | 29·66° |

*From Proceedings of N.S. Institute of Natural Science.*

## NOTES OF THE YEAR 186 .

*January* 5. Snow falls at night to depth of four inches, quite level, with a cold N.E. wind.

6. First good sleighing of the year in Halifax; thermometer ranges about 12° Fahr. throughout the day.

7. Clear and cold ; thermometer, −5°. A dense pall of vapour on the harbour, obscuring all but the tops of vessels, and coating the sides and rigging with ice. Large numbers of smelts and frost-fish (Morrhua pruinosa) brought to market ; the former taken with bait through holes cut in the ice in upper harbours or large lakes freely communicating with the sea ; the latter by bag-nets in rivers at the head of the tide, where they are now engaged in spawning. They are only taken at night, returning at daybreak to deep water. Trout, taken through the ice, and brought to market, dark and flabby, and quite worthless.

10. The north-west arm of the sea in rear of the city of Halifax frozen from head to the Chain Battery, two miles, and covered with light snow. Sleighing on roads excellent.

10—21. Mild, close weather, with southerly winds and occasional heavy rains ; snow nearly disappears, even in the woods to the eastward. This is an instance of the usual January thaw.

22. Ice on the lake twelve inches thick. Many moose killed during the thaw brought to market ; the bulls still retain their horns. Eels taken in harbours by spearing through holes in the ice on muddy bottoms, where they lie in a state of torpidity.

26. Four inches of snow fall during day.

27. Calm, clear weather ; excellent sleighing.

28—31. Very variable ; soft and mild, with rain from southward, changing to hard frost with N.W. wind ; three inches of snow from N.E. on 31st.

*February* 1. Thermometer, 0°, in the morning.

2—7. Very oppressive, unhealthy weather : dense fogs and occasional rains ; snow disappearing, except in the woods. The sap is commencing to flow in deciduous trees, owing to the mildness of the weather ; buds appear on maples and currant bushes.

8. Distant thunder heard.

10—13. Light frosts recommence. Ground bare of snow on roads ; good skating on lakes and arms of the sea, all the snow having been melted off the surface.

14. Wind shifts to N., with gale ; mercury falls at night to 0°.

18. Cold weather continues ; mercury, — 2°, at eight A.M. Good sleighing, considerable snow having fallen since the change.

22—24. A thaw ; rain, with thick sea fogs ; roads and streets deep with mud.

26—27. A little snow falls, succeeded by mild weather.

*March* 2. A heavy snow-storm from N.E. ; five inches fall ; the sleighing good. Smelts, caught through the ice, still brought to market, but becoming more scarce. The song sparrow (F. melodia), a few of which stay all winter, singing in gardens.

4. Snow disappearing under the sun.

5—10. Very variable ; much rain.

11. First salmon brought to market from the sea at Margaret's Bay. Several flocks of wild geese pass over to the eastward. A few robins (Turdus migratorius) seen. It is uncertain whether these are new comers, as many have remained all winter around the Halifax peninsula.

14. The fine, warm weather of past few days dispelled by a northerly snow-storm, with 14° of frost at night. Western salmon become more plentiful in the market. The fur of the hare assuming its summer colour, showing patches of light brown interspersed with the white.

19. Mild and clear, after rains. Ice on the lakes becomes very rotten, and unsafe for travelling. The rusty grakle (Quiscalus ferrugineus), locally termed blackbird, arrives. Immense quantities of sea-fish, comprising cod, haddock, and halibut, brought to market. Woodcock arrives. Robins frequently seen in open spots in the woods near the sea. Snowbird (Fringilla nivalis) arrives. A few have remained all winter.

23, 24. Easterly wind, with snow. Sleighs out again in the streets.

26. Fine and mild.

27. Very fine and pleasant. The song sparrow (F. melodia) is heard frequently. Grass on sloping banks becoming green. Robins find worms at the surface. Maple-trees (Acer saccharinum) tapped by sugar makers.

30—31. Cold rains, with N.E. wind. Many moose killed by settlers in woods near Annapolis, where the snow still continues deep.

## REMARKS ON THE ABOVE QUARTER.

The weather during the foregoing winter months was exceedingly unsettled. The mean temperatures of January, February, and March were 23°, 26°, and 28°, respectively; the minimum of cold in January, −5°, being unusually small. There are few instances of the two coldest months, January and February, passing over without −10° to −15° being registered. Even in the beginning of March, in some winters, the climate is still subject to the occurrence of one of those sudden passages of extreme cold, with strong N. and N.W. winds, which sweep uniformly over the continent from high latitudes, and form the most dreaded feature of the North American winter. On these occasions, and in severe visitations, the mercury will fall to −15°, and sometimes, though very rarely, to −20°, at Halifax, Nova Scotia, the minimum contemporary cold indicated at Sydney, (Cape Breton), Frederictown (New Brunswick), Bangor (Maine), and Kingston (Upper Canada), being −30° to −40°. In the beginning of March, 1863, a heavy snowstorm was followed by severe cold, the thermometer registering −6° at Halifax, and −30° at Sydney, Cape Breton. A similar late visitation of cold weather following a deep fall of snow occurred in March, 1859, when the mercury fell to −3° and −5° during the nights of the first three days of the month. The heaviest falls of snow occur in February and early in March, when sometimes nearly three feet of fresh snow is deposited, accumulating by road sides in immense drifts which almost hide small dwellings. On the 8th February, 1866, Halifax harbour was entirely frozen over, and bore large numbers of persons securely. The thermometer indicated only −7° when this occurred, but the cold was of some days' continuance, and favoured by a perfect calm. This harbour rarely freezes to impede navigation, as do those further to the eastward.

The roseate hue cast over the snow-covered surface of the country by the sun's rays on a fine March afternoon in the fine weather succeeding a storm imparts a beautiful effect to the wintry landscape ; in a steady winter this is the most busy time for sleds, snow-shoes, and the youthful sports of " trabogining " and coasting down the ice-clad hillocks and drifts of snow by the roadside.

As has been before observed, St. Patrick's Day (March 17) is looked upon generally as indicating the breaking-up of the winter at Halifax, Nova Scotia, when the wild geese pass over in large flights ; southerly weather, with soft rains and fogs, fast dissolving the snow, and rotting the ice on the lakes, which lingers a few days longer in dark, discoloured, and honeycombed patches, and finally sinks below the surface.

*April* 1. Cold N.E. wind, with rain ; large fields of ice drifting past the entrance of the harbour.

2—10. Fine, but with cold easterly winds. Common crow (C. Americanus) mated and building in tall spruces. Also ravens (C. corax) in tops of lofty pines and rocky precipices. Fox-coloured sparrow (F. iliaca) arrives. Trout take the fly in open water found in runs between lakes.

15. Wind veers to the westward after rain, with fine spring weather. Mayflowers (Epigæa repens) in flower abundantly ; occasional blossoms have been picked

during the last fortnight. The small marsh frog (Hylodes) is heard. Robins and song-sparrow sing frequently. Camberwell beauty (Vanessa antiopa) about. Ice disappeared from lakes.

20. Fine weather succeeded by cold N.E. wind and heavy snowstorm.

21. A few sleighs out in the streets in the morning ; snow disappears at noon, leaving a sea of mud on the roads.

22—30. Fine clear weather ; dust in the streets towards close of month. White-bellied martin (H. bicolæ) arrives on 23rd ; the gold-winged woodpecker (Picus auratus) on same date. Wood frog (R. sylvatica) and common spring frog (R. fontinalis) are heard to croak ; both are spawning. Trout take the artificial fly readily in lakes. Smelts ascend brooks to spawn, and are taken in great numbers by scoop nets. Dandelions picked in fields and sold as a vegetable.

*May* 1—3. Chilly, with rain ; all vegetation backward, owing to cold easterly weather till now prevailing. Wild gooseberry in leaf. Scarlet buds developing on maple. The Hylodes chirp in the evenings.

4. Bright and warm, with westerly wind. The kingfisher (Alcedo alcyon) arrives ; also the white-throated sparrow (F. Pennsylvanica), commonly called in Nova Scotia the "poor Kennedy bird." The hermit thrush (T. solitarius) is heard. The trilling note of the common toad is heard in the evening swelling the chorus of the frogs.

7—11. Cold easterly weather ; much ice off the coast. Green snake (Coluber vernalis) observed sunning on bank. Ferns (Lastreæ) sprouting. Blue wood-violet flowers, also white variety.

12. Clears up from westward for fine weather. Frogs and toads very noisy in the evening. Robins, white-throated sparrow, and hermit thrush sing till 8 P.M. The toad trills all day. May and stone flies (Ephemeræ and Phryganeæ) issue from the water, and are greedily devoured by trout. Black flies (Simulium molestum) make their appearance. The light green blossoms of the willow contrast prettily with the red bloom on maples (A. rubrum). Grass four or five inches high. Larches showing light green leaves and crimson blossoms. Waterlilies commencing to grow upwards from the bottom of ponds.

13—15. Fine weather continues. Gaspereaux (Alosa tyrannus) ascending stream to spawn in lakes. Ruffed and Canada grouse (Tetrao umbellus and T. Canadensis) incubating. Frog spawn hatching.

18. Fine weather continues. Trout gorged with Ephemeræ and refuse bait. Gold thread (Coptis trifolia) flowering. Ferns unfolding. Fir cones of A. picea of a delicate sea-green colour.

20. Atmosphere hazy from fires in the forest. Herons (Ardea Herodias) arriving in flights. Young leaves tipping the blossoms of the red-flowering maple. Poplar (P. tremuloides) in leaf.

21. The whip-poor-will (C. vociferus) is heard in copses on the banks of the north-west arm of the harbour ; the night hawk (C. Virginianus) on same evening. Rain at night.

22. Shad (Alosa sapidissima) ascends rivers to spawn, and will sometimes take the artificial fly. The moose-bush (Viburnum lantanoides) in flower ; also Indian

pear (Amelanchier) ; the young leaves of the latter of
a rich bronze tint. Light green leaves of birches unfolding. Pigeon berry (Cornus Canadensis) in flower ;
also wild Azalea (Rhodora Canadensis).

23—27. Variable weather, with rains. Blueberry
and whortleberry (Vacciniæ) in flower on open barrens.
Smilacina bifolia and S. borealis in flower in fir woods,
with Star of Bethlehem (Trientalis Americana). Profuse
blossoms on Indian pear and wild cherry (Cerasus Pennsylvanica).

28—31. Occasional showers, with thunder on the
31st. Leaves and seed-keys developed on maples. The
white death flower (Trillium pictum) in bloom. The
flower of the Rhodora now imparts a roseate hue to open
spots in the woods and by the roadside, contrasting most
pleasingly with the light green of birch and larch leaves
and young fern fronds.


*June* 1. Warm, pleasant weather. Blossoms of service
tree and wild cherry fading. Royal fern (Osmunda regalis)
in flower ; also O. cinnamomea and O. interrupta. Yellow-
throated frog assumes bright colour, and croaks all day.
Young hares (first brood) about. Labrador tea (Ledum
latifolium) and lady's slipper (Cypripedium) in flower.

2—6. Fine weather continues ; high winds from
westward. Leaves of trees nearly developed.

7. A splendid aurora at night. A corona formed a
little south of the zenith, to which streamers ascend
from all points of the compass, though their bases did
not approach the horizon to the southward. Hylodes,
frogs, and toads very noisy at nights. Young robins
leaving the nest.

11. Fine weather, but cold **for time of** year. The Bob o' Lincoln (Emberiza oryzivora) in full **song in** pasture fields.

15. Weather has become **very fine and warm ;** this day the thermometer indicates 87° in shade. Linnea borealis, the twin flower, out, and imparts much fragrance to the atmosphere under green woods. Pollack (Merlangus) arrive in bays and harbours, and take artificial fly on the surface greedily. Kalmia angustifolia **coming into bloom ; the** Rhodora **fading** off.

**16—20.** Warm sultry weather, with thunder showers on 20th. **Indian cup (Sarracenia purpurea) flowers with iris, cranberry, and sundew in swamps. Abundance of** salmon exposed for sale in the markets.

22. Fireflies (Lampyris corusca) are seen.

23—30. Variable weather : frequent incursions of **fog from the sea,** extending **many miles** inland. **Wild strawberries ripen and are brought to market in great** abundance. Withrod in flower.

*July* 5. Heavy rain succeeds fogs. **The** wood-sorrel **(Oxalis acetosella)** in flower. Wild **roses (R.** parviflora) **out.**

6—10. Very fine and warm ; atmosphere hazy, with strong smell **of** burning woods. **Grilse** numerous in the rivers. Haymaking commences.

12. Fireflies **very numerous** in evenings. **Water-**lilies, white and yellow, flowering ; also arrowhead (Sagittaria). Robins sitting **on** eggs of **second brood.** Balsam poplars (balsamifera) shedding their cotton.

13—21. Very fine and **dry.** Vegetation suffering **from** drought ; grass withering. Humming-birds numerous. Summer flowers going off. Orange lily (L. Canadense) flowering in intervale meadows, and fire-weed (Epilobium) in burnt woods.

24. Still fine, with high winds. Extensive fires in the woods fill the air with smoke and obscure the sun. Grasshoppers very numerous. Wild currants ripen. Young woodcock, partridge, and flappers of duck well grown. Wild cherries ripening; also blueberries (Vaccinium) on the barrens, with wild raspberries (Rubus idæus). Cargoes of sea-birds' eggs brought to market from the Gulf and sold for food. Garden cherries ripe and much visited by waxwings (Ampelis Americana).

25—31. Uninterruptedly fine weather. Albicore (Thynnus vulgaris) strike the N.W. arm, feeding on herring. House-flies become troublesome. The cicada sings continually in the woods.

*August* 1. Fine weather continues. Berries of Cornus Canadensis ripe and very plentiful; do. of blueberries and Indian pear. Great quantities of wild raspberries brought to market.

2—10. Weather changes to wet, commencing with thunder. The rivers, hitherto almost dry, swell, and salmon, delayed by drought, ascend.

11—17. Fine weather, with occasional showers. Passenger pigeons (Ectopistes migratorius) seen on barrens feeding on berries; these birds are more numerous westward from the coast. Cariboo (Cervus tarandus) commence to rut.

18. Golden plover (Charadrius marmoratus) arrives. Nights become cooler, and houseflies sluggish.

19—31. Fine weather. Tree frog (Hyla squirrella) pipes. Moose have their horns developed, and rub off deciduous skin. Trout recover from their summer lassitude, and again take the fly. Fungi very numerous in damp woods, with common mushroom (Agaricus campestris) on grass plots. Golden rods (Solidago), Michaelmas daisies, and spicries flowering in fields and barrens ; also the ground-nut (Apios tuberosa) in damp localities by margins of lakes and brooks. Blackberries (Rubus hispidus) ripen, and are brought to market. Maples and birches in damp spots are tinged with fall colours.

### REMARKS ON THE FOREGOING MONTHS.

The spring, comprising the months of April and May and part of June, was generally fine, though the long-continued easterly winds, coming over the ice-fields off the coast, greatly retarded vegetation. This feature was followed by a most unusual drought which prevailed through the summer over the whole continent. The prairies presented the appearance of an arid desert, and the large game suffered severely. On the Atlantic coast rivers and lakes were nearly dried up, and multitudes of eels and other fish were left dead on the banks. A large proportion of the migratory fish spawning in summer were prevented from reaching their grounds.

The mean temperature of April was 36°; of May 48°; of June 57°; of July 62° ; and of August 64°.

The summer in Canada, the Lower Provinces, and New England is characterised by the remarkable energy of growth of all vegetation and rapidity of maturing. Garden operations, begun late in May, will produce in a

few weeks the same results as if the seed had been sown
in England a month earlier; and the same rule applies
to general agriculture. The suitableness of the climate
to the growth of maize, tobacco, and the gourd family
attests its value in an agricultural light. The Jerusalem
artichoke flowers, and tomatoes and peppers produce
abundantly; and in Nova Scotia the vine succeeds so
well, that black Hamburg grapes will ripen in the
open air.

*September* 1—10. Fine autumnal weather. Apples
and fall fruits fast ripening. Berries of mountain ash
(Pyrus Americana) reddening. Rutting season of Cervus
Alces commences. Woodcock and snipe, partridges
(Tetrao), and hares brought to market, the latter being
principally snared. The whip-poor-will and night-hawk
leave. Gold-winged woodpeckers congregate before departure.

11—13. Heavy rain-storm, lasting two days, and
accompanied by thunder-storms.

14. Leaves of maples and other bushes resplendent,
with orange and scarlet appearing in splashes on the
green leaf. Brooks full and low lands inundated.
Porcupines' rutting season commences. Moose travelling
and calling. Scarlet berries of Trillium pictum and
blue of Smilacina borealis are very conspicuous in the
green woods. Large stops of fall mackarel made along
the coast. Apples and plums brought to market
abundantly.

20—30. Dull weather, but generally fine. Osmunda
cinnamomea assuming a beautiful golden-brown hue.
Willows turning yellow; also young poplars and birches.

Wild cherry leaves partially tinted with crimson. Sumach leaves parti-coloured : **green** and vivid orange-scarlet. Leaves of **Vaccineæ becoming tinted, especially those of** the whortleberry. Slight frosts at night. The young of the Gaspereau descend from the lakes (observed on 22nd). Large deciduous forest **trees** assume fall tints. The hill sides **are** now resplendent with colour.

*October* 3. Vegetable **decay in the forest** proceeding rapidly. **Ferns withering.** . The leaves of young **oaks turn dark brick** red.

10. Fall colours fading. **Distant** woods **appear of a** dull **brownish red. Fir cones** ripe. Robins and **hermit** thrush sing at sunrise, **the former** feeding **on berries in** flocks, and preparing **to depart.**

19. Leaves **of most deciduous trees** falling. **Poplars** nearly bare. **The huckleberry is now brilliant scarlet,** and the larch **turning golden.**

31. Migratory **birds depart.**

*November* 1. A beautiful day, **of the same** character as **the last of** October : **a soft west wind and** hazy atmosphere, **quite** Indian summer **weather.** The tints on the landscape are charming ; the distant hills show a light plum bloom ; the sky and **water** light apple green.

5—8. Cold rains. Leaves **all fallen from deciduous trees,** excepting the beech, **to** which many cling **all** winter.

11. Quantities of salmon **in the** market **in prime** condition. They continue **to** be brought **in** till the 20th.

12—31. Variable weather, with rain, sleet, and slight frosts. Salmon spawn.

*December* 1. Snow birds (Emberiza nivalis) arrive. A little snow falls from S.W.

2. Cold and wintry; minimum cold at night being 16° of frost. Large flights of wild geese passing over to the S.W.

5. Skating on ponds.

6—17. Damp, close, unseasonable weather.

19. Clear. Cold weather recommences.

20. The "Barber" appears on the harbour in the morning—a dense steam, due to the great difference of temperatures of air and water. The mercury in afternoon descends to 5° above zero, and during ensuing night to —10°.

21—31. Variable. Good skating on large lakes, and ice making on north-west arm of the sea, near the head.

### REMARKS ON THE FALL AND FIRST WINTER MONTH.

The mean temperature of September was 56°, of October 46°, of November 39°, and of December 27°. There were several days at the close of the fall when the attributes of Indian summer weather appeared; but no lengthened season of this delightful feature in the American autumn occurred in Nova Scotia. Nor is this weather ever prolonged here, as further westward, where (in Canada) a week or ten days is its frequent duration.

The song of birds in the early morning in the fall of the year has been generally ascribed to the resemblance of the temperature to that of spring. Perhaps from a similar cause is the occurrence of autumnal blossoms on spring-flowering plants. In the first week of October I have seen the wild strawberry in blossom in large patches in the woods, and also blossoms on the Kalmia and blueberry.

# APPENDIX.

THE following papers bearing upon the natural history of the Lower Provinces are selected from several read by the Author before the Nova Scotian Institute of Natural Science. The Institution referred to, of which the Author has had the honour of being a Member since its inauguration in 1863 (latterly a Vice-President), has done much in exposition of the resources and physical features of the colonies of Nova Scotia, New Brunswick, Newfoundland, and the Bermudas under the able management of the President, Mr. John M. Jones, F.L.S. The contributions of this careful observer to the natural history of the latter islands, comprised in "The Naturalist in Bermuda,"* and in several more recent notices, have been recognised as most valuable, both as a compendium of the Bermudan indigenous and permanent Fauna and Flora, and also for the observations therein contained on the migration of North American birds, and on meteorological subjects. The Society owes no less of its success to the indefatigable labours of Dr. J. Bernard Gilpin, M.R.C.S., Vice-President, whose papers on the food fishes of Nova Scotia have attracted much attention amongst American naturalists. To this gentleman I am indebted for the scientific descriptions of the game fish found in this work.

* "The Naturalist in Bermuda," Reeves & Turner, 238, Strand, 1859.

## ON THE NOCTURNAL LIFE OF ANIMALS IN THE FOREST.

In one of the most attractive of the works of Humboldt, entitled "Views of Nature,"—a collection of thoughts and personal observations in connection with some of the grandest objects of nature in various parts of the world, visited by the great naturalist—appears an interesting fragment, called "The Nocturnal Life of Animals in the Primeval Forest," suggesting to me comparative remarks on animal life in our own sombre woodlands.

The great writer, in the commencement of this chapter, describes the scene of his observations, coupled with some decisive remarks of his own on the nature of a primeval forest, which I think it well to introduce here. The scene is a boundless forest district which, in the torrid zone of South America, connects the river basins of the Orinoco and the Amazon. "This region," says Humboldt, "deserves, in the strictest sense of the term, to be called a primeval forest—a term that in recent times has been so frequently misapplied. Primeval (or primitive), as applied to a forest, a nation, or a period of time, is a word of rather indefinite signification, and generally but of relative import. If every wild forest, densely covered with trees on which man has never laid his destroying hand, is to be regarded as a primitive forest, then the phenomenon is common to many parts, both of the temperate and the frigid zones. If, however, this character consists in impenetrability, through which it is impossible to clear with the axe between trees measuring from 8 to 12 feet in diameter, a path of any length, primitive forests belong exclusively to tropical regions. This impenetrability is by no means, as is often erroneously supposed in Europe, always occasioned by the interlaced climbing 'lianes,' or creeping plants, for these often constitute but a very small portion of the underwood. The chief obstacles are the shrub-like plants which fill up every space between the trees in a zone where all vegetable forms have a tendency to become arborescent."

Now, our North American fir forests—especially in districts where woods predominate, and the growth of timber is large—have so frequently (generally) been termed "primeval," that we are bound to inquire into the justice of Humboldt's very decisive statement of his own views of the etymology of the word. He claims the title for the South American forest from its impenetrability, and not from, what would seem to me a much more distinguishing feature, the enormous diameter and **age of its** mighty trees. **In regard to the** latter attribute, we should **be** compelled to cede the **appellation as** inapplicable to our own woods, for, from the natural **duration of life** of our timber trees—even the giant "Pinus strobus" rarely **showing** over 1000 annular rings in section—the oldest members of the family of North American coniferæ cannot look back with those **ancient** trees which by some have been placed **coeval** with the builders of the pyramids. Still, **as it is** evident that in the heart of the great fir forests of the North, even in many wooded portions of this Province, **the** hand **of man has never stirred to remove** the existing giants, whilst the bones of their ancestors lie mouldering and moss-covered beneath, I cannot see why they do not merit the term primeval— **not in** Von Humboldt's acceptation, but according to the ordinary recognition of **its meaning, and as** "**original, such as** was at first," says Johnson.

To return to the subject more immediately before us. **Humboldt** next introduces a beautiful and eloquent description of the night life of creatures in the forest by the **Orinoco—the** wild cries of **a host of** apes and monkeys, terrified at the uproar occasioned **by the jaguar** pursuing crowds of peccaries and tapirs, which burst through **the** dense underwood with tremendous crashing; the voices of **com-** munities of birds, aroused by the long-continued conflict beneath, and the general commotion produced amongst the whole animal world, rendering sleep impossible of attainment on stormy nights, on which, especially, these carnivals appeared to be most frequent.

**What a contrast is** presented on entering the dreamy solitudes of the North American pine forest—sombre though it may be, but yet most attractive to the lover of nature—in the perfect harmony of its mysterious gloom and silence with **the** life of its animal tenants, their retiring and lonely habits, **and their** often plaintive and mournful voices! Our perceptions of the harmonies of nature as inseparably connect the **mournful hooting of the great owl with the** glooms of **the black spruce swamp, as we** can the tangled wildness **and tropical vegetation of the South** American forest with the dis- **cordant notes of** its gaudy parrots, and the screams of its monkeys. Although almost all of our mammalia are nocturnal in their habits, **and many** of them beasts of prey, their nightly wanderings and strife with their victims are conducted in the most orderly manner, compared with the scenes we have referred to. Quiet, noiseless stealth is the characteristic feature of all animal life in the forest; mutual distrust of the same species, and ever-present tendency to

z

alarm predominate even in the wildest districts, where the sight of man is unknown, or at least unremembered. At the slightest sound the ruminants and rodents cease feeding, remaining motionless either from fear or instinct; the rabbit or hare thus frequently avoiding detection, whilst the moose can so silently withdraw if suspecting an enemy, that I have on more than one occasion remained hours together on the stillest night, believing the animal to be standing within a few yards in a neighbouring thicket, to which he had advanced in answer to the call, and found at length that he had suspiciously retreated. The great creature had retired, worming his huge bulk and ponderous antlers through the entangled swamp, without detection of the straining ear to which the nibbling of a porcupine at the bark of a tree in the same grove was plainly audible.

The habits and sounds of animals at night are especially familiar to the hunter when calling the moose in the clear moonlight nights of September and October,—the season when this animal, forgetting his usual caution and taciturnity, finds a voice to answer the plaintive call of his mate, and often advances to sure destruction, within a few yards of his concealed foe. As the sun lowers beneath the horizon, and twilight is giving place to the uncertain light of the moon, we listen between the intervals of the Indian's calls (about twenty minutes is generally allowed) to the sounds indicating the movements of nocturnal animals and birds. The squirrels which have raced around us and angrily chirruped defiance from the surrounding trees, all through the twilight, have at last scuttled, one and all, into their holes and fastnesses, and the small birds drop, one by one—the latest being the common robin, who is loth to leave his rich pickings of ripe berries on the upland barren, on which he revels ere taking his annual departure—into the bushes. No longer annoyed by the multitudinous hum and bustle of diurnal animal life, the ear is now relieved, and anxiously criticises the nocturnal sounds which take their place. A little pattering amongst the leaves, and cracking of small sticks (often mistaken by the ambushed hunter when listening for sounds of moose, for the cautious movements of the latter animal), attests the presence abroad of the porcupine, come forth from rocky cavern or hollow tree to revel on berries, nuts, and the rind of young trees. A perfect "monitor" in his coat of protecting armour, he fears neither the talons of the swooping owl, or the spring of the wild cat. Woe to the peace of mind and bodily comfort of his adventurous assailant, for the barbed quills, once entering the **skin, slowly worm their** way through the system, and produce lingering suffering, if **not** death. Even **the moose** is lamed, if **not** for life, for a tedious time, **by accidentally** running over a "*maduis*," **as the** Indian calls him. **The porcupine is** essentially nocturnal in its habits, retiring at sunrise to its den to sleep off its midnight revels, till the "knell of parting day" **is again** tolled through the arches **of the forest** by the solemn war-cry of the horned **owl.**

All the *strigidæ* are now busily engaged in hunting mice, shrews, **and** even hares, through the darkest swamps, and uttering at intervals **their melancholy** hootings. **The call of the cat-owl, horned,** or eagle-**owl of America (B. Virginianus), is** one of the **most impressive sounds of the forest at night.** Coming on **the ear of the sojourner in the woods, most frequently just before daylight appears, and** emanating **from the dark recesses of a grove of hemlock spruce, from whose** massive **stems the sound re-echoes** through the forest, **the voice** of this bird is eminently suggestive of most melancholy **solitude and ghostliness, and** one instinctively awakens the dying embers of the camp **fire. Another** sound uttered by **this bird on its** nocturnal hunt is **positively** startling—a maniacal yell, terminating in mocking laughter, which **it is hard to believe can proceed from** the throat of a bird.

I believe there **is nothing of its own size that this fierce, powerful bird will not venture to attack under cover of the night.** The poor **hare constantly falls a prey;** the farmer **has a long score to settle with it,** frequently losing **his poultry—even geese—through its nocturnal visits. An** Indian recently told me that the **owl had carried off a favourite** little dog that was of great value in hunting **for partridges.** Whilst in confinement, these birds will prey on one **another.**

The great horned owl **is not so exclusively** nocturnal as some **of the other members of the family.** I have frequently started them sitting on a branch exposed **to open daylight, and noticed that they were perfectly** sure of **flight, and readily found their way to another hiding place. Passing the dark wooded banks of the Shubenacadie in a canoe, I have seen great numbers of them sitting in** the overhanging spruces and **hemlocks.**

Sometimes a curious whining sound, uttered at intervals, is noticeable at night in the woods. It is the note of the "*weluwaetch*," **as** the Indian calls it—Tengmalm's **owl.**

The **answer of** the bull moose **to the** Indian's plaintive ringing call on his cone trumpet of birch bark, if the animal is distant, is freely and quickly returned. Resembling, at first, the chopping of an axe far away in the woods, the sound, when nearer, becomes more distinctly guttural. It is well expressed by the monosyllable "Quoh!" uttered by the Indian through the bark cone.

Under the most favouring circumstances of a bright moon, and the death-like stillness of a clear frosty atmosphere, the too sanguine hunter is repeatedly doomed to disappointment ; the animal's appreciation of his own language frequently proves the best master of the craft to be but a sorry imitator. The moose on approaching the ambush, the imagined locality of his hoped-for mate, at length comes to a dead stand, maintaining the same attitude for sometimes a couple of hours without an audible movement ; when the impatient hunter once more ventures to allure him by another call, he is off in silent though hasty retreat.

As an instance, however, of departure from their usual cautious and quiet comportment at night on the part of these animals, I will introduce here one of my "Sporting Adventures," published some years since, and what I heard one cold October night in a very wild and (then) almost unhunted portion of the country.

"Though it was very cold, and my damped limbs were stiffening under me from crouching so long in the same posture, I could not but enjoy the calmness and beauty of the night. The moon was very low, but the columns of a magnificent aurora, shooting up to the zenith, threw a mellow light on the barren, which, covered by mist as by a sheet, appeared like a moonlit lake, and the numerous little clusters of dwarfish spruce as islands. We had not heard a moose answer to our call for nearly an hour, and were preparing to move, when the distant sound of a falling tree struck our ears. It appeared to come from the dim outline of forest which skirted the barren on our left, and at a great distance.

" Down we all drop again in our deeply impressed couches to listen. The sounds indicate that moose are travelling through the woods and close to the edge of the barren. Presently the foremost moose is abreast of our position, and gives vent to a wild and discordant cry. This is the signal for a general uproar amongst the procession of moose, for a whole troop of them are following at long and cautious intervals.

" The timber is crashing loudly opposite to our position, and distant reports show that more are still coming on from the same direction. A chorus of bellowings respond to the plaintive wail of the cow.

The branches are broken more fiercely, and horns are rapidly drawn across stems as if to whet them for the combat. Momentarily I expect to hear the crashing of rival antlers. One by one the bulls pass our position, and I long to get up and dash into the dark line of forest, and with a chance shot scatter the procession ; but to do so would entail wanton disturbance of the country ; so we patiently wait till the last moose has passed.

" Never before had I heard the calmness of the night in the Nova Scotia forest so disturbed ; they had passed as a storm ; and now the barren and the surrounding country were once more enveloped in the calm repose of an autumnal night, unbroken, save by the chirrup of the snake in the swamp."

Of all premonitors of the approach of a storm, the night voices of the barred owl (Syrnium nebulosum) and the loon are the surest. " The 'coogoquesk' is noisy again ; more rain comin'," says the Indian, and whether we hear the unwonted chorus of wild hootings soon after sundown or at daybreak, the storm will surely come within twelve hours. Such is likewise the case in summer, when from our fishing camps we hear the plaintive, quavering cry of the great northern diver echoing over the calm surface, and amongst the groups of islets of the forest lakes, and quickly repeated without intermission, during the night. In the autumn, in close damp weather, and especially before rain, the little tree frog (Hyla squir-rellus), rejoicing in the prospect of a relaxed skin, pipes vigorously his cheerful note throughout the night, and the Brek! B-r-rek! of the wood-frog (Rana sylvatica) is heard from pools of water standing in hollows in the forest. A sound that has always been pleasant to my ears when lying amongst the low bushes on the open barren, is the Chink! chink! chink! of the little chain mouse as he gambols around. It is a faint silvery tinkling, as might be produced by shaking the links of a small chain, whence his common name.

The little Acadian owl, commonly called the " saw-whet " (Ulula Acadica), is not uncommon in our woods, uttering morning and evening its peculiar and (until known) mysterious tinkling sound from the thickest groves of spruces. In one of these I once captured a specimen just about sundown, when proceeding to a barren to call moose. The Indian made a noose on the top of a long wattle, and after a little manœuvring, during which the bird kept hovering round ns, hissing and setting up its wings and feathers in great anger, he got it over its neck and secured it without injury. This little owl, just turning the scale at two ounces, will actually attack and kill a rat.

Wherever there is mystery there lies a charm; and to this effect expresses himself Mr. Gosse, who thus speaks of his acquaintance with the cry of the saw-whet in his "Romance of Natural History:"

"In the forests of Lower Canada and the New England States, I have often heard in spring a mysterious sound, of which, to this day, I do not know the author. Soon after night sets in, a metallic sound is heard from the most sombre forest swamps, where the spruce and the hemlock give a peculiar density to the wood, known as the black growth. The sound comes up clear and regular, like the measured tinkle of a cow bell, or gentle strokes on a piece of metal, or the action of a file upon a saw. It goes on, with intervals of interruption, throughout the hours of darkness. People attribute it to a bird which they call the whetsaw, but nobody pretends to have seen it, so that this can only be considered conjecture, though a highly probable one. The monotony and pertinacity of this note had a strange charm for me, increased, doubtless, by the uncertainty of its origin. Night after night it would be heard in the same spot, invariably the most sombre and gloomy recesses of the black timbered woods. I occasionally watched for it, resorting to the woods before sunset, and waiting till darkness; but, strange to say, it refused to perform under such conditions. The shy and recluse bird, if bird it was, was, doubtless, aware of the intrusion, and on its guard. Once I heard it under peculiarly wild circumstances. I was riding late at night, and, just at midnight, came to a very lonely part of the road, where the black forest rose on either side. Everything was profoundly still, and the measured tramp of my horse's feet on the frozen road was felt as a relief to the deep and oppressive silence; when suddenly, from the sombre woods, rose the clear metallic tinkle of the whetsaw. The sound, all unexpected as it was, was very striking, and though it was bitterly cold, I drew up for some time to listen to it. In the darkness and silence of the hour, that regularly measured sound, proceeding, too, from so gloomy a spot, had an effect on my mind solemn and unearthly, yet not unmixed with pleasure."

There is a bird that, long after sundown, and when the moose-caller begins to feel chilled by long watching on the frosty barren, will rush past him with such velocity as to leave no time to catch a certain view of its size or form. It passes close to the ground, and with the whizzing sound of an arrow. Almost every night, whilst thus watching, I have noticed this bird; can it be the night hawk?

But October is late for so tender a bird ; the latest day in which I have observed it in Nova Scotia, was the 28th September.

Another mysterious sound which many of the Indian hunters connect with superstition, and attribute to spirits of the Orpheonistic description, is that curious, rushing sound of music—an indescribable melodious rustling in the calm atmosphere of a still October night, with which the ear of the moose-hunter becomes so well acquainted. Most probably the cause exists in the tension of the nerves of that organ.

The fierce yell of the lucifee, and the short sharp bark of the fox, are often heard in wild parts of the country : they are both in pursuit of the unfortunate hare, which falls a frequent prey to so many of the carnivoræ and raptores. I once heard the startling cry of the former close to my head, whilst reposing in the open, after a night's moose-calling away from camp. Its bounds upon its prey, having stealthily crept to within sight, are prodigious : I have measured them as over twenty feet in the snow.

I have always noticed that in the small hours of the morning there appears to be a general cessation of movement of every living creature in the woods. Often as I have strolled from camp into the moonlight at this time, I never could detect the slightest sound— even the owls seemed to have retired. The approach of dawn, however, seems to call forth fresh exertions of the nocturnal animals in quest of food, and all the cries and calls are renewed—continuing till the first signs of Aurora send the owls flitting back into the thick tops of the spruces, and call forth the busy squirrels and small birds to their daily occupation.

Once, and only once, did I hear the little red squirrel utter his wrathful chirrup at night—a bad sign, say the Indians ; they firmly believe that it prognosticates the death of one of their friends. Neither does the chip-munk or striped ground squirrel come out at night ; the only member of the family of nocturnal habits is the flying squirrel, a rare but most beautiful little creature. Lying in an open camp, I once saw its form sail in a curved line from tree to tree in the moonlight.

Of night songsters amongst our small birds we have few examples. The whip-poor-will is our only systematic nightingale, if we may call him so. Arriving in June, and choosing the pleasantest retreat, in copses, by picturesque intervales, and generally preferring the neighbourhood of man, the plaintive song of this bird is strongly associated with the charms of a summer's evening in the country.

Occasionally, however, the white-throated sparrow, or the common peabiddy bird (F. Pennsylvanica) strikes up his piping note at various times of the night, and is often heard when the surrounding woods are suddenly lighted up by the application of fresh fuel to the camp fire. The Indians say that he sings every hour. The exquisite flute-like warblings of the hermit thrush (T. solitarius) are often prolonged far into the fine nights of early summer. As a general impression, however, the pleasing notes of song birds are foreign to the interior solitudes of the great fir forest, whose gloom is appropriately enhanced by the wilder and more mournful voices of predatory birds and animals. With these imperfect remarks, I close the present sketch on the night life of animals in the woods.

The following is a fragment of a Paper read by the Author before the Nova Scotian Institute of Natural Science on Acclimatisation. A large proportion of the matter contained therein has been omitted as irrelative to the objects of this work.

## ACADIAN ACCLIMATISATION.

Having thus adverted to the development of "Applied Natural History" in other parts of the world as a practical science, and the satisfactory results which have already attended such efforts, we now come to consider the proper subject of this paper—the question of Acclimatisation as applicable to Nova Scotia. I have so far drawn attention to the advances made by the antipodal colonists in this direction, to show how the objections of distance, expense, and uncertainty of results, have all been put aside for ends thought worthy of such sacrifices. But Australia was a country craving animal immigration, her large and wealthy population demanding many of the absent table luxuries of the old world, and her youth eager for the time when the boundless forests and grassy plains should abound with the stag or roe, in place of the monotonous marsupials which as yet had afforded the only material for the chase. In Atlantic America, on the contrary, instead of having to supplant the indigenous animals, we possess, in a state of nature, some of the noblest forms of animal life, which, no longer required to supply the aboriginal Indians with their sole means of subsistence, may be called on, with that moderation which should always characterise a civilised people, to afford both the invigorating pleasures of sport and luxuries for the market. Every stream and lake abounds with trout, and there are but few rivers from Cape Sable to the Labrador which the salmon does not annually attempt to ascend.

What, then, is to be desired? Has not America, receiving from the east all those useful animals which accompany man in his migrations, and which, returning to a state of nature in the plains of Mexico and South America, have multiplied so greatly as to afford a staple product for exportation, giving all imaginable luxuries to the new-coming nations in the produce of her forests, prairies, rivers, and sea coasts? Yes, but the gift has been abused. It is sad to contemplate the wanton destruction of game and game fish throughout the northern continent since its first settlement by Europeans: many animals, now on the verge of extinction, driven off their still large domains, not primarily by the approach of civilisation, but by ruthless, wholesale, and wanton modes of destruction. "One invariable peculiarity of the American people," says the author of "The Game Fish of the North," "is that they attack, overturn, and annihilate, and then laboriously reconstruct. Our first farmers chopped down the forests and shade trees, took crop after crop of the same kind from the land, exhausted the soil, and made bare the country; they hunted and fished, destroying first the wild animals, then the birds, and finally the fish, till in many places these ceased utterly from the face of the earth; and then, when they had finished their work, that race of gentlemen moved west to renew the same course of destruction. After them came the restorers; they manured the land, left it fallow, put in practice the rotation of crops, planted shade and fruit trees, discovered that birds were useful in destroying insects and worms, passed laws to protect them where they were not utterly extinct, as with the pinnated grouse of Pennsylvania and Long Island, and will, I predict, ere long re-stock the streams, rivers, and ponds, with the best of the fish that once inhabited them."

A home question for our subject would be,—In the hands of which class of men does this colony now find itself? And I fear the unhesitating answer of the impartial stranger and visitor would be, that in all regarding the preservation of our living natural resources, we were in the hands of the destroyers. The course of destruction so ably depicted by the author quoted, is being prosecuted throughout the length and breadth of Nova Scotia, and the settlers of this province, blind to their own interests, careless of their children's, and utterly regardless of restraint imposed by the laws of the country, worse than useless because not carried out, are bringing about the final depopulation of our large wild areas of land and water. It really becomes a question as to whether late interference shall arrest the tide of destruction ere the entire extermination of fish and game shall bring the country to a sense of its loss, and finally to a wish for their reproduction.

In such a state of affairs, provincial acclimatisation would prove an empty speculation, for any new animal or bird introduced into our woodlands requiring freedom from molestation for a term of years, would be quickly hunted down and destroyed.

Leaving, however, these important questions of protection or extinction of already-existing indigenous species in the hands of those who hold the means of ordering these matters, I will now call your attention to what might be done to increase our stock of useful wild or domestic animals, birds or fish, could they be ensured the necessary wardship. We will consider first whether our large woodland districts demand and would bear foreign colonisation, and for what types their physical conformation seems best adapted.

Even in its most undisturbed and wildest depths the North American forest has always been noted for its solitude ; the meaning being the great disproportion of the animal to the vegetable kingdom. It seems as if nature had exhausted her energies in shading the ground with the dense forest and the rank vegetation which everywhere seizes on the rough surface beneath. It is impossible to say to what extent animal life might have once existed in the primeval forest ; but no one who has taken a day's walk in the woods, either near to or far from the haunts of man, can fail being impressed with the apparent absence of animal life. The European visitor, in a suburban ramble through the bush, wonders at the scarcity of game birds, rabbits, or hares, but is astonished when told that in the deepest recesses of the wild country he will see but little increase of their numbers. A canoe paddled through lake after lake of our great highways of water communication, will startle but a few pairs or broods of exceedingly timid waterfowl, where in Europe they would literally swarm. Surely, then, here is room for the work of acclimatisation, in a country where so much toil is undergone in the often fruitless pursuit of sport.

The undergrowth of our wild forest lands, the field for acclimatisation which we have under immediate consideration, consists of an immense variety of shrubs, under-shrubs, and herbs, annual or perennial. The under-shrubs generally bear the various descriptions of berries, and with great profusion. There are, here and there, wild pastures, or intervales, by the edge of sluggish water, but they bear but a small proportion to the woodlands ; the bogs and barrens produce moss in abundance, and of the kind found in every part of the world where the reindeer is indigenous, or has been successfully introduced, as in Iceland.

We find, accordingly, that our largest ruminant, the moose-deer, is, in the strictest sense of the word, a wood-eater ; whilst our other animal representing this class, the American reindeer, or cariboo, is found in those portions of the province where large and seldom disturbed plains and bogs afford him his favourite moss, the lichen rangiferinus. As amongst the larger animals, ruminants alone offer a selection for introduction into a forest country with the physical attributes of Nova Scotia, we may ask if there is any other animal of the deer tribe which might be successfully acclimatised here. The answer comes through careful consideration of the fauna and flora of other regions compared with our own. The field naturally presenting itself for this research lies in the forest districts of America further west, and in northern Europe, which, under similar climatic influences, presents a strong analogy to this portion of the globe, especially on its western seaboard ; the forest trees and shrubs, the larger animals, the birds and the fish of Norway and Sweden, are almost reproduced in British North America ; indeed, distinction of species in many cases is far from established.

The common deer (Cervus Virginianus), then, of Maine and the Canadas, and more recently of New Brunswick by spontaneous acclimatisation, or perhaps rather through the instrumentality of the wolf, appears to be perfectly adapted for an existence in the Nova Scotian woods—a graceful species, but little inferior to the red deer of Europe, affording the excellent venison with which the New York and Boston markets are so well supplied. The climate of Nova Scotia, allowing so little snow to accumulate in the woods until the close of the winter, would prove a great safeguard against the wholesale destruction with which it meets in Maine and New Brunswick, where it is continually in a most helpless condition from the depth of snow throughout the winter. Indeed, it is already with us, for a small herd of healthy animals may now be seen at Mr. Downs' gardens, to whom the country is already indebted for many an unassisted attempt at real practical acclimatisation.*

* Mr. Andrew Downs, Naturalist, N. W. Arm, Halifax, Nova Scotia.

It is well known that both the buffalo and the elk (C. wapiti) formerly had an extensive range to the north-east. The latter animal, now mainly found on the Yellowstone and Upper Missouri rivers, once inhabited the forests of the Saguenay. Baird says it has a greater geographical distribution than any other American deer ; and, according to Richardson, it can exist as far as 57 deg. north. Doubtless it would thrive in the Nova Scotian or New Brunswick forests. The wapiti thrives in the Zoological Society's gardens in England, where it annually reproduces ; and large herds of this noble animal are being transported from America to the north of Italy by His Majesty King Victor Emmanuel. Thirty were recently awaiting departure from New York at the same time.

The only other ruminant on the list of this order, indigenous to climates similar to our own, is the hardy little roe-deer or roebuck, common in the beech woods of. northern Europe. I am confident that this animal would thrive in the extensive beech forests of Cumberland ; and as it seems to live and thrive close to civilisation, it would find ample room and food in our suburban copses and uncleared barrens. Descending in the scale of animal classification, the next selections for consideration of a future Acclimatisation Society in this country, as adapted to live and multiply and become profitable in the woodlands, seem to be offered in the prolific order Rodentia, of which many families are already indigenous—the squirrel, beaver, porcupine, and American hare, commonly known as the rabbit. The first of these might receive an interesting accession by the introduction of the black and grey squirrels of Canada and the States ; the beaver, porcupine, and woodchuck, are all prized by the hunter as food, lacking the supply of venison, and the hare, persecuted though it be by human, furred, and feathered foes, is still so prolific and common, as to form a great portion of the winter subsistence of both settlers and the poor of this city. Indeed, when we enumerate its enemies of the animal creation, which almost altogether live upon it, the lynx and wild cat, the foxes, the horned owl, the marten, and the weasel, and take into consideration the numbers which are taken by man, by snaring them in their easily discovered paths to and from their feeding grounds in the swamps, it is wonderful that they still remain so plentiful. A great objection to the flesh of the American hare, however, is its insipidity and toughness, except when taken young. Far more delicate and esteemed is that of the Spanish, or domestic, and common wild English rabbit (Lepus cuniculus), and it would seem that both are of a sufficiently hardy constitution to stand the rigours of our winter. The former is already an acclimatised inhabitant of the sandbanks of Sable Island, according to Dr. Gilpin, having been introduced by the Honourable Michael Wallace, and increased amazingly, affording the islanders many a fresh dinner when salt junk is plenty and fresh beef scarce. No easier experiment could be made in applied natural history than the extensive breeding of the common grey rabbit by some resident near town, whose premises bordered on uncleared bush or scrub. To commence, a large bank of loosely piled earth and stone might be made, here and there perforated by a length or so of suitable tubing, such as used for drains, the bank enclosed by wire netting, and a few pairs of rabbits turned in. They would soon tunnel the bank in all directions, and as the families increased they might be allowed to escape into the neighbourhood. A fair warren once established would be the means of a quick colonisation of the surrounding country. And the true rabbit, living so constantly under ground, would enjoy much greater security from animals and birds of prey than his indigenous congeners.

Still keeping in view the acclimatisation of creatures intended to exist in a state of nature; and not for domestication—a division of the subject which appears to be most feasible and best adapted to the condition of this province—let us next turn to the birds.

We have already existing in our woods as game birds, two species of Tetraonidæ—the T. umbellus, or the ruffed grouse, and the T. Canadensis, or spruce partridge—as permanent residents ; and, as summer visitors, the two North American Scolopacidæ, the woodcock and snipe. There is but one representative of the Phasianidæ in North America, the only gift of the new to the old world, whence the domestic race has sprung, and that is the wild turkey. It certainly would appear that our large woodland solitudes offer especial facilities for the introduction of some new members of the grouse family, birds especially formed for existence in cold climates. Formerly common in the Scotch pine forests, now only to be met with in abundance in the north of Europe, in Norway, Sweden, and Russia, the magnificent capercailzie, or cock of the wood (T. urogallus), equalling, in the case of the male bird, the turkey in size, presents so tempting an experiment that it should be almost introduced regardless of expense. A bird inhabiting so widely the fir woods of subarctic Europe and Asia, would surely succeed if transplanted to the corresponding region of North America. It appears to feed exclusively on pine shoots. Mr. Bernard, author of a recent work called "Sport in Norway," says it is still common in all large forest districts in that country. I believe this bird loves solitude, and surely he would find it, if essential to his existence, in some of the great expanses of coniferous forest which still prevail in most portions of Nova Scotia. Next in size and beauty might be selected the black game (T. tetrix) of the wilder portions of the British Isles, and numerous in Norway, where it is stated they not unfrequently cross with the capercailzie. This bird is known to subsist on the buds of the alder and birch, on the berries of the whortleberry, blueberry, and juniper, and on the bog cranberry, all of which are so abundant in our woods, and of almost identical species. A successful introduction of this bold, handsome grouse, would add great interest to the wild sports on the open barrens. The hazel hen of northern Europe (T. bonasia), reported to be the best fleshed bird of the grouse tribe, is another association of a country in which spruce woods abound. It is exceedingly like our birch partridge in appearance— a little smaller, and wanting the ruff ; like the latter, also, its flesh is white. There are many other northern grouse in both the old and new worlds, but none that I should import as so likely to succeed, and as such valuable acquisitions, as the capercailzie and the blackcock.

With the circumstance of the introduction and breeding of the English and gold and silver pheasants at Mr. Downs' establishment we are all acquainted ; and a most interesting fact is the well-ascertained capability of the English pheasant to live and find its own subsistence in our woods through a rigorous winter, whilst the latter birds, left out at night by accident, have apparently suffered little inconvenience by roosting in a fir tree, exposed to a strong wind, accompanied by the intense cold of —16°. Why should not this experiment be continued ?

It is to be feared that those troops of little songsters with which the fields of England abound, and which have been carefully acclimatised in Australia for old association sake, would die on the first near approach of the mercury to zero. Those that are imported, comprising thrushes, skylarks, finches, &c., are closely kept within doors. Mr. Downs has two pairs of the European jackdaw, which he hopes will increase in his neighbourhood. These interesting and garrulous little members of the family Corvidæ, whose young every English boy covets to obtain and educate to the acquisition of rudimentary speech, would find but few ivy-mantled towers or venerable steeples in which to build their nests ; but when Gilbert White informs us that for want of church steeples they will build under ground in rabbit burrows, the new-comers would **not be long in devising a** remedy for the defect. The **common English house-**sparrow, thoroughly acclimatised, and abundant **in New York,** would, doubtless, do as well in this neighbourhood.

As a second consideration in connection with this wide subject, let us inquire whether any good purpose could be **answered by an** attempt at domestication or semi-domestication **of** our indigenous ruminants, the moose and the cariboo. When we consider that these two species are found throughout the old world, under the same conditions of climate and vegetation **which attend them in the** new, it appears unaccountable that we have no **historic records of the** subjugation of the cariboo for **domestic purposes by** the primitive Indians of the northern coasts of America, **as this** animal has been applied from time immemorial by the Lapps.

An eminent naturalist, Dr. Gray, in delivering his **address in the** Nat. Hist. Section at the late meeting of the British **Association at** Bath, thus alludes to the latter fact :—"The inhabitants **of the arctic** or sub-arctic regions of Europe and Asia have partially domesticated the reindeer ; and either Asiatics have peculiar aptitude **for domesti-**cating animals, or the ruminants of that part of the **world are** peculiarly adapted for domestication ; "* and he then instances **a** variety of exemplifications, in their having domesticated the yak **in** the mountain regions of Thibet **and Siberia,** the camel and drome-dary in central Asia, in southern Asia the zebra, and in the Malayan archipelago various species of buffalo and wild cattle. It may be **stated, that modern** discovery has placed the original home of the reindeer in the high Alps of central Asia, whence these animals, followed by their ever-accompanying human associates, the Lapps, migrated to the north-west of **Europe.** As a beast of burden, how-ever, to traverse those treeless wastes **answering to** the snow-covered barrens of Lapland, the dog seems to have answered all the purposes of the Esquimaux and other **arctic-American** tribes, whilst in more southerly and wooded regions, a sledge-drawing animal would have no scope or sphere of employment. And, viewing **the** animals in this light, the horse and **the ox** which **have** accompanied Europeans,

---

* Erman in his Siberian travels frequently speaks of the passionate desire evinced by the reindeer for human urine as the acknowledged means of success adopted by the Ostyaks, Samoyeds and Tunguzes, in domesticating this animal, otherwise naturally so shy and averse to the presence of man. The new life apparently acquired by the deer on a journey, after gratifying this strange appetite, is attributed by the same author to the stimulus afforded by the ammoniacal salts.

have left no desideratum that could be supplied by either the moose
or the cariboo. There are, however, several undoubted instances of
the applicability of the moose to draught. A few years since a
settler on the Guysboro' road, named Carr, possessed a two-year old
bull moose, which was perfectly tractable in harness. For a wager,
he has been known to overtake and quickly distance the fastest
trotting horse on the road, drawing his master in a sleigh, the
guiding reins being fastened to a muzzle bound round the animal's
nose. Another instance was that of a very large moose kept by a
doctor in Cape Breton, which he would invariably employ in pre-
ference to his horse when wishing to make a distant visit to a
patient, and in the shortest time. It is very certain that in its
youth the moose is one of the most tractable of animals; but it is
in the rutting season of the third year that the males first become
unmanageable and dangerous.*

A point, however, on which I would engage attention, is not the
domestication of either of these animals in the state in which the
ordinary domesticated animals are associated with us, but a possible
state of semi-domestication, by which the moose might be caused to
multiply on uncleared land, and regularly bred, fattened, and turned
to profit without the smallest cost to the owner, except the expense
of maintaining his enclosures in an efficient state of security. My
attention was first drawn to this by reading an account of the
successful breeding of the American elk (C. wapiti) by an American
gentleman—a Mr. Stratton, of New York State. I quote from a
letter dated January 12, 1859 :—

" My desire to keep and breed them, without their becoming a tax
upon me, led to diligent inquiry in relation to what had been done
in the way of their domestication. I procured, as far as possible,
every paper, book, and document, which could give any light upon
the subject. I wrote to every part of the country whence any information could be obtained, and opened a correspondence with those
who had undertaken such an enterprise. The result of my efforts
was simply this : nearly every one who had owned an elk was a
gentleman amateur, and had left the care and direction to servants ;
the bucks, not having been castrated at the proper age, had
become unmanageable ; and when the novelty of the attempt was
over, the domestication in most cases was abandoned. But from my

* Formerly the European elk was used in Sweden to draw sledges, but its
use for this purpose was finally prohibited by government, as criminals used
it as a means of escape.

own inquiries, and a close personal observation of the habits of the
animal, I believed that a different course would produce a more
favourable result. The first requisite was a place to keep them in.
Now, they had always lived in the woods, summer and winter : why
not live in the forest again ? Acting upon this principle, I immediately set to work and fenced in about 150 acres of hill land,
which was steep and stony, covered with brushwood, and entirely
useless for agricultural purposes. In this lot I turned my elks,
where they have been six years. In the meantime, I purchased two
more does, and have reared eight fawns. Having emasculated the
older bucks as fast as the younger ones became adults, I have now a
herd so gentle, that a visitor at my farm would hardly imagine that
their ancestors, only three generations back, were wild animals.
And this has been done simply by visiting the park two or three
times a week, and always carrying them an ear of corn, some little
delicacy, or salt, and treating them with unvarying kindness.

" The facility for extending this business may easily be conceived.
New York alone might support 100,000 elks on land where our
domestic cattle could not subsist, furnishing an amount of venison
almost incredible ; while the adjoining State of Pennsylvania, to say
nothing of others, might sustain a still larger number without
encroaching upon an acre of land now used for stock-rearing, or any
other purpose connected with agriculture."*

Here, then, we have a modern precedent for an experiment which
I am convinced would answer in the case of the moose, a still larger
and more profitable animal than the wapiti. What an admirable
opportunity for utilising those barren wastes which surround us !
Take for example that large triangular piece of waste country in the
immediate vicinity of the city, commencing at Dartmouth, extending
along the shores of the Basin on one side, bounded by the Dartmouth lakes on the other, and skirted by the railroad from Bedford
to Grand Lake as its base. With the exception of a few clearings
on the shores of the Basin, the whole of this is a wilderness, containing some 15,000 acres of wild, undulating land, with here and
there thick spruce swamps, mossy bogs, and barrens covered with a
young growth of birch, poplar, and all the food on which the moose
delights to subsist. That they have an especial liking for this small
district may be gathered from the fact that I have never known it as

* In 1862, Mr. Stratton states that he had succeeded in raising thirty-seven
elk. He had trained a pair to harness, and had sold them for $1000. Whilst,
as an article of food he can now raise elk cheaper than sheep.

not containing two or three of these animals. There is no reason why an experimental farm, conducted on the principle indicated by Mr. Stratton, should not be able to breed and turn out in this district a very large number of moose, and in such a state of tameness, that they would be induced to remain within enclosed portions of the wilderness, furnishing, in proper season, a profitable supply of flesh for the market.

To the cariboo, on the other hand, these suggestions will not be applicable, as this animal requires, as a primary condition of its existence, a large and uninterrupted field for periodical migration.

As regards the introduction of new fish, a very good exchange might be made with the English Acclimatization Society, by sending the beautiful American brook trout (Salmo fontinalis), and receiving in return S. fario. Colonel Sinclair* has several times drawn my attention to the suitableness of many of our rivers for the reception of the true British trout—a fish quite different in its habits to our migratory, deep-frequenting S. fontinalis.

The Shubenacadie, and other rivers, steadily flowing through alluvial flats (*intervale*), present frequent gravelly reaches, with patches of waving weed, and soft overhanging banks—just the counterpart of many English trout-streams. With no predatory fish to harass the trout, these waters at once suggest the introduction of S. fario, more particularly as they are not the resort of our own species. As an association, and for purposes of food, the common English stream-minnow might be profitably turned in at the same time.

Our grayling (S. Gloverii), (the former a misnomer), is a lake-trout. The true grayling (Thymallus), as well as the common English perch, would be desirable additions to our waters. Even in lakes where the trout has almost disappeared, I should hesitate to recommend the introduction of any of the family Esocidæ, for fear of their spreading to damage more remunerative waters.

In conclusion, it is with the greatest pleasure that I welcome Colonel Sinclair's proposal to form a Society for the artificial propagation of fish in this Province. The Americans are already earnestly endeavouring by this means to restore their desolate rivers; and with the support of the Association for Protection of Game and Fish, and the advice and the experience of the English pisciculturists, the greatest results may be obtained in water-farming a country so prolific of lakes and streams as is Nova Scotia.

* Lieut.-Col. R. Bligh Sinclair, Adjt.-Gen. of N. S. Militia, late 42nd Highlanders.

## AUDACITY OF THE BULL MOOSE IN THE CALLING SEASON.

The following instances of the recklessness which characterises the bull moose in the fall are authentic :—

A sportsman, accompanied by an Indian, was moose-calling on Mosher's River, Nova Scotia, one morning in the autumn of 1867. They were on a barren, and near the margin of a heavy forest. A fine bull moose came up to the call, and fell to the Indian's gun, when instantly another bull emerged from the woods, and charged at the prostrate animal. A second bullet brought him over, and he fell on the body of what had most probably been his foe of the season.

A settler in the backwoods going out one October evening to chop firewood near his shanty in the forest, heard a bull moose "*handy.*" He returned for his gun, and, after a short stalk in the bushes, obtained a shot at the moose—an animal with superb antlers—and could distinctly see that he had hit him in the neck. There he stood for a considerable time, while the settler, who had only the one charge, lay in the bushes, and at length turned and leisurely walked away. The man was up betimes next morning, and away to the same spot. He saw blood ; and, following the trail for a short distance, heard sounds indicating the presence of moose. Having some faint idea of calling, he put a piece of bark to his mouth, and gave the note of the bull. Answering at once, a fine moose came in view, when he fired, and this time prostrated the animal—the identical one shot the evening before. He recognised the horns, and the wound was in his neck.

*Apropos* of this subject, the following extracts from his note-book, kindly placed at my disposal by "The Old Hunter," are highly interesting and illustrative. He says :—"I left my camp on Lake Mooin (the lake of the bear), Liscome River, September, 1866, in company with Peter, Joe, and Stephen, as my Indian hunters, intending to cross the next lake to the southward in a canoe which we had there secreted. On arriving at the lake we found the wind so high that it was considered altogether unsafe to trust ourselves on its waters in our frail bark. About five o'clock the wind moderated, but as I still thought that we could not reach my old calling-ground on the opposite side before the decline of the sun, I determined to cross to a narrow neck of rocky barren distant from us by water some seven hundred yards. After various perils we reached the spot, disembarked amongst the rocks, fixed a place for the calling-ground should the night be calm, collected our bedding of spruce boughs picked in a neighbouring swamp, and, releasing our blankets from their cordings, prepared for supper. Suddenly all was calm ; the wind had gone down, and the western sky was tinged with the gorgeous colouring denoting a moose-caller's delight—a calm and serene night. All at once a cracking of wood was heard away down on our side of the lake, and presently more noises, plainly determining the presence of moose thereabouts. A few minutes of hesitation, and I treed Peter to sound the love-note from aloft : and not long after he descried a moose at fully a mile's distance coming to the edge of the forest. The margin of the lake on our side had been burnt, and was barren of bush or tree except in a few spots. A few persuasive calls brought him out on the barren, from which, however, he soon returned to the cover of the green-woods—a fact, as we all knew, proving him to be either a coward or a beaten moose. We coaxed : he still came on, showing himself occasionally on the barren, though never answering, and at length was espied about three hundred yards off, peering around him and listening, his huge ears extended forwards to the utmost. We thought that he saw us, but he had cunning folks to deal with ; we did not move or call. Down he came, making directly for us, now *speaking* for the first time. I was lying in his route, and, when distant about fifteen yards, I bowled over one of the finest and most cautious of his species I had ever met with. He was cast and butchered before the twilight faded.

" We supped, and that night lay replete ; but my sleep not being of such a dead nature as that of my faithful followers, the crashings of trees and the bellowings of moose emanating from the same direction as that whence came the fallen monarch, struck frequently on my ears. At cock-crow I woke up the sleeping aborigines, and, severe as had been the cold of the past night, we listened long and with intense interest to the distant sounds, not the usual noise of the cow moose at this season, but a sort of unearthly roaring.

" We called, and presently observed two moose leave the woods, and approach us on the barrens. When about five hundred yards distant from us we lost sight of them in the alder bushes which grew thickly on the banks of a small brook flowing into the lake. Past this spot they would not come : we did not advance, as we determined to kill no more moose on that excursion. Our object was simply to watch ; I particularly wanted to ascertain from which animal the snorting and fierce bellowing came. We had perceived that they were male and female. They stopped in the alders for some fifteen minutes or so making a great row, breaking sticks and pawing the water in swamp holes with a loud splashing. At length we espied them beating a slow retreat on the route they had advanced upon, and I determined to take the canoe and follow them by water, leaving Stephen to prepare breakfast. The morning was perfectly calm, fog here and there rising from the lake and along the lines of the numerous brooks that emptied into it. I may here add, that though I have named it Lake Merganser, owing to the numbers of those birds frequenting it, it would have been fully entitled to have been called Rocky Lake, as I think that both below and above its surface rocks abound to a greater extent than in any other lake in Nova Scotia, and that is saying a good deal.

" Stealing over the lake's surface, and seated in the bottom of our canoe, we could not well scan the woods by the margin, for the rocks on the shore were fully eight feet high. However, at length we sighted two large black objects ascending a hill. Peter called like a bull, and this at once arrested them. They turned, and one, for a moment lost to sight, appeared on the edge of the barren : another step and he must have descended. It was a mighty bull moose. He peered at us, and we, motionless and with restrained breath, gazed upon him. After standing in that position for some minutes he turned and looked towards where we had slept. I did the same, and could plainly see the boy Stephen perched upon the rock beneath which we had lain. Then he walked five or six steps, turned, and gave us a full side view, twice picking some twigs from the bushes which we could hear him munching with his teeth, so close were we. During this wondrous sight the loud noise was made in the bush three times, when out walked a cow moose. She, like to her lord, looked hard at us, and I thought was " for off." Not a bit ; she stopped head on for fully five minutes ; then turned, and faced the hill, emitting several times the angry grunt so dreaded by the Indian as a sign of ill-luck. The bull quietly took his departure, and we watched them enter the forest. This bull had only one horn. Peter declared that the other was a small stump—a malformation—but I shall ever be of the opinion that he had lost it in battle, for on our return to our rocky home, and when butchering the dead moose, we found that he had been in the wars, and was much bruised about the neck and ribs on the near side.

" Parting with this most interesting couple, we paddled on to the foot of the lake, and called a few times at the head of a bog. We were quickly answered, and up came a rattling moose. He was astonished at first seeing us, I feel certain, and was for bolting, but continued walking along the dry edge of the bog. Peter imitated a bull's note, at which he turned fiercely round with mane, rump-hair, and ears erect, and answered angrily. This was repeated fully six

times to our great amusement. At length he walked away, making
constant ‘bockings,’ and rubbing his antlers against burnt trees.

“All at once we espied another pair of moose coming from the
opposite direction—a bull and a cow—and expected to see a meeting,
perhaps a combat ; but although there appeared every likelihood of
such an occurrence, it was avoided by the pair retreating into the
deep woods. The bulls ceasing to answer each other, we paddled
back to camp, where little Stephen, though he had observed all the
first part of the spectacle from the rock, had not neglected to provide
for his ‘ sacamow ’ and comrade red-skin a sumptuous repast of
kidneys, steaks, and coffee.

“I am a firm believer, and always was, that it is the cow moose
that makes the noise by some called a roar, and I was thus a witness
to the fact. Here was a glorious morning’s sport without bloodshed !
Alas ! last season upwards of fifty moose were killed about Lake
Merganser. It is a fact that now not a track can there be seen.”

---

## MOOSE CAUGHT IN A TREE.

Moose not unfrequently perish in the woods through becoming
entangled in some natural snare, or by breaking their legs amongst
the rents and holes in the rocks which strew the country, and are often
concealed by a carpet of moss. A few falls since I stumbled by
chance upon the body of a moose which had recently met with an
accidental death under the following curious circumstances. I was
crossing a deep still-water brook in the forest, on a log fallen from
bank to bank, when my attention was arrested by the disturbed
appearance of the bank, and by the bark being rubbed off the bottom
of a large spruce-tree which grew over the water on the opposite
side. Completely submerged below the surface was the body of a
large bull-moose, his antlers just peeping above the water A thick
root of the spruce grew out of the bank, and, curving round, re-
entered it, forming a strong loop. Into this the unfortunate moose,
in attempting to cross the brook at this point, had accidentally
slipped one of his hind legs up to the hock, and the looped root
being narrow, he was unable to extricate it. A prisoner, for who
can tell how long, the unhappy animal perished from starvation, and
at last sank into the stagnant brook. The denuded state of the stem
of the spruce, and the broken bushes around, showed with what
violence his struggles had been attended.

The following is an Indian’s story of a somewhat similar occurrence :—Being visited one winter by two of his tribe and the larder

nearly empty, the trio determined to have a hunt in search of moose-meat. It was February, and deep snow covered the country. On the evening of the first hunting day they came upon a fresh track, and their dogs, three in number, started the chase. Daylight failing, they renewed the hunt bright and early next morning, following until noon, when they finished the last morsel of their bread. Away again, and before nightfall the dogs had pressed the moose very hard. Taking up the trail next day, they pursued it with all the vigour left to them, and until two of the party gave in and deter-mined to strike out for some settlement. The other Indian, how-ever, resolving to stick to the trail to the last, went on, and, to his great delight, about an hour before sundown, he heard the dogs barking furiously. This was good ; on he dashed, and presently came up with the moose and dogs. It was a barren cow : she had crossed a bog bisected by a deep still-water stream thinly crusted with ice, and, having broken through, was struggling mightily to reach the opposite side. He shot the moose in the head, and found, on attempting to haul out the carcase, that he could not succeed in moving it ; so cutting off the mouffle and tongue, he lighted a fire and then and there feasted. In the morning he became aware that he was not far distant from a farm, as he heard the conk shell blow for breakfast, and proceeding to the spot he induced the settler to assist him by taking his two oxen and sled to the spot where the moose lay to haul out the meat. It was with the greatest difficulty that they extricated the beast from the hole. It appeared that a hard-wood tree had fallen across the still-water, and that the animal's hind leg had got fixed fast in a crutch of the tree. Whence the Indian's success. " Sartain good lucky this time," said he. He sold his meat well in the adjoining settlement.

---

## A BEAR SHOT WITH A HALFPENNY.*

" Not many years ago, when my head-quarters for fall hunting was on Lake Mooin (Anglicè, the lake of the bear), I had enjoyed most excellent sport, moose calling, and four superb sets of antlers hung around the camp. The skins of these animals, together with two of bears, stretched, surrounded the smoke place. This latter was our favourite daily resort ; for the camp was too hot a place by day, though a snug box enough at night, Jack Frost having come along with a late September moon. I had made up my mind to visit the

* From " The Old Hunter's " note-book.

lake which we had seen when out on the barrens ; it was studded with
islands, and not far from where a huge bear had fallen to our guns a
few days before when berry picking.  He came quietly along, licking
in the blue-berries, and when about twelve yards from us, who lay
behind a rock, I bowled him over with an eleven to the pound bullet.
My Indian, Peter, fired also, and terminated his death struggles by a
ball through the brain.  The other bear had likewise been stretched
in the same locality.  We had been calling on the barrens and had
heard moose several times, but wind arose and they got to leeward of
us.  Early next morning it became tolerably calm, though a few
light puffs of wind came from the westward.  A bull moose, accompanied by a cow, advanced, but winded us ; and we saw them spinning
over the barrens for a long time, making for the deep woods to the
west of our lake.  We kept a bright look-out for 'Mr. Mooin,' and a
black object was presently discerned in the distance, though whether
it was a bear or a moose we could not make out ; it seemed to keep
so much about the same spot, and seemed so large at times that we
thought it must be the latter animal.  Well, Peter and self started
for the locality ; the wind got up in our favour, and we advanced
with rapidity, though, at the same time, with caution.  Should it
prove to be a moose we were not to fire ; we had killed enough meat
at that time, and besides bore in mind the great distance we should
have to carry our load out of the woods.  On nearing the place
where we had seen the black object we crept to a large rock,
cautiously looked from its shelter, and at once sighted a bear.  We
could just see its shoulders and head ; it lay on its belly, and was
picking berries from a bush apparently held down by its fore paws.
I fired my right barrel, but missed my mark.  This brought the
monster to a sitting position, when, taking a second aim, my bullet
pierced his head, and tumbled over a full-grown he bear.  When we
examined the trees about, we found that what had given him such a
strange appearance to our eyes, when viewing him from a distance,
was, that he had been on his hind legs, pawing the bark on the tree
with his fore ; this was evident from the nature of the traces.

   "Well, now to my tale.  We got to camp about noon, and, as
before stated, were bound to see the lake of the islands.  There was
a good deal of talking and smoking over the matter, but early one
morning found us packed and in marching order.  Leaving my boat
capsized at the foot of Lake Mooin, we took to the woods, heading
for Lake Merganser ; found our little canoe, which had been concealed in the bushes by the shore ; crossed, and struck off for the

island lake. The difficulties were great ; and we had to pull up for the night, choosing a good place for calling of course, for one, though only one, more moose must fall to our party, and that one must carry the finest antlers. At night we called, and were answered from the direction in which we had come on our trail. Being fatigued, and somewhat indifferent from the reflection that a dead shot would necessitate some nine hundred-weight of meat being ' backed ' out of the woods, we gradually all slumbered. I was up very early. The rocks on which I had lain had pierced almost to my bones, and I felt particularly sore about the right hip. I smoked, then called, and was at once answered by what was in my opinion the moose of the previous evening. On he came dashingly—no signs of fear about his note. I roused up Peter, and after some fifteen minutes attentive listening, finding he was not far distant, sent him off to call from some bushes about one hundred yards away. The moose presently came in view. He was crippled in his gait, almost dead lame in the off fore leg. He carried just what I wanted, an A 1 pair of antlers. I shot him, and am persuaded that he was not more than ten yards from me at the time ; he was bound, with head erect, for the bushes wherein was secreted Peter. All the noise (my shot having been fired absolutely over the head of my other camp follower, the boy Stephen) had failed to arouse the slumbering son of the forest. There he lay until I hauled off his blanket, when he appeared quite annoyed at the close proximity of the antlered monarch. Upon examination we found that in the previous season this beast had got sadly mauled in a fight. Five ribs had been broken on one side, three on the other. His lameness was accounted for by the fact that the outside joint of his foot on the off side had been dislocated and had set out.

" The morning being very calm Peter proposed that we should leave the boy to get breakfast, and ourselves take up positions on two hills adjacent to look for bear. In case we saw any, the signal was to be the hat raised on the muzzle of the gun from the hill top. I had not been long on my look-out when I espied black objects moving, but not being certain of their genus, I started to ascertain, and soon came upon a fine cow moose with an attendant bull, a two-year-old. I strolled back to my look-out, and being tired, I suppose I " slept upon sentry." I was awakened by a shot, closely followed by another, again two more in quick succession. Now I knew that our party was alone in those deep woods, and that Peter had carried my smooth bore, for which I had handed him only four bullets, with what little powder remained, in a red half-pound canister of Curtis and Harvey's. I was alarmed, for I knew that my henchman would only fire at vermin, and I started helter-skelter in the direction of the firing. Fear accelerated my steps, for on my onward course I heard two more shots, and what that meant, except in sign of distress, I could not divine. On reaching the side of the hill, on the summit of which I well knew that Peter had perched himself, I saw an object which I readily recognised as a back view of the Indian actively engaged. I rushed on and found this wonderfully powerful and agile youth hauling along the carcase of a young bear. He was full of smiles, and chided me for not coming to the battle. He had seen a bear feeding on berries, and had given me the signal, but it must have been at the time I was off to the pair of moose, or—shall I write it ? yes, truth is best told—perhaps it was when I slumbered. He crawled down, and when about twenty yards distant had fired at the animal. A second shot seemed at first to have proved inefficacious, when the flying bear suddenly dropped dead in her tracks. It proved afterwards that the first shot had told, hitting high up in the lungs. Hearing a noise to his right he looked round, and espied two young bears in precipitate retreat. He made chase, when both treed simultaneously on the nearest 'ram-pikes'—huge naked stems of burnt pines, of which there was a bunch of five or six standing together. Peter halted and loaded. He missed the nearest youngster with shot number one, but the second brought it down dead from its perch. About fifteen yards from the spot there sat the other cub on a projecting branch, which, on the Indian's approach, it left, and clasped the trunk for a downward retreat. (Those who have not witnessed it can form but a faint idea of the rapidity with which a bear when scared can ascend or descend a tree.) Peter had no more bullets, so what was to be done ? Well, his first attempt to kill young 'mooin' was with the stopper, or rather charger of the powder horn, which he rammed down into the right-hand barrel. This was a failure and a miss. 'Mooin' still clasped the tree in desperation. Reflection made Peter search his pockets, when therein he found a halfpenny—a fitting remaining coin to be in an Indian's keeping. He sat down ; and underneath the tree where the poor victim clung, aided by the butt-end of the gun, which bears the well-indented marks to this day, he doubled up that copper, drove it down over the powder in the left-hand barrel, fired, and brought down the bear from its perch. He had broken its near thigh—a frightful fracture ; but, falling with three legs to work on, it took to the bush at a great pace. Scarcely a match at any time in point of speed for this agile young Indian, it was soon overtaken, and he had succeeded in beating it almost to fragments with a stick which he had snatched up in the wild chase when I arrived to see him hauling it out from the **thicket** in which he had captured it.

" Hearing his story, I went to the tree, and in it **could distinctly** see the end **of** the charger, and feel confident that it may **be still** seen there if the former is standing. That day we feasted gloriously at dinner-time on the roasted ribs of young bears, one of which had **been** shot with **a** halfpenny."

## THE CAPLIN.

### (*Mallotus villosus.*)

This **curious little Salmonoid, the smallest** known member of its family, and, perhaps, the most ancient in type,* plays a very important part in connection with the great cod fisheries on the banks and along the shores of Newfoundland, proving the most tempting bait on which to take the latter fish when it approaches the shores to **spawn.** This it does yearly in numbers baffling description, and the manner in which the operation is performed is one of the most singular and interesting facts in its character. It may be observed that the male and female differ so much in appearance at this season that **it** would be difficult to believe they were of the same species. The females are **very** like the common smelt, possessing, perhaps, more metallic lustre, but the males are adorned by lines or ridges of flaccid fringe, resembling velvet, which run just above the lateral line from the upper angle of the operculum to base of tail. It is stated by so many competent and credible authorities, that I think it deserves to be placed on record as an authenticated fact, that the following is the mode of proceeding. **The time for** the female depositing her spawn having arrived, she is **assisted by** two male fish, one on each

---

* Hugh Miller, **in** his **" Popular** Geology," thus speaks of the caplin as an inhabitant of the deep, **in the latter** days of the tertiary period :—" Clay nodules of the drift **period in** Canada and the United States, are remarkable for containing the only ichthyolite found by Agassiz among seventeen hundred species which still continue to exist, and that **can** be exhibited in consequence in duplicate specimens—the one fit for the table in the character of a palatable viand ; the other for the shelves of a geological museum, in the character of a curious ichthyolite. It is the *Mallotus villosus*, or **caplin.** "

side, and when the surf offers, they all force themselves with great swiftness on the beach, taking particular care that the female is kept in the middle, and by thus compressing her the object of their visit is accomplished. Many repetitions are undoubtedly required. The three caplin then separate, and struggle back into the ocean with a receding wave. It is difficult to say in what precise manner the processes or ridges of the male are used ; probably some amount of downward pressure is exerted through their aid in running on the sand, and the female is assisted thereby in exuding the ripe and readily expressed spawn.

The caplin arrives at its spawning beaches on the south-east coasts of Newfoundland, about the 20th June, and remains close inshore for about five weeks; beyond this period the fish is rarely seen or taken under any circumstances. The warm days with light fogs occurring at this season are looked upon by the expectant fishermen as favourable to their striking in; they call such days "caplin weather." Now all is rivalry as to who shall get the first haul for bait ; a bucket full would command any price—like new potatoes at Covent Garden or the first salmon at Boston. In a few days' time they will be rolled over the roads by strings of carts, selling at 3s. a load, and exported by thousands of barrels to the eager French fishermen on the Banks ; for now is the great banquet of the cod, and herring and clam, mackerel and sardine, are each refused for the new and delicate morsel. It was the height of the caplin season when I arrived in St. John's one summer. Caplin were being wheeled through the streets, caught in tubs, buckets, and ladled up in scoops by everybody from the wharves of the town ; the air was strongly impregnated with the smell of caplin ; they were scattered about in the streets, and you trod on or drove over them everywhere. The fish-flakes, roofs of houses, and little improvised stages attached to nearly every dwelling were strewn with caplin drying in the sun. In the country, on the roads to the out-harbours, a continual stream of carts was passing loaded with glittering cargoes of fish, the whole mass moving together like a jelly, and so likely to spill over the sides that division boards are placed across the cart to separate the fish into two masses, and thus keep them steadier. In the fields men were engaged in spreading them broadcast, or sowing them in drills with potatoes; whilst others were storing them for manure by burying enormous masses of fish in mounds of earth. But it is on the beach only that a just conception can be formed of the great multitudes in which this fish approaches the shore, when sometimes the surface of the water appears as a

living mass as far as the eye can reach ; with their heads towards
the land, they lie like a black line close in, each succeeding wave
dashing them on the beach, where, as the tide ebbs, they remain and
die. The seine, the cast-net, and the dip-net are being plied by the
busy fishermen, whose families are collecting the dead fish and
depositing them in heaps or in pits for manure. Sometimes the mass
is so dense that a boat is impeded in sailing through them, and in
dipping them up more fish than water are taken in a bucket. Numbers of the lively little tern wheel screaming through the air over the
school of fish, every now and then making a dash on their prey,
whilst out in the deep water lies the great army of codfish, ready to
feast on them as they return from the beach. In fact, as regards
their finny foes, every fish large enough to swallow them preys on the
caplin. Captain Murray, R.E., informed me that he had taken a
salmon with five, and a sea trout with two caplin in the stomach, the
latter being only 2 lbs. weight. A friend of his once thought he had
hooked a sea trout, but after a little play succeeded in landing a dead
caplin, to which the hook had affixed itself in the trout's mouth, the
latter being apparently too full to complete the act of swallowing.

A scene of this description is exceedingly interesting, as I saw it
one deliciously warm sunny afternoon in July on the pebbly beach at
Topsail, near the head of Conception Bay. As we approached the
village from the road leading to St. John's the prospect from the top
of the last hill was charming. The neat little village at our feet,
with its fish stages and patches of garden, bounded by the rough,
barren, sandstone cliffs of Portugal Cove ; a pebbly beach in front,
dotted with groups of fishermen throwing their cast-nets over the
black patches which indicate the approaching beds of caplin ; the
activity prevailing on board the boats and schooners moored a few
yards off ; the men dipping up the fish, and throwing them over their
shoulders into their boats, formed a pleasing and animated foreground
to a picture where the distance was formed of the lofty blue mountains across the bay, whilst in middle distance reposed the well
cultivated islands of Great and Little Belleisle. In the centre of the
bay was grounded a large iceberg, which lay melting away in torrents
under the influence of the hot July sun.

Nothing could exceed the beauty of the iridescent colours of the
fish as I handled them fresh caught. The back of the male between
the ridges flashed from deep blue to emerald green as it caught the
light. The absence of timidity on the part of the fish was wonderful :
it seemed as if no amount of splashing over them by the heavily

weighted cast-nets could frighten the remainder from the shore. They appeared impelled to push in by strong instinct, and even when wounded and dying from being struck by the lead weights of the net, their heads would still point to the beach. We could readily capture them with our hands as they swam close in, scarcely wetting our feet. The sand and gravel of the beach was mixed with a large proportion of spawn; I found the latter in the stomachs of several of the males which I opened.

As has been stated, the primary and most important use of the caplin in Newfoundland, Labrador, and the Gulf is as bait for the cod. During the spring the fish has been taken, both on the banks and along shore, by herring, but in inconsiderable numbers; now, however, they look for their great annual glut, and caplin alone will take them. Every shore boat must have its fresh caplin, as well as every Frenchman on the banks. It is the bait of the hook-and-line fisherman as well as for the destructive bultow. Were the supply of caplin withheld from the French, their great fishery fleet could do nothing, as, having exhausted the supply from their own islands of St. Pierre and Miquelon, by taking and wasting the fish with too great prodigality, they are now entirely dependent on the supply from the harbours of the main island.

It is evident that any material and permanent decrease of this bait must tell directly on the fisheries. The caplin may, as has been proved, be so thinned by wholesale destruction whilst spawning on the beach, whilst many are driven off and compelled to drop their spawn in deep water, where it will not vivify, as finally to desert a locality for ever. On many parts of the Newfoundland coast this has been the case, and Perley states that the cod fishery of the Bay of Chaleur has greatly fallen off since the caplin have almost ceased to visit parts of it, and many houses in consequence found it necessary to break up their establishments. The great complaints of the scarcity of bait along the western shore of Newfoundland are owing to the complete failure of a celebrated baiting place at Lamaline, where formerly the strand looked like a bed of spawn, but now is completely ruined, the caplin no sooner approaching the shore than they were hauled before they had time to spawn. In fact little argument is required to prove that the cod fishery must stand or fall with the supply of caplin. The wasteful practice of manuring the land with caplin is another incentive to taking the fish wantonly. Not only are the dead fish, which are strewn in myriads on the beaches, collected for manure, but live fish are hauled for the same purpose, and hundreds

of cartloads have I seen upset to form a heap of putrefaction, afterwards to be spread on the soil, every fish composing which was good
and wholesome food for man, eaten fresh on the spot, or simply dried
for exportation or winter use. But Newfoundland is shamefully
prodigal of the great natural resources afforded to her. It is true
that the fish is dried and exported to the markets of Europe—and a
more delicious dried fish than the caplin does not exist; but why this
shameful conversion of food into manure from sheer laziness? Neither
does the caplin manure prove so very beneficial after all. Though
very efficacious for one year for grass and all root crops except
potatoes, it then requires renewal; the land cannot do without the
stimulus, or it soon falls off. About five loads of earth are mixed
with one of caplin, which is bought at three to four shillings. The
fish, well covered, are allowed to decompose till October; then mixed
and ploughed in the land either that fall or the ensuing spring. On
the other hand, the caplin requires little or no attention in drying to
become an article of food. A few hours in pickle, and a few more
exposed to the sun, on a stage or roof, or even on the ground, and
they may be packed loosely in a barrel, without salt, and headed up.

Though its range is too great, and its spawning grounds far too
extended to render extinction of the species possible, yet, in the
baiting places whence it is obtained for the use of the neighbouring
cod fisheries, it has been in many instances rendered exceedingly
scarce; and its final total departure from these resorts must ensue
unless it is protected from being hauled before or in the act of
spawning, and for such a wasteful purpose as that of manuring the
land. The total absence of bait will at once ruin the fisheries, the
immediate effect of which must be the ruin, starvation, and abandon-
ment of their present residence on the part of thousands; and to
such a state of affairs the Newfoundland fisheries, including its very
vitality as a colony, seem rapidly drifting.

## THE GASPEREAU.
### (*Alosa tyrannus.*)

Another example of an important and interesting fish, affecting
the shores of Acadie as far north as the Miramichi river in New
Brunswick, is afforded by the Gaspereau, a true alosa allied to the
shad, which ascends all the streams and brooks of these provinces
to spawn in the parent lakes in the beginning of May, those with

clean sandy beaches being its most favoured resorts. Dr. Gilpin thus graphically describes its progress :—" The stream before us is crowded with a multitudinous marine army, coming up from the sea with the last of the flood, and running to reach the lakes to spawn. A little further up it becomes deep and smooth, and is crossed by the high road. Lying our length on the log bridge, we watch a continuous stream passing slowly up, two or three inches apart. Further up, and the river breaks over a smooth plane of slate stones too shallow for the depth of the fish. Arrived at this plane the gaspereau throws himself as far up as he can, and then commences a series of spasmodic flaps with his tail.

" Slowly and painfully he passes over and drops exhausted into the tranquil pool above. Utterly exhausted, they lie heads and tails in a confused mass. Presently recruiting, their heads all pointing up stream, they again commence their march. In countless hordes they sweep through lonely still waters, the home of the trout, cool and pellucid enough to tempt a weary way wanderer, but on and on his irresistible instinct drives him. A natural dam, some two or three feet elevation, and over which the waters fall with a perpendicular rush, now arrests his progress. He throws himself (no doubt with a vigorous sweep of tail) directly at it. That about two and a half to three feet is his utmost range, the many failures he makes before he drops into the pool above attest.

" He has now gained his lake, often a very small one in the heart of the forest, and perhaps at six hundred feet elevation from high water mark. And now commences his brief courtship, for, unlike the lordly salmon who dallies until November, our fish has but little time for delay. Camping on the lake-side of a moonlight night, you hear a swash in the water. " What fish in that ? " you ask your Indian ; " Gaspereau," is his answer. The trout-fisher by day sees the surface of the lake ruffled by a hundred fins, then the trout break all around him. " See the gaspereau hunting the trout," he says. But these are only his harmless gambols, coloured by the resistless instinct of reproduction. He has even been known to rise at a fly, and to take a bait on these waters. Although the salmon and trout are often seen spawning, I never met any one who has seen the Gaspereau in the act.

" In three or four weeks after leaving the salt water, his brief holiday over, our fish commences his return. Unnerved by the exhausting toil of reproduction, by the absence of food (on the lakes their stomachs are found empty), and perchance by the warming summer waters, he addresses himself to the perils and dangers of descent. Too poor for an object of capture, he slips down unnoticed, save by the idle or curious, where, a few weeks before, a whole population watched his ascent. It is said those marine wolves, the eels, follow the advancing and retreating armies in their rear, gobbling up many a weak fish, or unlucky little one on the march. A dry summer has emptied the lakes and turned the foaming torrents of the spring into dusty rills. He often gets caught in these lukewarm shallows and dies. Not unfrequently the hunter finds them in bushels in the fords; quite as often the bear secures a rich feast—dipping his hairy paws into the shallow pools. He may be seen approaching nervously and timidly a rapid, then striking up stream, and returning pass down tail first. Those which are seen in July or passing down in August, we must consider fish that have left the sea late in May, or that are caught by the dry season, and go down during the August freshets. Finally, October seems to be the last date for even the fry to be seen in fresh water."

The advent of this fish in fresh water just at the time when fly-fishing is at its best, often proves a source of vexation to the angler. It is so disappointing, just as one is commencing to ply the rod over some favourite pool for sea-trout, to see the sharp splash of the gaspereau, and the gleam of their silver sides as they dash round the pool in reckless gambols. The trout are quite cowed, and further fishing is useless; for, although this fresh-water herring will sometimes take the fly, it is a worthless fish when caught—thin, tasteless, and full of bones. Drenched in brine, and eaten as a relish with a mess of potatoes, it forms a common diet throughout the country; and as there is scarcely a brook too small for the gaspereau to ascend, provided it comes from a lake, the luxury is brought fresh from the sea to the very door of many a settler in the remote backwoods. Great fun to the youngsters is dipping for gaspereau. A noisy crew of juveniles, half-clothed in homespun, stand on opposite sides, or striding across a forest brook; presently there is a shout of "here they come!" and in go the dip-nets with which they are armed, working with the stream. At every scoop two or three bright silvery fish are brought out, and deposited in a tub or barrel behind. It is a picturesque scene—the brook dashing between the dark-brown rocks, the surrounding bushes tinged with the pale green of their young leaves, and laden with blossoms—the excited boys with their high-braced trousers tucked up over the knee, and tattered straw hats, and the gleam of the fish as they are quickly hoisted out.

B B

The damming up of many of these forest brooks to supply saw mills, and the disgraceful plan of stopping the now worthless fish on their return from spawning, by brushwood weirs stretched completely across the stream, is fast shortening the supply of these welcome visitors to the interior waters of the backwoods, thereby also depriving many of the harbours of the anxiously-sought visits of the mackerel, which come in vast shoals in search of the young fry of the gaspereau and the smelt. To enable this fish to ascend the rough waters and falls of the streams through which it must pass to get to the lake, it is provided with a horny ridge or keel, passing along the belly, and armed with recurved teeth like those of a saw, enabling it to hold its ground and rest on the rocky bottom in the roughest water.

## VOICES OF REPTILIA IN SPRING.

The subjoined passages from my note books advert to the multitudinous sounds emitted by reptile life in the warm nights of spring and early summer, which to a stranger appear one of the most striking features of New World natural history :—

*May* 10*th.*—Driving homewards this evening our ears were almost deafened by the chorus of frogs in the road-side swamps. For some days past we have been cheered by their welcome voices, but to-night they seemed to outdo themselves. The principal and noisiest performer is a little fellow, not more than three quarters of an inch in length, and so shy and acute that it is almost impossible to get a glimpse of him, even by the most artful approach. This is the common peeper or cricket frog (Hylodes Pickeringii). Its quickly repeated, chirping note is very like that of the common house cricket, and equally joyous. If we stand by to listen, they somehow or other slacken gradually, as if a warning of danger was being passed through the community: we remove a few paces, and a solitary peep of a bold frog announces that the danger is past, and away they all start again into the maddest chorus, each trying to outvie the others. At the edge of the swamp sits the common toad (B. americanus), and, with a distended throat, pours out that rapid and peculiar trilling note which may always be heard as an accompaniment to the frog chorus throughout the warm nights of spring. He is not quite such an ugly reptile as the English toad, though very similar in general appearance and form ; the colour is lighter and brighter, sometimes approaching an orange-yellow, and the spots and markings

e more conspicuous. At intervals we detect the solemn croak
? the large green-headed frog (Rana fontinalis), which seems to
it periods to the incessant rattle of the hylodes and toads. They
ent half afraid of this great handsome bully, and his authoritative
down, down !" comes from the undoubted monarch of the swamp.
his is a very pretty reptile—a dark brown skin barred with black,
ie head and upper portion of the back bright grass green, and the
iroat a glaring yellow. Their colours are most developed at mid-
mer, when they sit croaking in shallow ponds throughout the
s well as night, and pursue one another with prodigious leaps.
seen them clear eight feet at a jump. Returning from fishing,
tempted these frogs to spring on a red fly dangled over their
d a disagreeable business the releasing of the slimy monsters

scene for a Christmas pantomime would be a representation
our swamps, with an opening chorus of the little "peepers,"
...ghable representation of bull-frogs by agile humans meta-
orphosed into reptiles, whilst the staid old toad slowly waddles up
ie bank, and pours forth his monotonous trill. The hylodes might
shown clinging to the stems of rushes above the surface of the
ool (a position in which I have discovered them by the aid of a
ll's-eye lantern at night), inflating their immense throat bags to
roduce their shrill pipe, whilst an admirable scenic effect might be
ndered by imitation of the swamp vegetation—the tussacs of pink
hagnum perforated by the crimson and green vases of the pitcher
lant and covered by the creeping tendrils and great shining
pples of the cranberry, clumps of bulrush, purple iris, and other
aterside plants, arrow heads, and the two water lilies, white and
ellow.

THE END.

BRADBURY, EVANS, AND CO., PRINTERS, WHITEFRIARS.